NOTES ON THE BOOK

OF LEVITICUS

NOTES ON THE BOOK OF LEVITICUS

C H MACKINTOSH

CHAPTER TWO
LONDON • ENGLAND

NOTES ON THE BOOK OF LEVITICUS BY C. H. Mackintosh
UK ISBN 978 1 85307 222 2
Set of Six Notes on the Pentateuch ISBN 978 1 85307 219 2
This edition © Chapter Two 2007

The first edition of *Notes on the Book of Leviticus* was first published in 1860 by co-publishers Geo Morrish, 24 Warwick Lane, London, W H Broom, 112 Pentonville Road, London and G Herbert, 117 Grafton Street, Dublin. In 1861 the 2nd edition of *Notes on the Book of Leviticus* was published and numerous reprints followed.
First single volume edition of *Notes on the Pentateuch* by Loizeaux Bros. USA 1972

Translated into Amharic, Arabic, Bulgarian, Chinese, Croatian, Czech, Danish, Dutch, Finnish, French, German, Greek, Hindi, Hungarian, Italian, Japanese, Korean, Norwegian, Polish, Portuguese, Romanian, Russian, Spanish and Swedish.

All rights reserved. No part of this publication may be reproduced or transmitted in any form or by any means, electronic or mechanical, including photocopying, recording, or storage in any information retrieval system, without written permission from Chapter Two.

CHAPTER TWO
Fountain House, Conduit Mews, London SE18 7AP, UK
www.chaptertwobooks.org.uk

Distributors:
- Bible, Book and Tract Depôt, 23 Santarosa Avenue, Ryde, NSW 2112, Australia
- The Bible House, Gateway Mall, 35 Tudor Street, Bridgetown, Barbados, WI
- Believers Bookshelf, 5205 Regional Road 81, Unit 3, Beamsville, ON, L0R 1B3, Canada
- Bible Treasury Bookstore, 46 Queen Street, Dartmouth, Nova Scotia, B2Y 1G1, Canada
- El-Ekhwa Library, 3 Anga Hanem Street, Shoubra, Cairo 11231, Egypt
- Bibles & Publications Chrétiennes, 30 rue Châteauvert, 26000 Valence, France
- CSV, An der Schloßfabrik 30, 42499 Hückeswagen, Germany
- Christian Literature Service, PO Box GP 20872, Accra, Ghana
- Christian Truth Bookroom, Paddisonpet, Tenali 522 201, Andhra Pradesh, India
- Words of Life Trust, 3 Chuim, Khar, Mumbai, 400 052, India
- Words of Truth, 38-P.D.A Lamphelpat, Imphal 795 004, Manipur, India
- Uit het Woord der Waarheid, Postbox 260, 7120AG Aalten, Netherlands
- Bible and Book Depot, Box 25119, Christchurch 5, New Zealand
- Christian Literature Depot, PO Box 436, Ijeshatedo, Surulere, Lagos, Nigeria
- Believers Bookshelf, PO Box 777, Shadewell Heights, Basseterre, St. Kitts, WI
- Grace & Truth Book-room, 87 Chausee Road, Castries, St. Lucia, WI
- Chapter Two S.A., Box 2234, Alberton 1450, South Africa
- Beröa Verlag, Zellerstrasse 61, 8038 Zürich, Switzerland
- Éditions Bibles et Littérature Chrétienne, La Foge C, Case Postale, 1816 Chailly-Montreux, Switzerland
- Chapter Two Bookshop, 199 Plumstead Common Road, London, SE18 2UJ, UK
- HoldFast Bible & Tract Depôt, 41 York Road, Tunbridge Wells, Kent, TN1 1JX, UK
- Words of Truth, PO Box 147, Belfast, BT8 4TT, Northern Ireland, UK
- Believers Bookshelf Inc., Box 261, Sunbury, PA 17801, USA

Printed in The Netherlands by Van der Perk Printers

PREFACE

In the Person and work of the Lord Jesus Christ there is an infinite fullness, which meets every necessity of man, both as sinner and as a worshipper. The infinite dignity of His Person gives eternal value to His work. In the Book of Genesis we have seen "God's remedy for man's ruin" in the promised seed – the Ark of Salvation, and in the rich unfoldings of divine grace, to fallen and sinful man. There we have the *Bud,* the full-blown glories, and fragrance of which shall yet fill the heavens and the earth, with joy and gladness.

In the Book of Exodus we have seen "God's answer to man's question." There, man is not only outside of Eden, but he has fallen into the hands of a cruel and powerful enemy. He is the bond slave of the world. How is he to be delivered from Pharaoh's thraldom, from Egypt's furnace? How can he be redeemed, justified, and brought into the promised land? God only could answer such questions, and this He did in the blood of the slain Lamb. In the redemption-power of that blood, every question is settled. It meets Heaven's highest claims, and man's deepest necessities. Through its amazing efficacy, God is glorified, man is redeemed, saved, justified, and brought to God's holy habitation; while the enemy is completely overthrown, and his power destroyed.

And, now, in our meditations on the Book of Leviticus, we find most fully unfolded, what we may call, "God's provision for man's need;" or a Sacrifice, a Priest, and a Place of Worship. These are essentially necessary in drawing near unto God, as this book most abundantly proves. But everything therewith connected was appointed by God, and established by His law. Nothing was left to be supplied by man's fertile imagination, or his prudential arrangement. "So Aaron and his sons did *all things which the Lord commanded* by the hand of Moses" (8:36; 9:6, 7). Without the word of the Lord, neither priest nor people could take a single step in the right direction. *It is so still.* There is not a single ray of light in this dark world, but that which is shed from holy Scripture. "Thy word is a lamp unto my feet, and lamp unto my path" (Psalm 119:105). It is truly happy when the children of God so honour His word as to be guided by it in all things. We need *now*, as much as the Jew did *then*, divine direction and divine guidance for acceptable worship. "But the hour cometh, and now is, when the *true worshippers* shall worship the Father in spirit and in truth: for the Father seeketh such to worship him" (John 4:23, 24). More than sincerity or devoutness of feeling is required in the children's worship. It must be in the unction of the Spirit, and according to the truth of God. But we have all, blessed be His name, in the Person and work of our blessed Lord Jesus! He is both our sacrifice and priest, and our right of entrance into the holiest of all. Oh! to be kept near to His wounded side, and in the abiding sense, that He is the ground, the material, and the sweet incense of all our worship.

Let us now briefly notice the three points already mentioned.

I. In the first place, we would observe, that *sacrifice is the basis of worship*. Acceptable worship to God must be based on a sacrifice acceptable to Him. Man being in himself guilty and unclean, he needs a sacrifice to remove his guilt, cleanse him from his defilements, and fit him for the holy presence of God. "Without shedding of blood is no remission." And without remission, and the *knowledge* of remission, there can be no happy worship; no real, hearty praise, adoration and thanksgiving. Going to what is called "a place of worship," and worshipping God, are widely different things. God is holy, and man must approach Him in His own way, and according to what He is. As Moses said unto Aaron on the solemn occasion of the sin of Nadab and Abihu, "This is that the Lord spake, saying, *I will be sanctified in them that come nigh me,* and before all the people will I be glorified." The Lord alone could give directions as to how the people were to draw nigh unto Him. This is the great subject of the Book of Leviticus. The "NOTES" on the first seven, and the sixteenth chapters, will give the reader a very full and interesting view of the ordinance of sacrifice, and the character of Jewish worship.

It was on the ground of offered and accepted sacrifice that the children of Israel were constituted the worshipping people of God. It is on the same ground, namely, offered and accepted sacrifice, that believers in Jesus are constituted the worshipping people of God now. (Read carefully Lev. 16; Heb. 9; 10.) They have taken Israel's place, but after a much higher order, whether we look at the sacrifice, the priest, or the place of worship. The contrast between them is great, and strongly marked in Scripture, especially in the Epistle to the Hebrews. The Jewish sacrifices never reached the *conscience* of the offerer, and the Jewish priest could never pronounce him "clean every whit." The gifts and sacrifices which were offered under the law, as the apostle tells us, "could not make him that did the service perfect, as pertaining to the conscience." The conscience, observe, always being the *reflection* of the sacrifice, it could not be perfect, seeing that the sacrifice was not perfect. "For it is not possible that the blood of bulls and of goats should take away sins." Hence, Jewish worship was connected with inefficient sacrifices, a burdensome ritual, and an unpurged conscience, which gendered in the worshipper a spirit of bondage and fear.

But now, mark the contrast to all this in the once-offered and accepted sacrifice of Christ. He "put away sin by the sacrifice of himself." All is done. Having "by himself purged our sins, he sat down on the right hand of the Majesty on high." When the worshipper comes before God on the ground of this sacrifice, he finds that he has nothing to do save, as a priest, to show forth the praises of Him "who hath called us out of darkness into his marvellous light." Even Christ has nothing more to do as regards our justification and acceptance. "For by one offering he hath perfected for ever them that are sanctified." The Jew, by his sacrifice, was merely *ceremonially* clean, and that only for a moment, as it were; but the Christian, through the sacrifice of Christ, is *really* so, and that for ever. Oh! that sweet word, "FOR EVER." It is the common privilege of all believers to be perfected as worshippers before God, "through the offering of the body of Jesus Christ once for all." On this deeply-important point the testimony of Scripture is most full and explicit. For the worshippers once purged should have *"no more conscience of sins."* "The blood of Jesus Christ his Son cleanseth us from all sin." "And their sins and their iniquities will I remember no more" (1 John 1:7; Heb. 10). By the work of Christ *for us* our sins were all put away. And, now, by faith in God's word, we know that they are forgiven and forgotten. Hence, we can draw near to God, and stand in His holy presence, in the happy assurance that there is neither sin nor stain upon us. Our Great High Priest has pronounced us "clean every whit" (John 13). Believing this, the sense of guilt is taken away; we have "NO MORE CONSCIENCE OF SINS."

This deeply precious truth, observe, does not mean there is no more *consciousness* of sins. Far from it. Or that we may not get a bad conscience through failure – or that we need not be exercised "to have a conscience void of offence toward God and toward man." Not at all. It simply means that Christ, by the one, perfect, finished sacrifice of Himself, has for ever put away all our sins, root and branch. And having been led to know and believe this, how can there be sins on the conscience? Christ has put them all away. The precious blood of our once-offered and accepted sacrifice has cleansed us from every spot and stain of sin. There may be the deepest sense of indwelling sin, and of many sins and shortcomings in our every-day life, and the painful confession of them all to God. Still, there is the full assurance that Christ died for our sins, put them all away, and that not one of them can ever be put to our charge. This is indeed a most wonderful truth; but it is the great, the needed truth for a worshipper. How could we stand in God's presence, where all is perfection, if we were not as clean as He would have us to be? We must be clean enough for the eye of Infinite Holiness. But, blessed be God, all who believe in Jesus, and rest on His finished sacrifice, are forgiven and justified. They have eternal life, righteousness, and peace. The first cry for mercy of the guilty sinner is answered by the blood of the sacrifice. It penetrates to the deepest depths of his need – it raises him to the highest heights of heaven, and fits him to be there, a happy worshipper, in the immediate presence of the throne of God. "For Christ also hath once suffered for sins, the just for the unjust, that he might bring us to God." "For if the blood of bulls and of goats, and the ashes of an heifer, sprinkling the unclean, sanctifieth to the purifying of the flesh, how much more shall the blood of Christ, who, through the eternal Spirit, offered himself without spot to God, purge your conscience from dead works to serve the living God!" 1 Peter 3:18; Heb. 9:13, 14.

II. In the second place, we have, in the rich provisions of God's grace, *the Lord Jesus Christ as our Great High Priest in the presence of God for us.* He ministers there for us. "We have such an high priest who is set on the right hand of the throne of the Majesty in the heavens; a minister of the sanctuary, and of the true tabernacle, which the Lord pitched and not man" (Heb. 8:1, 2). His work of sacrifice having been fully completed, He sat down. Aaron is represented as being always in a standing position. His work was never finished. He stood "daily ministering, and offering oftentimes the same sacrifices which can never take away sin. But this man, after he had offered one sacrifice for sins, for ever sat down on the right hand of God." Immediately after the law of the Lord had been given as to sacrifice, the priesthood was established. (See "NOTES" on chapters 8, 9) The saints have both in Christ. He is our sacrifice and our priest. He appeared once on the cross *for us.* He now appears in heaven *for us.* Ere long He will appear in glory *with us.* To know what He accomplished on the cross, and what He is now doing in the sanctuary above, will nourish in our hearts the hope of His coming, and lead us to long for His appearing in glory.

In the New Testament we only read of two orders of Priests – namely, Christ as the Great High Priest in heaven, and the common priesthood of all believers on the earth. "Ye also, as lively stones, are built up a spiritual house, an holy priesthood, to offer up spiritual sacrifices, acceptable to God by Jesus Christ" (1 Peter 2:5). And, again, "Unto him that loved us, and washed us from our sins in his own blood, and hath made us kings and priests unto God and his Father" (Rev. 1:5, 6). These passages clearly prove the common standing of all believers as priests unto God. There is no mention in the New Testament of any peculiar class, or order of Christians who hold the office of priests, as distinct from other Christians. Christ is the *Great* High Priest over the house of God, and all His people are, in virtue of their connexion with Him, priests and privileged to enter, as once-purged worshippers, into the holiest of all. Even the apostles never took the place of priests, as distinct from, or superior to, the humblest child of God. They might know their privileges better than many, and enjoy them more. Their gifts and callings as to ministry of the word, were distinct and special, but as worshippers they stood on the same ground as all others, and, together with them, worshipped God through Jesus Christ, the Great High Priest of all His people.

In the priestly ministry of our blessed Lord there are many points of special interest; we only notice the two following:

1. As our Great High Priest, He *represents* us in the sanctuary above. And, oh! what a Representative! God's beloved Son, the glorified Man, whose name is above every name. "For Christ is not entered into the holy place made with hands, which are the figures of the true, but into heaven itself, now to appear in the presence of God *for us*" (Heb. 9:24). Oh! what dignity! what nearness to God is ours! Oh! that our hearts appreciated it more! When Aaron appeared before the Lord in his garments of glory and beauty, he represented the children of Israel. Their names were engraven in precious stones in the beautiful breastplate. Blessed type of our real and everlasting place in the heart of Christ, who appears, not

annually, like Aaron of old, but *continually* in the presence of God *for us*. The name of each believer is kept continually before the eye of God, in all the glory and beauty of Christ, His well-beloved Son. We stand in His righteousness, possess His life, enjoy His peace, are filled with His joy, and radiate His glory. Although without right, title, or privilege in ourselves, we have all in Him. He is there *for us* and *as us*. His name be for ever praised.

> "He stands in heaven their great Priest,
> And bears their names upon His breast."

It is by His continual intercession in heaven that saints on earth are succoured and sustained in their wilderness journey, and, at the same time, upheld as worshippers within the veil, in all the sweet fragrance of His own divine excellencies. And neither their ignorance, nor their lack of enjoyment of these things, alters or affects their blessed, glorious, and eternal reality. "Seeing he ever liveth to make intercession for them." Heb. 7: 25.

2. As our Great High Priest, He presents to God the gifts and sacrifices of His worshipping people. Under the law, the worshipper brought his offering to the priest, and by him it was presented to the Lord, on His own altar. Everything was arranged by the priest, according to the word of the Lord. How perfectly all this is done for the worshipper now by his High Priest in Heaven! Our prayers, praises, and thanksgiving, all pass through His hands before they reach the throne of God. What a wonderful mercy this is, when we think of our confused and mixed services! So much that is of the flesh mixes with that which is of the Spirit. But the blessed Lord knows how to divide and separate between them. That which is of the flesh must be rejected, and consumed as wood, hay, and stubble, while that which is of the Spirit is precious, preserved, and presented to God in the value and sweet savour of His own perfect sacrifice. *"By Him* therefore let us offer the sacrifice of praise to God continually, that is, the

fruit of our lips, giving thanks unto His name" (Heb. 13:15). The kindness of the Philippians to Paul was "an odour of a sweet smell, a sacrifice acceptable, well pleasing to God." Hence the importance of the exhortation, "Whatsoever ye do in word or deed, do all in the name of the Lord Jesus, giving thanks to God and the Father by him." Col. 3:17.

III. In the third place, we observe, that *the Christian's only place of worship is inside the veil*, "whither the forerunner is for us entered." Outside the camp is his place as a witness; inside the veil is his place as a worshipper. In both positions Christ is surely with him. "Let us go forth therefore unto him without the camp, bearing his reproach." "Having therefore, brethren, *boldness to enter into the holiest* by the blood of Jesus" (Heb. 13; 10:19). To know these two positions in communion with Christ Himself, through the teaching of the Spirit, is unspeakable blessedness. The Church has no divinely-consecrated place of worship on earth. Our place is in heaven, in virtue of the sacrifice and of the priestly ministry of Christ there for us. Whatever may be the character of the building in which Christians are gathered together in the name of the Lord Jesus, their true and only sphere of worship is the heavenly sanctuary. Through faith in God's word, and by the power of His Holy Spirit, they worship Him in "the true tabernacle, which the Lord pitched and not man."

Israel had "a worldly sanctuary," and accordingly, the character of their worship was worldly, "the way into the holiest of all was not yet made manifest, while as the first tabernacle yet still standing." But the way has been opened by the blood of Jesus. The same stroke that slew the Lamb rent the veil from top to bottom. The way into the holiest of all was then laid open, and Christ, with all His blood-washed ones, entered into the immediate presence of God, without a veil. There is no *outer* court-worship now for the people, and *temple*-worship for the priest, as under the law. These distinctions are unknown in the Church of the living God. It is all priestly worship and temple worship now. All are equally near – all have equal liberty – all are equally acceptable, through the presence and intervention of the Great High Priest of His people. The same precious blood that cleansed us from all sin, has brought us near to God as children, and as worshipping priests. And if we really know the wondrous efficacy and power of that blood in the heavenly places, we shall be at home and happy there in all the liberty and dignity of sonship, and in all the official nearness and standing of once-purged worshippers, in the most holy place.

Oh! that our hearts may be kept in the sweet remembrance, knowledge, and power of the rich provisions of God's grace for all our need! Oh! that we may never lose sight of the blood on the mercy-seat, the minister of the sanctuary, and of our holy, heavenly, and eternal place of worship.

We must now leave the dear reader, earnestly commending to his most prayerful and diligent study this precious Book of Leviticus. The light which it sheds on the Person and work of Christ – the ground and character of our communion with God, is deeply blessed to the heart that desires to live in the enjoyment of these eternal realities. He will find the "NOTES" most helpful in unfolding the text, and in giving an interesting and practical view to many of the ceremonies which we are prone to pass over as uninteresting and uninstructive to us. See, for example, the eleventh chapter.

And now, may the Lord graciously own, use, and bless, this little volume for the glory of His own name, and for the comfort and blessing of many precious souls.

A.M.
London, May, 1860

PREFACE TO THE SECOND EDITION

The rapid sale of a large edition of this volume evidences an amount of interest in the study of the Book of Leviticus, for which I unfeignedly bless the Lord. Too many, even of the people of God, seem to think that this section of inspiration contains nothing of any interest or value to them. They regard it as a detail of rites and ceremonies with which they have nothing to do – a record of by-gone institutions, affording no instruction or edification for them. That this is a great mistake, thousands are now discovering. Very many who, for years, looked upon the Book of Leviticus as little more than a dry catalogue of Jewish ordinances, are now discovering in it an exhaustless mine of spiritual wealth for which they cannot be too thankful. They have brought its marvellous pages under the light of the New Testament scriptures, and they can only wonder at that which is now unfolded to their gaze. That they may discover yet more of the precious treasure, is my earnest desire on their behalf.

I have carefully revised the following pages, and, I may say, I have left them very much as I found them. An expression, here and there, which seemed likely to be misunderstood, I have slightly touched. I have also added a brief note or two. These trifling matters excepted, the Second Edition is a reprint of the First, and, as such, it is again committed to the care of Him from whom all blessings flow. May He be graciously pleased to crown it, still further, with the stamp of His approval.

His seal and sanction are all that any book requires to make it useful; and, truly, we may say, the book that has not these, has nothing.

The Lord grant a more abundant blessing, and His name shall have all the praise.

C. H. M.
47, Mountjoy St., Dublin.
August, 1861.

Chapter 1

THE SACRIFICES - INTRODUCTION

God speaks out of the tabernacle

Ere entering upon the details of the chapter before us, there are two things which demand our careful consideration; namely, first, Jehovah's position; and, secondly, the order in which the offerings are presented.

"And the Lord called unto Moses, and spake unto him out of the tabernacle of the congregation." Such was the position from which Jehovah made the communications contained in this book. He had been speaking from Mount Sinai, and his position, there, gave marked character to the communication. From the fiery mount "went a fiery law;" but, here, He speaks "out of the tabernacle of the congregation." This was an entirely different position. We have seen this tabernacle set up, at the close of the preceding book. "And he reared up the court round about the tabernacle and the altar, and set up the hanging of the court gate. So Moses finished the work. Then a cloud covered the tent of the congregation, and the glory of the Lord filled the tabernacle . . . For the glory of the Lord was upon the tabernacle, by day, and fire was on it, by night, in the sight of all the house of Israel, throughout all their journeys" (Exod. 40:33-38).

Now, the tabernacle was God's dwelling place, in grace. He could take up His abode there, because He was surrounded, on all sides, by that which vividly set forth the ground of His relationship with the people. Had He come into their midst, in the full display of the character revealed upon Mount Sinai, it could only have been to "consume them in a moment," as a "stiff-necked people." But He retired within the veil –

type of Christ's flesh, (Heb. 10:20) – and took His place on the mercy seat where the blood of atonement, and not the "stiff-neckedness" of Israel, was that which met His view, and satisfied the claims of His nature. The blood which was brought into the sanctuary, by the high priest, was the type of that precious blood which cleanses from all sin; and, although Israel, after the flesh, saw nothing of this, it, nevertheless, justified God in abiding amongst them – it "sanctified to the purifying of the flesh" (Heb. 9:13).

Thus much as to Jehovah's position in this Book, which must be taken into account, in order to a proper understanding of the communications made therein. In them we shall find inflexible holiness united with the purest grace. God is holy, no matter from whence He speaks. He was holy on Mount Sinai, and holy above the mercy-seat; but, in the former case, His holiness stood connected with "a devouring fire;" in the latter, it was connected with patient grace. Now, the connexion of perfect holiness with perfect grace is that which characterizes the redemption which is in Christ Jesus, which redemption is, in various ways, shadowed forth in the Book of Leviticus. God must be holy, even though it should be in the eternal condemnation of impenitent sinners; but the full display of His holiness, in the salvation of sinners, calls forth heaven's loudest and loftiest note of praise. "Glory to God in the highest, and on earth peace, good-will toward men" (Luke 2:14). This doxology could not have been sung in connexion with "the fiery law." No doubt, there was "glory to God in the highest," but there was no "peace on earth" nor "good pleasure in men," inasmuch as it was the declaration of what men ought to be, ere God could take pleasure in them. But when "the Son" took His place, as a man, on the earth, the mind of Heaven could express its entire delight in Him as the One whose Person and work could combine, in the most perfect manner, divine glory with human blessedness.

The order of the different offerings

And, now, one word, as to the order of the offerings, in the opening chapters of the Book of Leviticus. The Lord begins with the burnt offering, and ends with the trespass offering. That is to say, He leaves off where we begin. This order is marked and most instructive. When, first, the arrow of conviction enters the soul, there are deep searchings of conscience, in reference to sins actually committed. Memory casts back its enlightened eye over the page of one's past life, and sees it stained with numberless trespasses against God and man. At this point of the soul's history, it is not so occupied with the question of the root from whence those trespasses have sprung, as with the stern and palpable fact that such and such things have actually been committed; and, hence, it needs to know that God has provided a sacrifice through which "all trespasses" can be "frankly forgiven." This is presented to us in the trespass offering.

But, as one advances, in the divine life, he becomes conscious that those *sins* which he has committed are but branches from a root, streams from a fountain; and, moreover, that *sin* in his nature is that fountain – that root. This leads to far deeper exercise, which can only be met by a deeper insight into the work of the cross. In a word, the cross will need to be apprehended by that in which God Himself has "condemned *sin in the flesh*" (Rom. 8:3). My reader will observe, it does not say, "*sins* in the *life*," but the root from whence these have sprung, namely, "*sin* in the *flesh*." This is a truth of immense importance. Christ not merely "died for our *sins*, according to the scriptures," but He was "made *sin* for us" (2 Cor. 5:21). This is the doctrine of the sin offering.

Now, it is when the heart and conscience are set at rest, through the knowledge of Christ's work, that we can feed upon Himself as the ground of our peace and joy, in the presence of God. There can be no such thing known as peace or joy, until we see all our trespasses forgiven and our sin judged. The trespass offering and the sin offering must be known, ere the peace offering, joy offering, or thanksgiving offering can be appreciated. Hence, therefore, the order in which the peace offering stands, corresponds with the order of our spiritual apprehension of Christ.

The same perfect order is observable in reference to the meat offering. When the soul is led to taste the sweetness of spiritual communion with Christ – to feed upon Him, in peace and thankfulness, in the divine presence, it is drawn out in earnest desire to know more of the wondrous mysteries of His Person; and this desire is most blessedly met in the meat offering, which is the type of Christ's perfect manhood.

Then, in the burnt offering, we are conducted to a point beyond which it is impossible to go, and that is, the work of the cross, as accomplished under the immediate eye of God, and as the expression of the unswerving devotion of the heart of Christ. All these things will come before us, in beauteous detail, as we pass along; we are here only looking at the order of the offerings, which is truly marvellous, whichever way we travel, whether *outward* from God to us, or *inward* from us to God. In either case, we begin with the cross and end with the cross. If we begin with the burnt offering, we see Christ, on the cross, doing the will of God – making atonement, according to the measure of His perfect surrender of Himself to God. If we begin with the trespass offering, we see Christ, on the cross, bearing our sins, and putting them away, according to the perfection of His atoning sacrifice; while, in each and all, we behold the excellency, the beauty, and the perfection of His divine and adorable Person. Surely, all this is sufficient to awaken in our hearts the deepest interest in the study of those precious types which we shall now proceed to consider in detail. And may God the Holy Ghost, who penned the Book of Leviticus, expound its contents in living power to our hearts; that so, when we have reached the close, we may have abundant cause to bless His name for many thrilling and soul-stirring views of the Person and work of our blessed Lord and Saviour Jesus Christ, to whom be glory, now, henceforth, and for evermore. Amen.

THE BURNT OFFERING

Christ's offering of Himself to God

In the burnt offering, with which our book opens, we have a type of Christ "offering himself without spot to God." Hence the position which the Holy Ghost assigns to it. If the Lord Jesus Christ came forth to accomplish the glorious work of atonement, His highest and most fondly-cherished object, in so doing, was the glory of God. "Lo, I come, to do thy will, O God," was the grand motto in every scene and circumstance of His life, and in none more markedly than in the work of the cross. Let the will of God be what it might, He came to do it. Blessed be God, we know what our portion is in the accomplishment of this "will;" for by it "we are sanctified, through the offering of the body of Jesus Christ once" (Heb. 10:10). Still, the primary aspect of Christ's work was to God-ward. It was an ineffable delight to Him to accomplish the will of God on this earth. No one had ever done this before. Some had, through grace, done "that which was right in the sight of the Lord;" but no one had ever, perfectly, invariably, from first to last, without hesitation, and without divergence, done the will of God. But this was, exactly, what the Lord Jesus did. He was "obedient unto death, even the death of the cross" (Phil. 2:8). "He steadfastly set his face to go to Jerusalem." And as He walked from the garden of Gethsemane to the cross of Calvary, the intense devotion of His heart told itself forth in these accents: "The cup which my Father hath given me, shall I not drink it?'

Now, in all this self-emptied devotedness to God, there was truly a sweet savour. A perfect Man on the earth accomplishing the will of God, even in death, was an object of amazing interest to the mind of Heaven. Who could fathom the profound depths of that devoted heart, which displayed itself, under the eye of God, on the cross? Surely, none but

God; for in this, as in everything else, it holds good that "no man knoweth the Son, but the Father;" and no one can know anything about Him, save as the Father reveals Him. The mind of man can, in some measure, grasp any subject of knowledge "under the sun." Human science can be laid hold of by the human intellect; but no man knoweth the Son, save as the Father reveals Him, by the power of the Holy Ghost, through the written word. The Holy Ghost delights to reveal the Son – to take of the things of Jesus, and show them unto us. These things we have, in all their fullness and beauty, in the word. There can be no new revelation, inasmuch as the Spirit brought "*all* things" to the apostles' memory, and led them into "*all* truth." There can be nothing beyond "all truth;" and, hence, all pretension to a new revelation, and the development of new truth, – meaning thereby truth not contained in the sacred canon of inspiration – is an effort, on man's part, to add to what God calls "all truth." No doubt, the Spirit may unfold and apply, with new and extraordinary power, truth contained in the word; but this is, obviously, a very different thing from our travelling outside the range of divine revelation, for the purpose of finding principles, ideas, or dogmas, which shall command the conscience. This latter can only be regarded in the light of impious presumption.

The types in Leviticus

In the gospel narrative, we have Christ presented to us in the varied phases of His character, His Person, and His work. To those precious documents the people of God in all ages have rejoiced to betake themselves, and drink in their heavenly revelations of the object of their love and confidence – the One to whom they owed everything, for time and eternity. But very few, comparatively, have ever been led to regard the rites and ceremonies of the Levitical economy as fraught with the most minute instruction in reference to the same commanding theme. The offerings of Leviticus, for example, have been too much regarded as so many antiquated records of Jewish customs, conveying no intelligible voice to our ears – no spiritual light to our understandings. However, it must be admitted that the apparently abstruse records of Leviticus, as well as the sublime strains of Isaiah, take their place amongst the "things which were written aforetime," and they are, therefore, "for our learning." True, we shall need to study those records, as indeed all Scripture, with an humble, self-emptied spirit; with reverent dependence upon the teaching of Him who graciously penned them for us; with sedulous attention to the general scope, bearing, and analogy of the entire body of divine revelation; with an effectual curb on the imagination, that it may not take unhallowed flights; but if thus, through grace, we enter upon the study of the types of Leviticus, we shall find in them a vein of the richest and finest ore.

The essential glory of Christ

We shall now proceed to examine the burnt offering, which, as we have remarked, presents Christ, offering Himself, without spot, to God.

"If his offering be a burnt sacrifice of the herd, let him offer a male, without blemish." The essential glory and dignity of Christ's Person form the basis of Christianity. He imparts that dignity and glory to every thing He does, and to every office He sustains. No office could possibly add glory to Him who is "God over all, blessed for ever" – "God manifest in the flesh" – the glorious "Immanuel" – "God with us" – the eternal Word – the Creator and Sustainer of the universe. What office could add to the dignity of such an One? In point of fact, we know that all His offices are connected with His humanity; and in assuming that humanity, He stooped from the glory which He had with the Father, before the world was. He thus stooped, in order to glorify God perfectly, in the very midst of a scene where all was hostile to Him. He came to be "eaten up" by a holy, unquenchable zeal for the glory of God, and the effectual carrying out of His eternal counsels.

The value of the cross of Christ to God

The unblemished male, of the first year, was a type of the Lord Jesus Christ offering Himself for the perfect accomplishment of the will of God. There should be nothing expressive either of weakness or imperfection. "A male of the first year" was required. We shall see, when we come to examine the other offerings, that "a female" was, in some cases, permitted; but that was only expressive of the imperfection which attached to the worshipper's apprehension, and in nowise of any defect in the offering, inasmuch as it was "unblemished" in the one case, as well as in the other. Here, however, it was an offering of the very highest order, because it was Christ offering Himself to God. Christ, in the burnt offering, was exclusively for the eye and heart of God. This point should be distinctly apprehended. God alone could duly estimate the Person and work of Christ. He alone could fully appreciate the cross as the expression of Christ's perfect devotedness. The cross, as foreshadowed by the burnt offering, had an element in it which only the divine mind could apprehend. It had depths so profound that neither mortal nor angel could fathom them. There was a voice in it which was intended exclusively for, and went directly to, the ear of the Father. There were communications between the cross of Calvary and the throne of God, which lay far beyond the highest range of created intelligence.

A *voluntary offering*

"He shall offer it of his own voluntary will at the door of the tabernacle of the congregation before the Lord." The use of the word "*voluntary*," here, brings out, with great clearness, the grand idea in the burnt offering. It leads us to contemplate the cross in an aspect which is not sufficiently apprehended. We are too apt to look upon the cross merely as the place where the great question of sin was gone into and settled, between eternal Justice and the spotless victim

– as the place where our guilt was atoned for, and where Satan was gloriously vanquished. Eternal and universal praise to redeeming love! The cross was all this. But it was more than this. It was the place where Christ's love to the Father was told out in language which only the Father could hear and understand. It is in the latter aspect that we have it typified, in the burnt offering; and, therefore, it is that the word "voluntary" occurs. Were it merely a question of the imputation of sin, and of enduring the wrath of God on account of sin, such an expression would not be in moral order. The blessed Lord Jesus could not, with strict propriety, be represented as *willing* to be "made sin" – *willing* to endure the wrath of God, and the hiding of His countenance; and, in this one fact, we learn, in the clearest manner, that the *burnt offering does not foreshadow Christ, on the cross, bearing sin* but Christ on the cross, accomplishing the will of God. That Christ Himself contemplated the cross in these two aspects of it, is evident from His own words. When he looked at the cross as the place of sin-bearing – when He anticipated the horrors with which, in this point of view, it stood invested, He exclaimed, "Father, if thou be willing, remove this cup from me" (Luke 23:42). He shrank from that which His work, as a sin-bearer, involved. His pure and holy mind shrank from the thought of contact with sin; and His loving heart shrank from the thought of losing, for a moment, the light of God's countenance.

But, then, the cross had another aspect. It stood before the eye of Christ as a scene, in which He could fully tell out all the deep secrets of His love to the Father – a place in which He could, "of his own voluntary will," take the cup which the Father had given Him, and drain it to the very dregs. True it is that the whole life of Christ emitted a fragrant odour, which ever ascended to the Father's throne – He did always those things which pleased the Father – He ever did the will of God; but the burnt offering does not typify Him in His life – precious, beyond all thought, as was every act of that life – but in His death, and in that, not as one "made a curse for us," but as one presenting to the heart of the Father an odour of incomparable fragrance.

This truth invests the cross with peculiar charms for the spiritual mind. It imparts to the sufferings of our blessed Lord an interest of the most intense character. The guilty sinner, no doubt, finds in the cross a divine answer to the deepest and most earnest cravings of heart and conscience. The true believer finds in the cross that which captivates every affection of his heart, and transfixes his whole moral being. The angels find in the cross a theme for ceaseless admiration. All this is true; but there is that, in the cross, which passes far beyond the loftiest conceptions of saints or angels; namely, the deep-toned devotion of the heart of the Son presented to, and appreciated by, the heart of the Father. This is the elevated aspect of the cross, which is so strikingly shadowed forth in the burnt offering.

And, here, let me remark that the distinctive beauty of the burnt offering must be entirely sacrificed, if we admit the idea that Christ was a sin-bearer all His life. There would then be no force, no value, no meaning in the word "voluntary." There could be no room for voluntary action in the case of one who was compelled, by the very necessity of his position, to yield up his life. If Christ were a sin-bearer, in His life, then, assuredly, His death must have been a *necessary*, not a voluntary, act. Indeed, it may be safely asserted that there is not one of the offerings the beauty of which would not be marred, and its strict integrity sacrificed, by the theory of *a life* of sin-bearing. In the burnt offering, this is especially the case, inasmuch as it is not, in it, a question of sin-bearing, or enduring the wrath of God, but entirely one of voluntary devotedness, manifested in the death of the cross. In the burnt offering we recognise a type of God the Son, accomplishing, by God the Spirit, the will of God the Father. This He did "of His own voluntary will." "Therefore doth my Father love me, because I lay down my life, that I might take it again" (John 10:17). Here we have the burnt offering aspect of the death of Christ. On the other hand, the prophet, contemplating Him as the sin offering, says, "his life *is taken* from the earth" (Acts 8:33, which is the LXX version of Isaiah 53:8). Again, Christ says, "No one (*ou deis*) taketh it from me, but I lay it down of myself." Was He a sin-bearer when He said this? Observe, it is "no one" man, angel, devil, or else. It was His own voluntary act, to lay down His life that He might take it again. "I delight to do thy will, O my God." Such was the language of the divine burnt offering – of Him who found His unutterable joy in offering Himself without spot to God.

Now, it is of the last importance to apprehend, with distinctness, the primary object of the heart of Christ, in the work of redemption. It tends to consolidate the believer's peace. The accomplishment of God's will, the establishment of God's counsels, and the display of God's glory, occupied the fullest, deepest, and largest place in that devoted heart which viewed and estimated everything in reference to God. The Lord Jesus never once stopped to inquire how any act or circumstance would affect Himself. "He humbled himself" – "He made himself of no reputation" – He surrendered all. And, hence, when He arrived at the close of His career, He could look back upon it all, and say, with His eyes lifted up to heaven, "I have glorified thee on the earth; I have finished the work which thou gavest me to do" (John 17:4). It is impossible to contemplate the work of Christ, in this aspect of it, without having the heart filled with the sweetest affections toward His Person. It does not detract, in the smallest degree, from our sense of His love to us, to know that He made God His primary object, in the work of the cross. Quite the opposite. His love to us, and our salvation in Him, could only be founded upon God's established glory. That glory must form the solid base of everything. "As truly as I live, all the earth shall be filled with the glory of the Lord" (Num. 14:21). But we know that God's eternal glory, and the creature's eternal blessedness, are, in the divine counsels, inseparably linked together, so that if the former be secured, the latter must needs be so likewise.

The identification of the worshipper with the burnt offering

"And he shall put his hand upon the head of the burnt offering; and it shall be accepted for him, to make atonement for him." The act of laying on of hands was expressive of full identification. By that significant act, the offerer and the offering became one; and this oneness, in the case of the burnt offering, secured for the offerer all the acceptableness of his offering. The application of this to Christ and the believer sets forth a truth of the most precious nature, and one largely developed in the New Testament; namely, the believer's everlasting identification with, and acceptance in, Christ. "As he is, so are we, in this world." "We are in him that is true" (1 John 4:17; 5:20). Nothing, in any measure, short of this could avail. The man who is not in Christ is in his sins. There is no middle ground. You must be either in Christ or out of Him. There is no such thing as being *partly* in Christ. If there is a single hair's-breadth between you and Christ, you are in an actual state of wrath and condemnation. But, on the other hand, if you are in Him, then are you "as he is" before God, and so accounted in the presence of infinite holiness. Such is the plain teaching of the Word of God. "Ye are complete in him" – "accepted in the beloved" – "members of his body, of his flesh, and of his bones." "He that is joined to the Lord, is one Spirit" (1 Cor. 6:17; Eph. 1:6; 5:30; Col. 2:10) Now, it is not possible that the Head can be in one degree of acceptance and the members in another. No; the Head and the members are one. God counts them one; and, therefore, they are one. This truth is, at once, the ground of the loftiest confidence, and of the most profound humility. It imparts the fullest assurance of "boldness in the day of judgment," inasmuch as it is not possible that anything can be laid to the charge of Him with whom we are united. It imparts the deep sense of our own nothingness, inasmuch as our union with Christ is founded upon the death of nature and the utter abolition of all its claims and pretensions.

Since, therefore, the Head and the members are viewed in

the same position of infinite favour and acceptance, before God, it is perfectly evident that all the members stand in one acceptance, in one salvation, in one life, in one righteousness. There are no degrees in justification. The babe in Christ stands in the same justification as the saint of fifty years' experience. The one is in Christ, and so is the other; and this, as it is the only ground of life, so it is the only ground of justification. There are not two kinds of life, neither are there two kinds of justification. No doubt, there are various measures of enjoyment of this justification – various degrees in the knowledge of its fullness and extent – various degrees in the ability to exhibit its power upon the heart and life; and these things are frequently confounded with the justification itself, which, as being divine, is, necessarily, eternal, absolute, unvarying, entirely unaffected by the fluctuation of human feeling and experience.

But, further, there is no such thing as progress in justification. The believer is not more justified to-day than he was yesterday; nor will he be more justified tomorrow than he is today; yea, a soul who is "in Christ Jesus" is as completely justified as if he were before the throne. He is "*complete* in Christ." He is "*as*" Christ. He is, on Christ's own authority, "clean every whit" (John 13:10). What more could he be, at this side of the glory? He may, and – if he walks in the Spirit – will, make progress in the sense and enjoyment of this glorious reality; but, as to the thing itself, the moment he, by the power of the Holy Ghost, believed the gospel, he passed from a positive state of unrighteousness and condemnation into a positive state of righteousness and acceptance. All this is based upon the divine perfectness of Christ's work; just as, in the case of the burnt offering, the worshipper's acceptance was based upon the acceptableness of his offering. It was not a question of what he was, but simply of what the sacrifice was. "*It* shall be accepted *for him,* to make atonement for him."

The place of the priests

"And he shall kill the bullock before the Lord: and the priests, Aaron's sons, shall bring the blood, and sprinkle the blood round about upon the altar that is by the door of the tabernacle of the congregation." It is most needful, in studying the doctrine of the burnt offering, to bear in mind that the grand point set forth therein is not the meeting of the sinner's need, but the presentation to God of that which was infinitely acceptable to Him. Christ, as foreshadowed by the burnt offering, is not for the sinner's conscience, but for the heart of God. Further, the cross, in the burnt offering, is not the exhibition of the exceeding hatefulness of sin, but of Christ's unshaken and unshakable devotedness to the Father. Neither is it the scene of God's out-poured wrath on Christ the sin-bearer; but of the Father's unmingled complacency in Christ, the voluntary and most fragrant sacrifice. Finally, "atonement," as seen in the burnt offering, is not merely commensurate with the claims of man's conscience, but with the intense desire of the heart of Christ, to carry out the will and establish the counsels of God – a desire which stopped not short of surrendering up His spotless, precious life, as "a voluntary offering" of "sweet savour" to God.

From the carrying out of this desire, no power of earth or hell, men or devils, could shake Him. When Peter ignorantly sought to dissuade Him, by words of false tenderness, from encountering the shame and degradation of the cross – "Pity thyself, Lord! this shall not be unto thee" – what was the reply? "Get thee behind me, Satan; thou art an offence unto me; for thou savourest not the things that be of God, but those that be of men" (Matt. 16:22, 23). So also, on another occasion, He says to His disciples, "Hereafter, I will not talk much with you, for the prince of this world cometh, and hath nothing in me: but that the world may know that *I love the Father*, and as the Father hath given me commandment, even so I do" (John 14:30). These and numerous other kindred scriptures, bring out the burnt offering phase of Christ's work, in which, it is evident, the primary thought is His "offering himself without spot to God."

In full keeping with all that has been stated, in reference to the special point in the burnt offering, is the place which Aaron's sons get, and the functions assigned them therein. They "sprinkle the blood" – they "put the fire upon the altar" – they "lay the wood in order upon the fire" – they "lay the parts, the head and the fat, in order upon the wood that is on the fire which is upon the altar" These are very prominent actions, and they form a marked feature of the burnt offering, as contrasted with the sin offering, in which Aaron's sons are not mentioned at all. "The sons of Aaron" represent the church, not as "one body," but as a priestly house. This is easily apprehended. If Aaron was a type of Christ, then Aaron's house was a type of Christ's house, as we read, in Heb. 3, "But Christ as a Son over his own house, whose house are we." And, again, "Behold I and the children whom God hath given me." Now, it is the privilege of the Church, as led and taught by the Holy Ghost, to gaze upon, and delight in, that aspect of Christ, which is presented in this opening type of Leviticus. "Our fellowship is with the Father," who graciously calls us to participate, with Him, in His thoughts about Christ. True, we can never rise to the height of those thoughts; but we can have fellowship therein, by the Holy Ghost who dwells in us. It is not, here, a question of having the conscience tranquillised, by the blood of Christ, as the sin-bearer, but of communion with God in the matter of Christ's perfect surrender of Himself on the cross.

"*The priests,* Aaron's sons, shall bring the blood, and sprinkle the blood round about upon the altar that is by the door of the tabernacle of the congregation." Here, we have a type of the Church, bringing the memorial of an accomplished sacrifice, and presenting it in the place of individual approach to God. But, we must remember, it is the blood of the burnt offering, and not of the sin offering. It is the Church, in the power of the Holy Ghost, entering into the stupendous thought of Christ's accomplished devotedness to God, and not a convicted sinner, entering into the value of the blood of the sin-bearer. I need hardly say that the Church is composed of sinners, and convicted sinners, too; but "Aaron's sons" do not represent convicted sinners, but worshipping saints. It is as *"priests"* they have to do with the burnt offering. Many err as to this. They imagine that, because one takes the place of a worshipper – being invited by the grace of God, and fitted by the blood of Christ, so to do – he, thereby, refuses to acknowledge himself a poor worthless sinner. This is a great mistake. The believer is, in himself, "nothing at all." But in Christ, he is a purged worshipper. He does not stand, in the sanctuary, as a guilty sinner, but as a worshipping priest, clothed in "garments of glory and beauty." To be occupied with my guilt, in the presence of God, is not humility, as regards myself, but unbelief, as regards the sacrifice.

Atonement

However, it must be very evident to my reader, that the idea of sin-bearing – the imputation of sin – the wrath of God, does not appear in the burnt offering. True, we read, "it shall be accepted for him, *to make atonement* for him;" but, then, it is "atonement" not according to the depths and enormity of human guilt, but according to the perfection of Christ's surrender of Himself to God, and the intensity of God's delight in Christ. This gives us the very loftiest idea of atonement. If I contemplate Christ as the sin offering, I see atonement made according to the claims of divine justice, with respect to sin. But when I see atonement, in the burnt offering, it is according to the measure of Christ's willingness and ability to accomplish the will of God; and according to the measure of God's complacency in Christ and His work. What a perfect atonement must that be which is the fruit of Christ's devotion to God! Could there be anything beyond this? Assuredly not. The burnt offering aspect of atonement is that about which the priestly household may well be occupied in the courts of the Lord's house, for ever.

The preparation of the sacrifice

"And he shall flay the burnt offering, and cut it into his pieces." The ceremonial act of "flaying" was peculiarly expressive. It was simply the removing of the outward covering, in order that what was *within* might be fully revealed. It was not sufficient that the offering should be, outwardly, "without blemish," "the hidden parts" should be all disclosed, in order that every sinew and every joint might be seen. It was only in the case of the burnt offering that this action was specially named. This is quite in character, and tends to set forth the depth of Christ's devotedness to the Father. It was no mere surface-work with Him. The more the secrets of His inner life were disclosed, the more the depths of His being were explored, the more clearly was it made manifest that pure devotion to the will of His Father, and earnest desire for His glory, were the springs of action in the great Antitype of the burnt offering. He was, most assuredly, a whole burnt offering.

"And cut it into his pieces." This action presents a somewhat similar truth to that taught in the "sweet incense *beaten small*" (Lev. 16). The Holy Ghost delights to dwell upon the sweetness and fragrance of the sacrifice of Christ, not only as a whole, but also in all its minute details. Look at the burnt offering, as a whole, and you see it without blemish. Look at it in all its parts, and you see it to be the same. Such was Christ; and as such He is shadowed forth in this important type.

"And the sons of Aaron the priest shall put fire upon the altar, and lay the wood in order upon the fire. And the priests, Aaron's sons, shall lay the parts, the head and the fat, in order upon the wood that is on the fire which is upon the altar." This was a high position for the priestly family. The burnt offering was wholly offered to God. It was all burnt upon the altar;[1] Man did not partake of it; but the sons of Aaron the priest, themselves being likewise priests, are here seen standing round the altar of God, to behold the flame of an acceptable sacrifice ascending to Him – an odour of sweet smell. This was a high position – high communion – a high order of priestly service – a striking type of the Church having fellowship with God, in reference to the perfect accomplishment of His will in the death of Christ. As convicted sinners, we gaze on the cross of our Lord Jesus Christ, and behold therein that which meets all our need. The cross, in this aspect of it, gives perfect peace to the conscience. But, then, as priests, as purged worshippers, as members of the priestly family, we can look at the cross in another light, even as the grand consummation of Christ's holy purpose to carry out, even unto death, the will of the Father. As convicted sinners, we stand at the brazen altar, and find peace through the blood of atonement; but, as priests, we stand there, to behold and admire the completeness of that burnt offering – the perfect surrender and presentation of the spotless One to God.

We should have a very defective apprehension of the mystery of the cross, were we only to see in it that which meets man's need as a sinner. There were depths in that mystery, which only the mind of God could fathom. It is, therefore, important to see that when the Holy Ghost would furnish us with foreshadowings of the cross, He gives us, in the very first place, one which sets it forth in its aspect to Godward. This alone would be sufficient to teach us that there are heights and depths in the doctrine of the cross which man never could reach. He may approach to "that one well-spring of delight," and drink for ever – he may satisfy the utmost longings of his spirit – he may explore it with all the powers of the renewed nature; but, after all, there is that in the cross which only God could know and appreciate. Hence it is that the burnt offering gets the first place. It typifies Christ's death as viewed and valued by God alone. And surely, we may say, we could not have done without such a type as this, for, not only does it give us the highest possible aspect of the death of Christ, but it also gives us a most precious thought in reference to God's peculiar interest in that death. The very fact of His instituting a type of Christ's death, which was to be exclusively for Himself, contains a volume of instruction for the spiritual mind.

But though neither man nor angel can ever fully sound the amazing depths of the mystery of Christ's death, we can, at least, see some features of it which would needs make it precious, beyond all thought, to the heart of God. From the cross, He reaps His richest harvest of glory. In no other way could He have been so glorified, as by the death of Christ. In Christ's voluntary surrender of Himself to death, the divine glory shines out in its fullest brightness. In it, too, the solid foundation of all the divine counsels was laid. This is a most comforting truth. Creation never could have furnished such a basis. Moreover, the cross furnishes a righteous channel through which divine love can flow. And, finally, by the cross, Satan is eternally confounded, and "principalities and powers made a show of openly." These are glorious fruits produced by the cross; and, when we think of them, we can see just reason why there should have been a type of the cross exclusively for God Himself, and also a reason why that type should occupy the leading place – should stand at the very top of the list. Again, let me say, there would have been a grievous blank among the types had the burnt offering been lacking; and there would be a grievous blank in the page of inspiration had the record of that type been withheld.

A sacrifice by fire: a sweet savour

"But his inwards and his legs shall he wash in water: and the priest shall burn all on the altar, to be a burnt sacrifice, an offering made by fire, of a sweet savour unto the Lord." This action rendered the sacrifice, typically, what Christ was essentially – pure, both inwardly and outwardly, pure. There was the most perfect correspondence between Christ's inward motives and His outward conduct. The latter was the index of the former. All tended to the one point, namely, the glory of God. The members of His Body perfectly obeyed and carried out the counsels of His devoted heart – that heart which only beat for God, and for His glory, in the salvation of men. Well, therefore, might the priest "burn *all* on the altar." It was all typically pure, and all designed only as food for the altar of God. Of some sacrifices the priest partook; of some, the offerer; but the burnt offering was "all" consumed on the altar. It was exclusively for God. The priests might arrange the wood and the fire, and see the flame ascend; and a high and holy privilege it was so to do. But they did not eat of the sacrifice. God alone was the object of Christ, in the burnt offering aspect of His death. We cannot be too simple in our apprehension of this. From the moment that the unblemished male was voluntarily presented at the door of the tabernacle of the congregation, until it was reduced to ashes, by the action of the fire, we discern in it Christ offering Himself, by the Eternal Spirit, without spot to God.

This makes the burnt offering unspeakably precious to the soul. It gives us the most exalted view of Christ's work. In that work God had His own peculiar joy – a joy into which no created intelligence could enter. This must never be lost sight of. It is unfolded in the burnt offering, and confirmed by "the law of the burnt offering," to which we shall just refer.

The law of the burnt offering

"And the Lord spake unto Moses, saying, Command Aaron and his sons, saying, this is the law of the burnt offering: it is the burnt offering, because of the burning upon the altar all night unto the morning, and the fire of the altar shall be burning in it. And the priest shall put on his linen garment, and his linen breeches shall he put upon his flesh, and take up the ashes which the fire hath consumed with the burnt offering on the altar, and he shall put them beside the altar. And he shall put off his garments, and put on other garments, and carry forth the ashes without the camp unto a clean place. And the fire upon the altar shall be burning in it, it shall not be put out: and the priest shall burn wood on it every morning, and lay the burnt offering in order upon it, and he shall burn thereon the fat of the peace offering. The fire shall ever be burning upon the altar: it shall never go out" (Lev. 6:8-13). The fire on the altar consumed the burnt offering, and the fat of the peace offering. It was the apt expression of divine holiness which found in Christ, and His perfect sacrifice, a proper material on which to feed. That fire was never to go out. There was to be the perpetual maintenance of that which set forth the action of divine holiness. Through the dark and silent watches of the night, the fire blazed on the altar of God.

"And the priest shall put on his linen garment," &c. Here, the priest takes, in type, the place of Christ, whose personal righteousness is set forth by the white linen garment. He, having given Himself up to the death of the cross, in order to accomplish the will of God, has entered, in His own eternal righteousness, into heaven, bearing with Him the memorials of His finished work. The ashes declared the completion of the sacrifice, and God's acceptance thereof. Those ashes, placed beside the altar, indicated that the fire had consumed the sacrifice – that it was not only a completed, but also an accepted, sacrifice. The ashes of the burnt offering declared the acceptance of the sacrifice. The ashes of the sin offering declared the judgment of the sin.

Many of the points on which we have been dwelling will, with the divine blessing, come before us with increasing clearness, fullness, precision, and power as we proceed with the offerings. Each offering is, as it were, thrown into relief, by being viewed in contrast with all the rest. All the offerings, taken together, give us a full view of Christ. They are like so many mirrors, arranged in such a manner, as to reflect, in various ways, the figure of that true and only perfect Sacrifice. No one type could fully present Him. We needed to have Him reflected in life and in death – as a Man and as a Victim – to God-ward and to us-ward; and we have Him thus, in the offerings of Leviticus. God has graciously met our need: and may He give us an enlarged capacity to enter into and enjoy His provision.

---

[1] It may be well, at this point, to inform the reader that the Hebrew word which is rendered "burn," in the case of the burnt offering is wholly different from that which is used in the sin offering. I shall, because of the peculiar interest of the subject, refer to a few of the passages in which each word occurs. The word used in the burnt offering signifies "incense," or to "burn incense," and occurs in the following passages, in some one or other of its various inflections. Lev. 6:15; "and all the *frankincense*, . . . and shall *burn* it upon the altar." Deut. 33:10; "they shall put *incense* before thee, and whole *burnt* sacrifice upon thine altar. Exod. 30:1; "and thou shalt make an altar to *burn incense* upon." Ps. 66:15; "with the *incense* of rams." Jer. 44:21 "The *incense* that ye *burned* in the cities of Judah." Cant. 3:6 "Perfumed with myrrh and *frankincense.*" Passages might be multiplied, but the above will suffice to show the use of the word which occurs in the burnt offering.

The Hebrew word which is rendered "burn," in connexion with the sin offering, signifies to burn, in general, and occurs in the following passages. Gen. 11:3; "let us make brick, and *burn* them thoroughly." Lev. 10:16; "And Moses diligently sought the goat of the *sin* offering and, behold, it was *burnt*." 2 Chr. 16:14; "And they made a very great *burning* for him."

Thus, not only was the sin offering burnt in a different place, but a different word is adopted by the Holy Ghost to express the burning of it. Now, we cannot imagine, for a moment, that this distinction is a mere interchange of words, the use of which is indifferent. I believe the wisdom of the Holy Ghost is as manifest in the use of the two words, as it is in any other point of difference in the two offerings. The spiritual reader will attach the proper value to the above most interesting distinction.

Chapter 2

THE MEAL OFFERING

Christ in His life

We, now, come to consider the meat offering which presents, in a very distinct manner, "the man Christ Jesus." As the burnt offering typifies Christ in *death*, the meat offering typifies Him in *life*. In neither the one nor the other, is there a question of sin-bearing. In the burnt offering, we see atonement but no sin bearing[2] – no imputation of sin – no outpoured wrath on account of sin. How can we know this? Because it was all consumed on the altar. Had there been anything of sin-bearing, it would have been consumed outside the camp (comp. Lev. 4:11, 12 with Heb. 13:11).

But, in the meat offering, there was not even a question of blood shedding. We simply find, in it, a beauteous type of Christ, as He lived and walked and served, down here, on this earth. This one fact is, of itself, sufficient to draw the spiritual mind to the close and prayerful consideration of this offering. The pure and perfect manhood of our blessed Lord is a theme which must command the attention of every true Christian. It is to be feared that great looseness of thought prevails, in reference to this holy mystery. The expressions which one sometimes hears and reads are sufficient to prove that the fundamental doctrine of incarnation is not laid hold of as the word presents it. Such expressions may, very probably, proceed from misapprehension as to the real nature of His relations, and as to the true character of His sufferings; but, from what cause soever they arise, they should be judged in the light of holy scripture, and rejected. Doubtless, many who make use of those expressions, would recoil, with just horror and indignation, from the real doctrine contained in them, were it put before them in its broad and true characters; and, for this reason, one should be sorry to attribute unsoundness as to fundamental truth, where it may merely be inaccuracy of statement.

The humanity of Christ

There is, however, one consideration which should weigh heavily in the estimation of every Christian, and that is, the vital nature of the doctrine of Christ's humanity. It lies at the very foundation of Christianity; and, for this reason, Satan has diligently sought, from the beginning, to lead people astray in reference to it. Almost all the leading errors which have found their way into the professing church disclose the Satanic purpose to undermine the truth as to the Person of Christ. And even when earnest, godly men have sought to combat those errors, they have, in many cases, plunged into errors on the opposite side. Hence, therefore, the need of close adherence to the veritable words which the Holy Ghost has made use of in unfolding this profound and most sacred mystery. Indeed, I believe that, in every case, subjection to the authority of holy scripture, and the energy of the divine life in the soul, will prove effectual safeguards against every complexion of error. It does not require high theological attainments to enable a soul to keep clear of error with respect to the doctrine of Christ. If only the word of Christ be dwelling richly, and "the Spirit of Christ" be in energy, in the soul, there will be no room for Satan to thrust in his dark and horrible suggestions. If the heart be delighting in the Christ which Scripture unfolds, it will, assuredly, shrink from the false Christs which Satan would introduce. If we are feeding upon God's reality, we shall unhesitatingly reject Satan's counterfeit. This is the best possible way in which to escape the entanglements of error, in every shape and character. "The sheep *hear his voice,* and . . . follow him: for they *know His voice.* And a stranger will they not follow, but will flee from him; *for they know not the voice of strangers"* (John 10:4,

5). It is not, by any means, needful to be acquainted with the voice of a stranger, in order to turn away from it; all we require is to know the voice of "the good Shepherd." This will secure us against the ensnaring influence of every strange sound. While, therefore, I feel called upon to warn the reader against strange sounds, in reference to the divine mystery of Christ's humanity, I do not deem it needful to discuss such sounds, but would rather seek, through grace, to arm him against them, by unfolding the doctrine of Scripture on the subject.

There are few things in which we exhibit more failure than in maintaining vigorous communion with the perfect manhood of the Lord Jesus Christ. Hence it is that we suffer so much from vacancy, barrenness, restlessness, and wandering. Did we but enter, with a more artless faith, into the truth that there is a real Man, at the right hand of the Majesty in the heavens – One whose sympathy is perfect, whose love is fathomless, whose power is omnipotent, whose wisdom is infinite, whose resources are exhaustless, whose riches are unsearchable, whose ear is open to our every breathing, whose hand is open to our every need, whose heart is full of unspeakable love and tenderness towards us – how much more happy and elevated we should be, and how much more independent of creature streams, through what channel soever they may flow! There is nothing the heart can crave which we have not in Jesus. Does it long for genuine sympathy? Where can it find it, save in Him who could mingle His tears with those of the bereaved sisters of Bethany? Does it desire the enjoyment of sincere affection? It can only find it in that heart which told forth its love in drops of blood. Does it seek the protection of real power? It has but to look to Him who made the world. Does it feel the need of unerring wisdom to guide? Let it betake itself to Him who is wisdom personified, and "who of God is made unto us wisdom." In one word, we have all in Christ. The divine mind and the divine affections have found a perfect object in "the man Christ Jesus;" and, surely, if there is that in the Person of Christ which can perfectly satisfy God, there is that which ought to satisfy us, and which will satisfy us, in proportion as, by the grace of the Holy Ghost, we walk in communion with God.

The perfect man

The Lord Jesus Christ was the only perfect man that ever trod this earth. He was all perfect – perfect in thought, perfect in word, perfect in action. In Him every moral quality met in divine and, therefore, perfect proportion. No one feature preponderated. In Him were exquisitely blended a majesty which overawed, and a gentleness which gave perfect ease in His presence. The Scribes and the Pharisees met His withering rebuke; while the poor Samaritan and "the woman that was a sinner," found themselves unaccountably, yet irresistibly, attracted to Him. No one feature displaced another, for all was in fair and comely proportion. This may be traced in every scene of His perfect life. He could say, in reference to five thousand hungry people, "Give ye them to eat;" and, when they were filled, He could say, "Gather up the fragments that remain, that nothing be lost." The benevolence and the economy are both perfect and neither interferes with the other. Each shines in its own proper sphere. He could not send unsatisfied hungry away; neither could He suffer a single fragment of God's creatures to be wasted. He would meet, with a full and liberal hand, the need of the human family, and, when that was done, He would carefully treasure up every atom. The self-same hand that was widely open to every form of human need was firmly closed against all prodigality. There was nothing niggardly nor yet extravagant in the character of the perfect, the heavenly Man.

What a lesson for us! How often, with us, does benevolence resolve itself into an unwarrantable profusion! And, on the other hand, how often is our economy marred by the exhibition of a miserly spirit! At times, too, our niggard hearts refuse to open themselves to the full extent of the need which presents itself before us; while, at other times, we squander, through a wanton extravagance, that which might satisfy many a needy fellow-creature. Oh! my reader, let us carefully study the divine picture set before us in the life of the "Man Christ Jesus." How refreshing and strengthening to "the inward man" to be occupied with Him who was perfect in all His ways, and who "in all things must have the pre-eminence!"

See Him in the garden of Gethsemane. There, He kneels in the profound depths of a humility which none but Himself could exhibit; but yet, before the traitor's band, He exhibits a self-possession and majesty which cause them to go backward and fall to the ground. His deportment before God is prostration; before His judges and accusers, unbending dignity. All is perfect. The self-emptiness and the self-possession, the prostration and the dignity, are all divine.

So also, when we contemplate the beauteous combination of His divine and human relations, the same perfectness is observable. He could say, "How was it that ye sought me? Wist ye not that I must be about my Father's business?" And, at the same time, He could go down to Nazareth, and there set an example of perfect subjection to parental authority (see Luke 2:49-51). He could say to His mother, "Woman, what have I to do with thee?" And yet, when passing through the unutterable agony of the cross, He could tenderly commit that mother to the care of the beloved disciple. In the former case, He separated Himself in the spirit of perfect Nazariteship to accomplish His Father's will; while, in the latter, He gave expression to the tender feelings of the perfect human heart. The devotion of the Nazarite and the affection of the man were both perfect. Neither was permitted to interfere with the other. Each shone with undimmed lustre in its proper sphere.

Now, the shadow of this perfect man passes before us in the "fine flour" which formed the basis of the meat offering. There was not so much as a single coarse grain. There was nothing uneven – nothing unequal – nothing rough to the touch. No matter what pressure came from without, there was always an even surface. He was never ruffled by any circumstance or set of circumstances. He never had to retrace a step, or recall a word. Come what might, He always met it in that perfect evenness which is so strikingly typified by the "fine flour."

In all these things, it is needless to say, He stands in marked contrast with His most honoured and devoted servants. For example, Moses, though "the meekest man in all the earth," yet "spoke unadvisedly with his lips." In Peter, we find a zeal and an energy which, at times, proved too much for the occasion; and, again, a cowardice which shrank from the place of testimony and reproach. There was the assertion of a devotedness which, when the time for action arrived, was not forthcoming. John, who breathed so much of the atmosphere of the immediate presence of Christ, exhibited, at times, a sectarian and an intolerant spirit. In Paul, the most devoted of servants, we observe considerable unevenness. He uttered words to the high priest which he had to recall. He sent a letter to the Corinthians, of which at first he repented, and afterwards repented not. In all, we find some flaw, save in Him who is "the fairest among ten thousand, and altogether lovely."

In the examination of the meat offering, it will give clearness and simplicity to our thoughts to consider, first, the materials of which it was composed; secondly, the various forms in which it was presented; and, thirdly, the persons who partook of it.

Fine flour mingled with oil

As to the materials, the "fine flour" may be regarded as the basis of the offering; and, in it, we have a type of Christ's humanity, wherein every perfection met. Every virtue was there, and ready for effectual action, in due season. The Holy Ghost delights to unfold the glories of Christ's Person, to set Him forth in all His peerless excellence – to place Him before us in contrast with all beside. He contrasts Him with Adam, even in his very best and highest state; as we read, "the first man is of the earth, earthy: the second man is the Lord from heaven" (1 Cor. 15:47). The first Adam, even in his unfallen condition, was "of the earth;" but the second Man was "the Lord from heaven."

The "oil," in the meat offering, is a type of the Holy Ghost. But, inasmuch as the oil is applied in a twofold way, so we have the Holy Ghost presented in a double aspect, in *connexion* with the *incarnation* of the Son. The fine flour was "*mingled*" with oil; and there was oil "*poured*" upon it. Such was the type; and, in the Antitype, we see the blessed Lord Jesus Christ, first, "*conceived*," and then "*anointed*," by the Holy Ghost (comp. Matt. 1:18, 23, with chap. 3:16). This is divine! The accuracy, which is here so apparent, draws forth the soul's admiration. It is one and the same Spirit which records the ingredients of the type, and gives us the facts in the Antitype. The one who has detailed for us, with such amazing precision, the types and shadows of the Book of Leviticus, has also given us the glorious subject thereof, in the gospel narratives. The same Spirit breathes through the pages of the Old and those of the New Testament, and enables us to see how exactly the one corresponds with the other.

The conception of Christ's humanity, by the Holy Ghost, in the womb of the Virgin, unfolds one of the most profound mysteries, which can possibly engage the attention of the renewed mind. It is most fully set forth in Luke's Gospel; and this is entirely characteristic, inasmuch as, throughout that Gospel, it would seem to be the special object of the Holy Ghost to unfold, in His own divinely-touching manner, "the Man Christ Jesus." In Matthew, we have "the Son of Abraham – the Son of David." In Mark, we have the Divine Servant – the Heavenly Workman. In John, we have "the Son of God" – the Eternal Word – the Life – the Light, by whom all things were made. But the great theme of the Holy Ghost in Luke is "the Son of man."

When the angel Gabriel had announced to Mary the dignity which was about to be conferred upon her, in connexion with the great work of incarnation, she, not in a spirit of scepticism, but of honest ignorance, enquired, "How shall this be, seeing I know not a man?" It, manifestly, seemed to her that the birth of this glorious Person who was about to appear should be according to the ordinary principles of generation; and this her thought is made the occasion, in the exceeding goodness of God, of developing much valuable light, in reference to the cardinal truth of incarnation. The angel's reply to the virgin's question is unspeakably interesting, and cannot be too closely considered. "And the angel answered and said unto her, The Holy Ghost shall come upon thee, and the power of the Highest shall overshadow thee; *therefore* also that *holy thing* which shall be born of thee shall be called the Son of God." (Luke 1:35)

From this magnificent passage, we learn that the human body into which the eternal Son entered, was formed by "the power of the Highest." "A body hast *thou* prepared me" (comp. Psalm 40:6 with Heb. 10:5). It was a real human body – real "flesh and blood." There is no possible foundation here, on which Gnosticism or mysticism can base its vapid and worthless theories – no warrant for the cold abstractions of the former, or the misty fancies of the latter. All is deep, solid, and divine reality. The very thing which our hearts needed – the very thing which God has given. The early promise had declared that "the seed of the woman shall bruise the serpent's head," and none but a real man could accomplish this prediction – one whose nature was as real as it was pure and incorruptible. "Thou shalt conceive in thy womb," said the angelic messenger, "and bring forth a son."[3] And, then, lest there should be any room for an error, in reference to the mode of this conception, he adds such words as prove unanswerably, that "the flesh and blood" of which the Eternal Son "took part," while absolutely real, was absolutely incapable of receiving, of retaining, or of communicating a single taint. The humanity of the Lord Jesus was, emphatically, *"that holy thing."* And, inasmuch as it was wholly without taint, it was wholly without a seed of mortality. We cannot think of mortality, save in connexion with sin; and Christ's humanity had nought to do with sin, either personally or relatively. Sin was imputed to Him, on the cross, where He was "made sin for us." But the meat offering is not the type of Christ as a sin-bearer. It foreshadows Him in His perfect life, here below – a life in which He suffered, no doubt, but not as a sin-bearer – not as a substitute – not at the hand of God. Let this be distinctly noted. Neither in the burnt offering, nor in the meat offering, have we Christ as a sin-bearer. In the latter, we see Him *living*; and, in the former, we see Him *dying*; but, in neither, is there a question of the imputation of sin, nor of enduring the wrath of God, on account of sin. In short, to present Christ as the sinner's substitute any where else save on the cross, is to rob His life of all its divine beauty and excellency, and to displace the cross altogether. Moreover, it would involve the types of Leviticus in hopeless confusion.

The truth concerning the person of Christ

I would, at this point, solemnly admonish my reader, that he cannot be too jealous in reference to the vital truth of the Person and the relations of the Lord Jesus Christ. If there be error as to this, there is no security as to anything. God cannot give the sanction of His presence to anything that has not this truth for its foundation. The Person of Christ is the living – the divine centre round which the Holy Ghost carries on all His operations. Let slip the truth as to Him, and you are like a vessel broken from its moorings, and carried, without rudder or compass, over the wild watery waste, and in imminent danger of being dashed to fragments upon the rocks of Arianism, Infidelity, or Atheism. Question the eternal Sonship of Christ – question His Deity – question His unspotted humanity, and you have opened the floodgate for a desolating tide of deadly error to rush in. Let no one imagine, for a moment, that this is a mere matter to be discussed by learned theologians – a curious question – a recondite mystery   a point about which we may lawfully differ. No; it is a vital, fundamental truth, to be held in the power of the Holy Ghost, and maintained at the expense of all beside – yea, to be confessed, under all circumstances, whatever may be the consequences.

What we want is simply to receive into our hearts, by the grace of the Holy Spirit, the Father's revelation of the Son, and, then, our souls shall be effectually preserved from the snares of the enemy, let them take what shape they may. He may speciously cover the trap of Arianism or Socinianism with the grass and leaves of a most plausible and attractive system of interpretation; but directly the devoted heart discovers what this system attempts to make of the Blessed One to whom it owes everything, and where it attempts to put Him, it finds but little difficulty in sending it back to where it manifestly came from. We can well afford to do without human theories; but we can never do without Christ – the Christ of God – the Christ of God's affections – the Christ of God's counsels – the Christ of God's word.

The Lord Jesus Christ, God's eternal Son, a distinct Person in the glorious Trinity, God manifest in the flesh, God over all, blessed for ever, assumed a body which was inherently and divinely pure, holy, and without the possibility of taint – absolutely free from every seed or principle of sin and mortality. Such was the humanity of Christ, that He could at any moment, so far as He was personally concerned, have returned to heaven, from whence He had come, and to which He belonged. I speak not here of the eternal counsels of redeeming love, or of the unswerving love of the heart of Jesus – His love to God – His love to God's elect, or of the work that was needful to ratify God's everlasting covenant with the seed of Abraham, and with the whole creation. Christ's own words teach us that "it behoved Him to suffer, and to rise from the dead the third day" (Luke 24:46). It was necessary that He should suffer, in order to the full manifestation and perfect accomplishment of the great mystery of redemption. It was His gracious purpose to "bring many sons unto glory." He would not "abide alone," and, therefore, He, as the "corn of wheat," should "fall into the ground and die." The more fully we enter into the truth of His Person, the more fully do we apprehend the grace of His work.

When the apostle speaks of Christ's being "made perfect through suffering," it is as "the Captain of our salvation" that he contemplates Him, and not as the eternal Son who, as regards His own abstract Person and nature, was divinely perfect and could not possibly have anything added to Him. So, also, when He Himself says, "Behold I cast out devils, and I do cures today and tomorrow, and the third day I shall be perfected" (Luke 13:32), He refers to His being perfected, in the power of resurrection, as the Accomplisher of the entire work of redemption. So far as He was personally concerned, He could say, even on His way forth from the garden of Gethsemane, "Thinkest thou that I cannot now pray to my Father, and he shall presently give me more than twelve legions of angels? But how then shall the scriptures be fulfilled, that thus it must be?" (Matt. 26:53, 54).

It is well that the soul be clear as to this – well to have a divine sense of the harmony which exists between those scriptures which present Christ in the essential dignity of His Person, and the divine purity of His nature, and those which present Him in His relation with His people, and as accomplishing the great work of redemption. At times we find both these things combined, in the same passage, as in Heb. 5:8, 9: "Though *he were a Son,* yet learned he obedience by the things which he suffered; and being made perfect, he became the author of eternal salvation to all them that obey him." We must, however, bear in mind that not one of those relations into which Christ, voluntarily, entered – whether as the expression of divine love to a lost world, or the Servant of the divine counsels – not one of these could possibly interfere with the essential purity, excellency, and glory of His Person. "The Holy Ghost came upon" the virgin, and "the power of the Highest overshadowed her;" and "therefore that holy thing which was born of her was called the Son of God." Most magnificent unfolding, this, of the deep secret of

Christ's pure and perfect humanity – the great antitype of the *"fine flour mingled with oil!"*

And here, let me observe, that, between humanity, as seen in the Lord Jesus Christ, and humanity, as seen in us, there could be no union. That which is pure could never coalesce with that which is impure. That which is incorruptible could never unite with that which is corruptible. The spiritual and the carnal – the heavenly and the earthly – could never combine. Hence, therefore, it follows that incarnation was not, as some have attempted to teach, Christ's taking our fallen nature into union with Himself. If He could have done this, there would have been no need of the death of the cross. He needed not, in that case, to feel "straitened" until the baptism was accomplished – the corn of wheat did not need to "fall into the ground and die." This is a point of grave moment. Let the spiritual mind ponder it deeply. Christ could not possibly take sinful humanity into union with Himself. Hear what the angel saith to Joseph, in the first chapter of Matthew's gospel. "Joseph, thou son of David, fear not to take unto thee Mary thy wife; *for that which is conceived in her is of the Holy Ghost.*" See now Joseph's natural sensibilities, as well as Mary's pious ignorance, are made the occasion of a fuller unfolding of the holy mystery of Christ's humanity; and also of guarding that humanity against all the blasphemous attacks of the enemy!

How, then, is it that believers are united to Christ? Is it in incarnation or resurrection? In resurrection, assuredly. How is this proved? "Except a corn of wheat fall into the ground and die, it abideth *alone*" (John 12:24). At this side of death, there could be no union between Christ and His people. It is in the power of a new life that believers are united to Christ. They were dead *in sin,* and He, in perfect grace, came down, and, though Himself pure and sinless, was "made sin" – "died *unto sin*" – put it away – rose triumphant over it, and all pertaining to it, and, in resurrection, became the Head of a new race. Adam was the head of the old creation, which fell with him. Christ, by dying, put Himself under the full weight of His people's condition, and having perfectly met all that was against them, rose, victorious over all, and carried them with Him into the new creation, of which He is the glorious Head and Centre. Hence, we read, "He that is joined unto the Lord is one spirit" (1 Cor. 6:17). "But God, who is rich in mercy, for his great love wherewith he loved us, even when we were *dead in sins*, hath quickened us *together with Christ*, (by grace ye are saved;) and hath raised us up together, and made us sit together in heavenly places in Christ Jesus" (Eph. 2:4-6). "For we are members of his body, of his flesh, and of his bones." (Eph. 5:30.) "And you *being dead in your sins,* and the uncircumcision of your flesh, *hath he quickened together with him,* having forgiven you all trespasses." (Col. 2:13.)

Passages might be multiplied, but the above are amply sufficient to prove that it was not in incarnation, but in death, that Christ took a position in which His people could be "quickened together with him." Does this seem unimportant to the reader? Let him examine it in the light of Scripture. Let him weigh all the consequences. Let him view it in its bearing upon Christ's Person, upon His life, upon His death, upon our condition, by nature, in the old creation, and our place, through mercy, in the new. Let him consider it thus, and, I feel persuaded, he will no longer regard it as a light matter. Of one thing, at least, he may rest assured, that the writer of these pages would not pen a single line to prove this point, did he not consider it to be fraught with the most momentous results. The whole of divine revelation so hangs together – is so adjusted by the hand of the Holy Ghost – is so consistent in all its parts, that, if one truth be disturbed, the entire arch is injured. This consideration should suffice to produce, in the mind of every Christian, a holy caution lest, by some rude touch, he mar the beauteous superstructure. Every stone must be left in its divinely appointed place; and, unquestionably, the truth as to Christ's Person is the keystone of the arch.

Fine flour anointed with oil

Having thus endeavoured to unfold the truth typified by the

"fine flour *mingled* with oil," we may remark another point of much interest in the expression, "He shall *pour* oil upon it." In this we have a type of the anointing of the Lord Jesus Christ, by the Holy Ghost. The body of the Lord Jesus was not merely formed, mysteriously, by the Holy Ghost, but that pure and holy vessel was also anointed for service, by the same power. "And it came to pass when all the people were baptised, and Jesus also being baptised and praying, the heaven was opened, and the Holy Ghost descended in a bodily shape, as a dove, upon him, and there was a voice from heaven, saying, Thou art my beloved Son, in thee I am well pleased" (Luke 3:21, 22).

The anointing of the Lord Jesus, by the Holy Ghost, previous to His entrance upon His public ministry, is of immense practical importance to every one who really desires to be a true and an effectual servant of God. Though conceived, as to His manhood, by the Holy Ghost; though, in His own proper Person, "God manifest in the flesh;" though embodying, in Himself, all the fullness of the Godhead; yet, be it well observed, when coming forth, as man, to do the will of God, on the earth, whatever that will might be, whether preaching the gospel, teaching in the synagogues, healing the sick, cleansing the leper, casting out devils, feeding the hungry, or raising the dead, He did all by the Holy Ghost. That holy and heavenly vessel in which God the Son was pleased to appear in this world, was formed, filled, anointed, and led by the Holy Ghost.

What a deep and holy lesson for us! A most needful and salutary lesson! How prone are we to run unsent! How prone to act in the mere energy of the flesh! How much of that which looks like ministry is only the restless and unhallowed activity of a nature which has never been measured and judged in the divine presence! Truly, we need to contemplate, more closely, our divine "meat offering" – to understand, more fully, the meaning of the "fine flour anointed with oil." We need to meditate, more deeply, upon Christ Himself, who, though possessing, in His own Person, divine power, nevertheless, did all His work, wrought all His miracles, and, finally, offered himself without spot to God, by the eternal Spirit. He could say, "I, by the Spirit of God, cast out devils."

Nothing is of any value save that which is wrought by the power of the Holy Ghost. A man may write; but, if his pen be not guided and used by the Holy Ghost, his lines will produce no permanent result. A man may speak; but, if his lips be not anointed by the Holy Ghost, his word will not take permanent root. This is a solemn consideration, and, if properly weighed, would lead to much watchfulness over ourselves, and much earnest dependence upon the Holy Ghost. What we need is thorough self-emptiness, so that there may be room left for the Spirit to act by us. It is impossible that a man full of himself can be the vessel of the Holy Ghost. Such an one must, first, be emptied of himself, and, then, the Spirit can use him. When we contemplate the Person and ministry of the Lord Jesus, we see how that, in every scene and circumstance, He acted by the direct power of the Holy Ghost. Having taken His place, as man, down here, He showed that men should not only live by the Word, but act by the Spirit of God. Even though, as man, His will was perfect – His thoughts, His words, His acts, all perfect, yet would He not act, save by the direct authority of the Word, and by the direct power of the Holy Ghost. Oh! that in this, as in every thing else, we could, more closely, more faithfully, follow in His steps. Then, indeed, would our ministry be more effective, our testimony more fruitful, our whole course more entirely to the glory of God.

Frankincense

The next ingredient in the meat offering demanding our consideration is "the frankincense." As has been remarked, the "fine flour" was the basis of the offering. The "oil" and "frankincense" were the two leading adjuncts; and, truly, the connexion between these two latter is most instructive. The "oil" typifies the *power* of Christ's ministry; the "frankincense" typifies the *object* thereof. The former teaches us that He did everything by the Spirit of God; the latter that He did everything to the glory of God. The frankincense presents that in the life of Christ, which was, exclusively, for God. This is evident from the second verse: "And he shall bring it (the meat offering) to Aaron's sons, the priests: and he shall take thereout his handful of the flour thereof, and of the oil thereof, with *all the frankincense thereof;* and the priest shall burn the memorial of it upon the altar, to be an offering made by fire, of a sweet savour unto the Lord." Thus was it in the true meat offering – the Man Christ Jesus. There was that in His blessed life which was exclusively for God. Every thought, every word, every look, every act of His, emitted a fragrance which went up, immediately, to God. And, as in the type, it was "the fire of the altar" that drew forth the sweet odour of the frankincense; so, in the Antitype, the more he was "tried," in all the scenes and circumstances of His blessed life, the more fully was it manifested that, in His manhood, there was nothing that could not ascend, as an odour of a sweet smell, to the throne of God. If, in the burnt offering, we behold Christ "offering himself, without spot, to God;" in the meat offering, we behold Him presenting all the intrinsic excellence and perfect actings of His human nature to God. A perfect, a self-emptied, an obedient man, on the earth, doing the will of God, acting by the authority of the Word, and by the power of the Spirit, had a sweet odour which could only be for divine acceptance. The fact that "all the frankincense" was consumed on the altar, fixes its import in the simplest manner.

Salt

It now only remains for us to consider an ingredient which was an inseparable adjunct of the meat offering, namely, "*salt*." "And every oblation of thy meat offering shalt thou season with salt; neither shalt thou suffer the salt of the covenant of thy God to be lacking from thy meat offering: with all thine offerings thou shalt offer salt." The expression, "salt of the covenant," sets forth the enduring character of that covenant. God Himself has so ordained it, in all things, that nought can ever alter it – no influence can ever corrupt it. In a spiritual and practical point of view, it is impossible to over-estimate the value of such an ingredient. "Let your conversation be always with grace, seasoned with *salt*." The whole conversation of the Perfect Man exhibited the power of this principle. His words were not merely words of grace, but words of pungent power – words divinely adapted to preserve from all taint and corrupting influence. He never uttered a word which was not redolent with "frankincense" and seasoned with salt. The former was most acceptable to God, the latter most profitable for man.

Sometimes, alas! man's corrupt heart and vitiated taste could not tolerate the pungency of the divinely salted meat offering. Witness, for example, the scene in the synagogue of Nazareth (Luke 4:16-29). The people could "bear him witness, and wonder at the *gracious* words which proceeded out of his mouth;" but when He proceeded to season those words with *salt,* which was so needful, in order to preserve them from the corrupting influence of their national pride, they would fain have cast Him over the brow of the hill whereon their city was built.

So, also, in Luke 14, when His words of "grace" had drawn "great multitudes" after Him, He instantly throws in the "salt," by setting forth, in words of holy faithfulness, the sure results of following Him. "Come, for all things are now ready." Here was the "grace." But, then, "whosoever forsaketh not all that he hath, cannot be my disciple." Here was the "salt." Grace is attractive; but "salt is good." Gracious discourse may be popular; but salted discourse never will. The pure gospel of the grace of God may, at certain times, and under certain circumstances, be run after by "the multitude" for a while; but when the "salt" of a fervid and faithful application is introduced, it will soon thin the benches of all save such as are brought under the power of the word.

Leaven

Having thus considered the ingredients which composed the meal offering, we shall now refer to those which were excluded from it.

The first of these was "leaven." "No meat offering which ye shall bring unto the Lord, shall be made with leaven." This ingredient is used throughout the inspired volume, without so much as a single exception, as the symbol of *evil*. In chap. 23 of our book, which will be noticed in due course, we find leaven admitted in the two loaves which were offered on the day of Pentecost; but from the meat offering, leaven was most sedulously excluded. There was to be nothing sour: nothing that would puff up, nothing expressive of evil in that which typified "the Man Christ Jesus." In Him, there could be nothing savouring of nature's sourness, nothing turgid, nothing inflated. All was pure, solid, and genuine. His word might, at times, cut to the quick; but it was never sour. His style never rose above the occasion. His deportment ever exhibited the deep reality of one walking in the immediate presence of God.

In those who bear the name of Jesus, we know, too well, alas! how leaven shows itself in all its properties and effects. There has been but one untainted sheaf of human fruit – but one perfectly unleavened meat offering; and, blessed be God, that one is ours – ours to feed upon in the sanctuary of the divine presence, in fellowship with God. No exercise can be more truly edifying and refreshing for the renewed mind than to dwell upon the unleavened perfectness of Christ's humanity – to contemplate the life and ministry of One who was, absolutely and essentially, unleavened. In all His springs of thought, affection, desire, and imagination, there was not so much as a particle of leaven. He was the sinless, spotless, perfect Man. And the more we are enabled, by the power of the Spirit, to enter into all this, the deeper will be our experience of the grace which led this perfect One to place Himself under the full consequences of His people's sins, as

He did when He hung upon the cross. This thought, however, belongs entirely to the sin-offering aspect of our blessed Lord. In the meat offering, sin is not in question. It is not the type of a sin-bearer, but of a real, perfect, unblemished Man, conceived and anointed by the Holy Ghost, possessing an unleavened nature, and living an unleavened life, down here; emitting, ever, to God-ward, the fragrance of His own personal excellency, and maintaining, amongst men, a deportment characterised by "grace seasoned with salt."

Honey

But there was another ingredient, as positively excluded from the meat offering as "leaven," and that was "honey." "For ye shall burn no leaven, *nor any honey,* in any offering of the Lord made by fire" (ver. 11). Now, as "leaven" is the expression of that which is positively and palpably *evil,* in nature, we may regard "honey" as the significant symbol of that which is apparently *sweet* and attractive. Both are disallowed of God – both were carefully excluded from the meat offering – both were unfit for the altar. Men may undertake, like Saul, to distinguish between what is "vile and refuse," and what is not; but the judgment of God ranks the delicate Agag with the vilest of the sons of Amalek. No doubt, there are some good moral qualities in man which must be taken for what they are worth. "Hast thou found *honey,* eat so much as is convenient;" but, be it remembered, it found no place in the meat offering, nor in its Antitype. There was the fullness of the Holy Ghost; there was the fragrant odour of the frankincense; there was the preservative virtue of "the salt of the covenant." All these things accompanied the "fine flour," in the Person of the true "meat offering;" but "no honey."

What a lesson for the heart is here! yea, what a volume of wholesome instruction! The blessed Lord Jesus knew how to give nature and its relationships their proper place. He knew how much "honey" was "convenient." He could say to His mother, "Wist ye not that I must be about my Father's business?" And yet He could say, again, to the beloved disciple, "Behold thy mother." In other words, nature's claims were never allowed to interfere with the presentation to God of all the energies of Christ's perfect manhood. Mary and others too might have thought that her human relation to the blessed One gave her some peculiar claim or influence, on merely natural grounds. "There came, then, his brethren ('after the flesh') and his mother, and standing without, sent unto him, calling him. And the multitude sat about him; and they said unto him, Behold, thy mother and thy brethren without seek for thee." What was the reply of the true Meat Offering? Did He, at once, abandon His work, in order to respond to nature's call? By no means. Had He done so, it would have been to mingle "honey" with the meat offering, which could not be. The honey was faithfully excluded, on this, as on every occasion, when God's claims were to be attended to, and instead thereof, the power of the Spirit, the odour of the "frankincense," and the virtues of the "salt" were blessedly exhibited. "And he answered them, saying, Who is my mother, or my brethren? And he looked round about on them which sat about him, and said, Behold my mother and my brethren! For whosoever shall do the will of God, the same is my brother, and my sister, and my mother"[4] (Mark 3:31-35).

There are few things which the servant of Christ finds more difficult than to adjust, with spiritual accuracy, the claims of natural relationship, so as not to suffer them to interfere with the claims of the Master. In the case of our blessed Lord, as we know, the adjustment was divine. In our case, it often happens that divinely-recognised duties are openly neglected for what we imagine to be the service of Christ. The doctrine of God is constantly sacrificed to the apparent work of the gospel. Now, it is well to remember that true devotedness always starts from a point within which all godly claims are fully secured. If I hold a situation which demands my services from ten till four every day, I have no right to go out to visit or preach, during those hours. If I am in business, I am bound to maintain the integrity of that business, in a godly manner. I have no right to run hither and thither preaching, while my business, at home, lies in sixes and sevens, bringing great reproach on the holy doctrine of God. A man may say, "I feel myself called to preach the gospel, and I find my situation, or my business, a clog." Well, *if you are divinely called and fitted* for the work of the gospel, and that you cannot combine the two things, then resign your situation, or wind up your business, in a godly manner, and go forth, in the name of the Lord. But, clearly, so long as I hold a situation, or carry on a business, my work in the gospel must begin from a point within which the godly claims of such business or situation are fully responded to. This is devotedness. Anything else is confusion, however well intended. Blessed be God, we have a perfect example before us in the life of the Lord Jesus, and ample guidance, for the new man, in the word of God; so that we need not make any mistakes, in the varied relationships which we may be called, in the providence of God, to fill, or as to the various claims which God's moral government has set up, in connexion with such relationships.

A sweet savour

II. The second point, in our theme, is the mode in which the meat offering was prepared. This was, as we read, by the action of fire. It was "baken in an oven" – "baken in a pan" – or "baken in a frying pan." The process of baking suggests the idea of suffering. But inasmuch as the meat offering is called "a sweet savour" – a term which is never applied to the sin offering, or trespass offering – it is evident that there is no thought of suffering for sin – no thought of suffering the wrath of God on account of sin – no thought of suffering at the hand of infinite Justice, as the sinner's substitute. The two ideas of "sweet savour" and suffering for sin, are wholly incompatible, according to the Levitical economy. It would completely destroy the type of the meat offering, were we to introduce into it the idea of suffering for sin.

In contemplating the *life* of the Lord Jesus, which, as we have already remarked, is the special subject foreshadowed in the meat offering, we may notice three distinct kinds of suffering; namely, suffering for righteousness; suffering by the power of sympathy; and suffering, in anticipation.

Suffering for righteousness' sake

As the righteous Servant of God, He suffered in the midst of a scene in which all was contrary to Him; but this was the very opposite of suffering for sin. It is of the utmost importance to distinguish between these two kinds of suffering. The confounding of them must lead to serious error. Suffering as a righteous One, standing amongst men, on God's behalf, is one thing; and suffering instead of men, under the hand of God, is quite another. The Lord Jesus suffered for righteousness, during His *life*. He suffered for sin, in His *death*. During His life, man and Satan did their utmost; and, even at the cross, they put forth all their powers; but when all that they could do was done – when they had travelled, in their deadly enmity, to the utmost limit of human and diabolical opposition, there lay, far beyond a region of impenetrable gloom and horror into which the Sin-bearer had to travel, in the accomplishment of His work. During His life He ever walked in the unclouded light of the Divine countenance; but, on the cursed tree, the dark shadow of sin intervened, and shut out that light, and drew forth that mysterious cry, "My God, my God, why hast thou forsaken me?" This was a moment which stands absolutely alone, in the annals of eternity. From time to time, during the life of Christ, down here, heaven had opened to give forth the expression of divine complacency in Him; but on the cross God forsook Him, because He was making His soul an offering for sin. If Christ had been a sin-bearer all His life, then what was the difference between the cross and any other period? Why was He not forsaken of God during His entire course? What was the difference between Christ on the cross, and Christ on the holy mount of transfiguration? Was

He forsaken of God, on the mount? Was He a sin-bearer there? These are very simple questions, which should be answered by those who maintain the idea of a life of sin-bearing.

The plain fact is this, there was nothing either in Christ's humanity, or in the nature of His associations, which could possibly connect Him with sin, or wrath, or death. He was "made sin" on the cross; and there He endured the wrath of God, and there He gave up His life, as an all-sufficient atonement for sin; but nothing of this finds a place in the meat offering. True, we have the process of baking – the action of fire; but this is not the wrath of God. The meat offering was not a sin offering, but a "sweet savour" offering. Thus, its import is definitely fixed; and, moreover, the intelligent interpretation of it must ever guard, with holy jealousy, the precious truth of Christ's spotless humanity, and the true nature of His associations. To make Him, by the necessity of His birth, a sinbearer, or to place Him, thereby, under the curse of the law, and the wrath of God, is to contradict the entire truth of God, as to incarnation – truth announced by the angel, and repeated, again and again, by the inspired apostle. Moreover, it destroys the entire character and object of Christ's life, and robs the cross of its distinctive glory. It lowers the sense of what sin is, and of what atonement is. In one word, it removes the keystone of the arch of revelation, and lays all in hopeless ruin and confusion around us.

Suffering in sympathy

But, again, the Lord Jesus suffered by the power of sympathy; and this character of suffering unfolds to us the deep secrets of His tender heart. Human sorrow, and human misery ever touched a chord in that bosom of love. It was impossible that a perfect human heart could avoid feeling, according to its own divine sensibilities, the miseries which sin had entailed upon the human family. Though, personally free, both from the cause and the effect – though belonging to heaven, and living a perfect heavenly life, on the earth, yet did He descend, by the power of an intense sympathy, into the deepest depths of human sorrow; yea, He felt the sorrow, more keenly by far, than those who were the direct subjects thereof, inasmuch as His humanity was perfect. And, further, He was able to contemplate both the sorrow and its cause, according to their just measure and character, in the presence of God. He felt as none else could feel. His feelings – His affections – His sensibilities – His whole moral and mental constitution were perfect; and, hence, none can tell what such an One must have suffered, in passing through such a world as this. He beheld the human family struggling beneath the ponderous weight of guilt and wretchedness; He beheld the whole creation groaning under the yoke; the cry of the prisoner fell upon His ear; the tear of the widow met His view; bereavement and poverty touched His sensitive heart; sickness and death made Him "groan in the spirit;" His sympathetic sufferings were beyond all human conception.

I shall quote a passage for my reader, illustrative of that character of suffering to which we are now referring. "When the even was come, they brought unto him many that were possessed with devils: and he cast out the spirits with his word, and healed all that were sick; that it might be fulfilled which was spoken by Isaiah the prophet, saying, *Himself took our infirmities, and bare our sicknesses*" (Matt. 8:16, 17). This was entirely sympathetic – the power of fellow-feeling, which in Him was perfect. He had no sicknesses or infirmities of His own. Those things which are sometimes spoken of as "sinless infirmities," were, in His case, but the evidences of a veritable, a real, a perfect manhood. But by sympathy, by perfect fellow feeling, "He *took* our infirmities, and *bare* our sicknesses." None but a perfect man could have done this. We may feel for, and with, each other; but only Jesus could make human infirmity and sickness His own.

Now, had He been bearing all these things by the necessity of His birth, or of His relations with Israel and the human family, we should have lost all the beauty and preciousness of His voluntary sympathy. There could be no room for voluntary action when absolute necessity was laid upon Him. But, on the other hand, when we see His entire freedom, both personally and relatively, from human misery and that which produced it, we can enter into that perfect grace and compassion which led Him to "take our infirmities, and bear our sicknesses," in the power of true sympathy. There is, therefore, a very manifest difference between Christ's suffering as a voluntary sympathiser with human misery, and His sufferings as the sinner's substitute. The former are apparent throughout His entire *life*; the latter are confined to His *death*.

Suffering by anticipation

Finally, we have to consider Christ's sufferings, by anticipation. We find the dark shadow of the cross casting itself athwart His path, and producing a very keen order of suffering which, however, must be as clearly distinguished from His atoning suffering, as either His suffering for righteousness, or His suffering by sympathy. Let us take a passage, in proof: "And he came out, and went, as He was wont, to the mount of Olives; and his disciples also followed him. And when he was at the place, he said unto them, Pray that ye enter not into temptation. And he was withdrawn from them about a stone's cast, and kneeled down, and prayed, saying, Father, if thou be willing, remove this cup from me: nevertheless, not my will but thine, be done. And there appeared an angel unto him from heaven strengthening him. And being in an agony, he prayed more earnestly: and his sweat was as it were great drops of blood falling down to the ground" (Luke 22:39-44.). Again, we read, "And he took with him Peter and the two sons of Zebedee, and began to be sorrowful and very heavy. Then saith he unto them, My soul is exceeding sorrowful, even unto death: tarry ye here, and watch with me . . . he went away again the second time, and prayed, saying, O my Father, if this cup may not pass away from me, except I drink it, thy will be done" (Matt. 26:37-42.).

From these verses, it is evident, there was a something,

in prospect, which the blessed Lord had never encountered before. There was a "cup" being filled out for Him of which He had not yet drunk. If He had been a sin-bearer all His life, then why this intense "agony" at the thought of coming in contact with sin and enduring the wrath of God on account of sin? What was the difference between Christ, in Gethsemane, and Christ, at Calvary, if He were a sin-bearer all His life? There was a material difference! but it is because He was not a sin-bearer all His life. What is the difference? In Gethsemane, He was *anticipating* the cross! at Calvary, He was actually *enduring* it. In Gethsemane, "there appeared an angel unto him from heaven strengthening him;" at Calvary, He was forsaken of all. There was no angelic ministry there. In Gethsemane He addresses God as *"Father,"* thus enjoying the full communion of that ineffable relationship; but at Calvary, He cries, "My *God*, my *God,* why hast thou forsaken me?" Here the sin-bearer looks up, and beholds the throne of eternal Justice enveloped in dark clouds, and the countenance of inflexible Holiness averted from Him because He was being "made sin for us."

Communion with the sufferings of Christ

The reader will, I trust, find no difficulty in examining this subject for himself. He will be able to trace, in detail, the three characters of the *life*-sufferings of our blessed Lord, and to distinguish between them and His *death*-sufferings – His sufferings for sin. He will see how that, when man and Satan had done their utmost, there yet remained a character of suffering which was perfectly unique, namely, suffering, at the hand of God, on account of sin – suffering as the sinner's substitute. Until He came to the cross, He could ever look up and bask in the clear light of His Father's countenance. In the darkest hour, He found a sure resource above. His path down here was a rough one. How could it be otherwise, in a world where all was directly contrary to His pure and holy nature? He had to "endure the contradiction of singers against himself." He had to endure "the reproach of them that reproached God." What had He not to endure? He was misunderstood, misinterpreted, abused, maligned, accused of being mad, and of having a devil. He was betrayed, denied, deserted, mocked, buffeted, spit upon, crowned with thorns, cast out, condemned, and nailed between two malefactors. All these things He endured at the hand of man, together with all the unutterable terrors which Satan brought to bear upon His spirit; but let it be, once more, emphatically repeated, when man and Satan had exhausted their power and enmity, our blessed Lord and Saviour had to endure a something compared with which all the rest was as nothing, and that was the hiding of God's countenance – the three hours of darkness and awful gloom, during which He suffered what none but God could know.

Now, when scripture speaks of our having fellowship with Christ's sufferings, it refers, simply, to His sufferings for righteousness – his sufferings at the hand of man. Christ suffered for sin, that we might not have to suffer for it. He endured the wrath of God, that we might not have to endure it. This is the ground of our peace. But, as regards suffering from man, we shall always find that the more faithfully we follow in the footsteps of Christ, the more we shall suffer in this respect; but this is a matter of gift, a matter of privilege, a favour, a dignity (see Philip. 1:29, 30). To walk in the footsteps of Christ – to enjoy companionship with Him – to be thrown into a place of sympathy with Him, are privileges of the very highest order. Would that we all entered, more fully, into them! But, alas! we are too well content to do without them – too well satisfied, like Peter, to "follow afar off" – to keep aloof from a despised and suffering Christ. All this is, undoubtedly, our heavy loss. Had we only more fellowship with His sufferings, the crown would glisten, far more brightly, in our soul's vision. When we shrink from fellowship with Christ's sufferings, we rob ourselves of the deep joy of His present companionship, and also of the moral power of the hope of His future glory.

The priests' portion

III. Having considered the ingredients which composed the meat offering, and the various forms in which it was presented, it only remains for us to refer to the persons who partook of it. These were the head and members of the priestly house. "And that which is left of the meat offering shall be Aaron's and his sons: it is a thing most holy of the offerings of the Lord made by fire" (ver. 10). As in the burnt offering, we observed the sons of Aaron introduced as types of all true believers, not as convicted sinners, but as worshipping priests; so, in the meat offering, we find them feeding upon the remnant of that which had been laid, as it were, on the table of the God of Israel. This was a high and holy privilege. None but priests could enjoy it. This is set forth, with great distinctness, in "the law of the meat offering," which I shall here quote at length. "And this is the law of the meat offering: the sons of Aaron shall offer it before the Lord, before the altar. And he shall take of it his handful, of the flour of the meat offering, and of the oil thereof, and *all the frankincense* which is upon the meat offering, and shall burn it upon the altar for a sweet savour, even the memorial of it unto the Lord. And the remainder thereof shall Aaron and his sons eat: with *unleavened bread* shall it be eaten, *in the holy place;* in the court of the tabernacle of the congregation they shall eat it. It shall not be baken with leaven. I have given it unto them for their portion of my offerings made by fire; it is most holy, as is the sin offering, and as the trespass offering. *All the males* among the children of Aaron shall eat of it: it shall be a statute for ever in your generations, concerning the offerings of the Lord made by fire: *every one that toucheth them shall be holy"* (Lev. 6:14-18).

Here, then, we are furnished with a beauteous figure of the Church, feeding, "in the holy place," in the power of practical holiness, upon the perfections of "the Man Christ Jesus." This is our portion, through the grace of God; but, we must remember, it is to be eaten "with unleavened bread."

We cannot feed upon Christ if we are indulging in anything evil. "Every one that toucheth them shall be holy." Moreover, it must be "in the holy place." Our position, our practice, our persons, our associations, must be holy, ere we can feed upon the meat offering. Finally, it is, "all the males among the children of Aaron shall eat of it." That is to say, real priestly energy, according to the divine idea of it, is required, in order to enjoy this holy portion. Aaron's "*sons*" set forth the idea of *energy* in priestly action. His *"daughters," feebleness* therein (comp. Num. 18:8-13). There were some things which the sons could eat which the daughters could not. Our hearts should earnestly desire the highest measure of priestly energy, so that we may discharge the highest priestly functions, and partake of the highest order of priestly food.

In conclusion, let me add that, inasmuch as we are made, through grace, "partakers of the divine nature," we can, if living in the energy of that nature, walk in the footsteps of Him who is foreshadowed in the meat offering. If only we are self-emptied, our every act may emit a sweet odour to God. The smallest as well as the greatest services may, by the power of the Holy Ghost, present the fragrance of Christ. The paying of a visit, the writing of a letter, the public ministry of the word, giving a cup of cold water to a disciple, giving a penny to a pauper, yea, the common-place acts of eating and drinking – all may emit the sweet perfume of the name and grace of Jesus.

So, also, if only nature be kept in the place of death, there may be, in us, the exhibition of that which is not corruptible, even a conversation seasoned with the "salt" of abiding communion with God. But, in all these things, we fail and come short. We grieve the Holy Spirit of God in our ways. We are prone to self-seeking or men-pleasing, in our very best services, and we fail to "season" our conversation. Hence, our constant deficiency in the "oil," the "frankincense," and the "salt;" while, at the same time, there is the tendency to suffer the "leaven" or the "honey" of nature to make its appearance. There has been but one perfect "meat offering;" and, blessed be God, we are accepted in Him. We are the "sons" of the true Aaron; our place is in the sanctuary, where we can feed upon the holy portion. Happy place! Happy portion! May we enjoy them more than ever we have done! May our retirement of heart from all but Christ be more profound. May our gaze at Him be so intense, that we shall have no heart for the attractions of the scene around us, nor yet for the ten thousand petty circumstances, in our path, which would fret the heart and perplex the mind. May we rejoice in Christ, in the sunshine and in the darkness; when the gentle breezes of summer play around us, and when the storms of winter rage fiercely abroad; when passing over the surface of a placid lake, or tossed on the bosom of a stormy ocean. Thank God! "we have found him" who is to be our satisfying portion for ever. We shall spend eternity dwelling upon the divine perfections of the Lord Jesus. Our eyes shall never be averted from Him, when once we have seen Him as He is.

May the Spirit of God work mightily in us, to strengthen us, "in the inner man." May He enable us to feed upon that perfect Meat Offering, the memorial of which has been fed upon by God Himself! This is our holy and happy privilege. May we realise it, yet more fully!

---

[2] That is to say sin-bearing is not prominent. Of course, where there is atonement, sin must be in question.

[3] "But when the fullness of the time was come, God sent forth his Son, made of a woman, made under the law." (*genomenon ek gunaikos, genomenon hupo nomon.*) This is a most important passage inasmuch as it sets forth our blessed Lord as Son of God, and Son of man. "God sent forth *his* Son, made of a woman." Precious testimony.

[4] How important to see, in the above beautiful passage, that doing God's will brings the soul into a relationship with Christ, of which His brethren according to the flesh knew nothing, on merely natural grounds. It was as true, with respect to those brethren, as any one else, that "except a man be born again, he cannot see the kingdom of God." Mary would not have been saved by the mere fact of her being the mother of Jesus. She needed personal faith in Christ as much as any other member of Adam's fallen family. She needed to pass, by being born again, out of the old creation into the new. It was by treasuring up Christ's words in her heart that this blessed woman was saved. No doubt, she was "highly favoured" in being chosen as a vessel,

to such a holy office; but, then, as a lost sinner, she needed to "rejoice in God her Saviour," like any one else. She stands on the same platform, is washed in the same blood, clothed in the same righteousness, and will sing the same song, as all the rest of God's redeemed.

This simple fact will give additional force and clearness to a point already stated, namely, that incarnation was not Christ's taking our nature into union with Himself. This truth should be carefully pondered. It is fully brought out in 2 Cor. 5, "For the love of Christ constraineth us; because we thus judge, that if one died for all, then were all dead: and that he died for all that they which live should not henceforth live unto themselves, but unto him which died for them, and rose again. Wherefore henceforth know we no man after the flesh, yea, *though we have known Christ after the flesh, yet now henceforth know we him no more.* Therefore if any man be *in Christ*, he is a new creation: old things are passed away; behold all things are become new" (Ver. 14-17).

Chapter 3

THE PEACE OFFERING

The more closely we contemplate the offerings, the more fully do we see how that no one offering furnishes a complete view of Christ. It is only by putting all together, that anything like a just idea can be formed. Each offering, as might be expected, has features peculiar to itself. The peace offering differs from the burnt offering, in many points; and a clear understanding of the points in which any one type differs from the others, will be found to help much in the apprehension of its special import.

What distinguishes this sacrifice from the burnt offering

Thus, in comparing the peace offering with the burnt offering, we find that the threefold action of "flaying," "cutting it into its pieces," and "washing the inwards and legs" is entirely omitted; and this is quite in character. In the burnt offering, as we have seen, we find Christ offering Himself to, and accepted by God, and hence, the completeness of His self-surrender, and also the searching process to which He submitted Himself, had to be typified. In the peace offering, the leading thought is the communion of the worshipper. It is not Christ as enjoyed, exclusively, by God, but as enjoyed by the worshipper, in communion with God. Therefore it is that the whole line of action is less intense. No heart, be its love ever so elevated, could possibly rise to the height of Christ's devotedness to God, or of God's acceptance of Christ. None but God Himself could duly note the pulsations of that heart which throbbed in the bosom of Jesus; and, therefore, a type was needed to set forth that one feature of Christ's death, namely, His perfect devotedness therein to God. This type we have in the burnt offering, in which, alone, we observe the threefold action above referred to.

So, also, in reference to the character of the sacrifice. In the burnt offering, it should be "a male without blemish;" whereas, in the peace offering, it might be "a male or female," though equally "without blemish." The nature of Christ, whether we view Him as enjoyed exclusively by God, or by the worshipper in fellowship with God, must ever be one and the same. There can be no alteration in that. The only reason why "a female" was permitted in the peace offering, was because it was a question of the worshipper's capacity to enjoy that blessed One, who, in Himself, is "the same yesterday, today, and for ever" (Heb. 13).

Again, in the burnt offering, we read, "The priest shall burn *all;*" whereas, in the peace offering, *a part* only was burnt, that is, "the fat, the kidneys, and the caul." This makes it exceedingly simple. The most excellent portion of the sacrifice was laid on God's altar. The inward parts – the hidden energies – the tender sensibilities of the blessed Jesus, were devoted to God as the only One who could perfectly enjoy them. Aaron and his sons fed upon "the wave breast" and "the heave shoulder" (see carefully Lev. 7:28-36).[5] All the members of the priestly family, in communion with their head, had their proper portion of the peace offering. And now, all true believers constituted, by grace, priests unto God, can feed upon the *affections* and the *strength* of the true Peace Offering – can enjoy the happy assurance of having His loving heart and powerful shoulder to comfort and sustain them continually.[6] "This is the portion of the anointing of Aaron, and of the anointing of his sons, out of the offerings of the Lord made by fire, in the day when he presented them to minister unto the Lord in the priest's office; which the Lord commanded to be given them of the children of Israel, in the day that he anointed them by a statute for ever throughout their generations" (chap. 7:35, 36).

A portion in communion with God

All these are important points of difference between the burnt offering and the peace offering; and, when taken together, they set the two offerings, with great clearness, before the mind. There is something more in the peace offering than the abstract devotedness of Christ to the will of God. The worshipper is introduced; and that, not merely as a spectator, but as a participator – not merely to gaze, but to feed. This gives very marked character to this offering. When I look at the Lord Jesus in the burnt offering, I see Him as One whose heart was devoted to the one object of glorifying God and accomplishing His will. But when I see Him in the peace offering, I find One who has a place in His loving heart, and on His powerful shoulder, for a worthless, helpless sinner. In the burnt offering, the breast and shoulder, legs and inwards, head and fat, were all burnt on the altar – all went up as a sweet savour to God. But in the peace offering, that very portion that suits me is left for me. Nor am I left to feed, in solitude, on that which meets my individual need. By no means. I feed in communion – in communion with God, and in communion with my fellow priests. I feed, in the full and happy intelligence, that the selfsame sacrifice which feeds my soul has already refreshed the heart of God; and, moreover, that the same portion which feeds me feeds all my fellow worshippers. Communion is the order here – communion with God – the communion of saints. There was no such thing as isolation in the peace offering. God had His portion, and so had the priestly family.

Thus it is in connection with the Antitype of the peace offering. The very same Jesus who is the object of heaven's delight, is the spring of joy, of strength, and of comfort to every believing heart; and not only to every heart, in particular, but also to the whole church of God, in fellowship. God, in His exceeding grace, has given His people the very same object that He has Himself. "Truly our fellowship is with the Father, and with his Son Jesus Christ" (1 John 1). True, our thoughts of Jesus can never rise to the height of God's thoughts. Our estimation of such an object must ever fall far short of His; and, hence, in the type, the house of Aaron could not partake of the fat. But though we can never rise to the standard of the divine estimation of Christ's Person and sacrifice, it is, nevertheless, the same object we are occupied with, and, therefore, the house of Aaron had "the wave breast and the heave shoulder." All this is replete with comfort and joy to the heart. The Lord Jesus Christ – the One "who was dead, but is alive for evermore," is now the exclusive object before the eye and thoughts of God; and, in perfect grace, He has given unto us a portion in the same blessed and all-glorious Person. Christ is our object too – the object of our hearts, and the theme of our song. "Having made peace by the blood of his cross," He ascended into heaven, and sent down the Holy Ghost, that "other Comforter," by whose powerful ministrations we feed upon "the breast and shoulder" of our divine "Peace Offering." He is, indeed, our peace; and it is our exceeding joy to know that such is God's delight in the establishment of our peace that the sweet odour of our peace offering has refreshed His heart. This imparts a peculiar charm to this type. Christ, as the burnt offering, commands the admiration of the heart; Christ, as the peace offering, establishes the peace of the conscience, and meets the deep and manifold necessities of the soul. The sons of Aaron might stand around the altar of burnt offering; they might behold the flame of that offering ascending to the God of Israel; they might see the sacrifice reduced to ashes; they might, in view of all this, bow their heads and worship; but they carried nought away for themselves. Not so in the peace offering. In it they not only beheld that which was capable of emitting a sweet odour to God, but also of yielding a most substantial portion for themselves on which they could feed, in happy and holy fellowship.

The joy of communion

And, assuredly, it heightens the enjoyment of every true

priest to know that God (to use the language of our type) has had His portion, ere he gets the breast and the shoulder. The thought of this gives tone and energy, unction and elevation to the worship and communion. It unfolds the amazing grace of Him who has given us the same object, the same theme, the same joy with Himself. Nothing lower – nothing less than this could satisfy Him. The Father will have the prodigal feeding upon the fatted calf, in fellowship with Himself. He will not assign him lower place than at His own table, nor any other portion than that on which He feeds Himself. The language of the peace offering is, "it is meet that *we* should make merry and be glad" – "Let *us* eat and be merry." Such is the precious grace of God! No doubt, we have reason to be glad, as being the partakers of such grace; but when we can hear the blessed God saying, "Let *us* eat and be merry," it should call forth from our hearts a continual stream of praise and thanksgiving. God's joy in the salvation of sinners, and His joy in the communion of saints, may well elicit the admiration of men and angels throughout eternity.

The peace offering and the meat offering

Having, thus, compared the peace offering with the burnt offering, we may, now, briefly glance at it, in connexion with the meat offering. The leading point of difference, here, is that, in the peace offering, there was blood-shedding, and in the meat offering, there was not. They were both "sweet savour" offerings; and, as we learn, from chap. 7:12, the two offerings here very intimately associated. Now, both the connexion and the contrast are full of meaning and instruction.

It is only in communion with God that the soul can delight itself in contemplating the perfect humanity of the Lord Jesus Christ. God the Holy Ghost must *impart*, as He must also *direct*, by the word, the vision by which we can gaze on "the Man Christ Jesus." He might have been revealed "in the likeness of sinful flesh;" He might have lived and laboured on this earth; He might have shone, amid the darkness of this world, in all the heavenly lustre and beauty which belonged to His Person; He might have passed rapidly, like a brilliant luminary, across this world's horizon; and, all the while, have been beyond the range of the sinner's vision.

Man could not enter into the deep joy of communion with all this, simply because there would be no basis laid down on which this communion might rest. In the peace offering, this necessary basis is fully and clearly established. "He shall lay his hand upon the head of his offering, and kill it at the door of the tabernacle of the congregation: and Aaron's sons, the priests, shall sprinkle the blood upon the altar round about" (chap. 3:2). Here, we have that which the meat offering does not supply, namely, a solid foundation for the worshipper's communion with all the fullness, the preciousness, and the beauty of Christ, so far as he, by the gracious energy of the Holy Ghost, is enabled to enter thereunto. Standing on the platform which "the precious blood of Christ" provides, we can range, with tranquillised hearts, and worshipping spirits, throughout all the wondrous scenes of the manhood of the Lord Jesus Christ. Had we nought save the meat offering aspect of Christ, we should lack the title by which, and the ground on which, we can contemplate and enjoy Him therein. If there were no blood-shedding, there could be no title, no standing place for the sinner. But Leviticus 7:12 links the meat offering with the peace offering, and, by so doing, teaches us that, when our souls have found peace, we can delight in the One, who has "made peace," and who is "our peace."

But let it be distinctly understood that while, in the peace offering, we have the shedding and sprinkling of blood, yet sin-bearing is not the thought. When we view Christ, in the peace offering, He does not stand before us as the bearer of our sins, as in the sin and trespass offerings; but (having borne them) as the ground of our peaceful and happy fellowship with God. If sin-bearing were in question, it could not be said, "It is an offering made by fire of a sweet savour unto the Lord" (chap. 3:5 comp. with chap. 4:10-12). Still, though sin-bearing is not the thought, there is full provision for one who knows himself to be a sinner, else he could not have any portion therein. To have fellowship with God we must be "in the light;" and how can we be there? Only on the ground of that precious statement, "the blood of Jesus Christ His Son cleanseth us from *all* sin" (1 John 1). The more we abide in the light, the deeper will be our sense of everything which is contrary to that light, and the deeper, also, our sense of the value of that blood which entitles us to be there. The more closely we walk with God, the more we shall know of "the unsearchable riches of Christ."

It is most needful to be established in the truth that we are in the presence of God, only as the partakers of divine life, and as standing in divine righteousness. The Father could only have the prodigal at his table, clothed in "the best robe," and in all the integrity of that relationship in which He viewed him. Had the prodigal been left in his rags, or placed "as a hired servant" in the house, we never should have heard those glorious words, "Let us eat and be merry: for this *my son* was dead, and is alive again; he was lost, and is found." Thus it is with all true believers. Their old nature is not recognised as existing, before God. He counts it dead, and so should they. It is dead, to God – dead, to faith. It must be kept in the place of death. It is not by improving our old nature that we get into the divine presence; but as the possessors of a new nature. It was not by repairing the rags of his former condition that the prodigal got a place at the Father's table, but by being clothed in a robe which he had never seen, or thought of before. He did not bring this robe with him from the "far country," neither did he provide it as he came along; but the father had it for him in the house. The prodigal did not make it, or help to make it; but the father provided it for him, and rejoiced to see it on him. Thus it was they sat down together, to feed in happy fellowship, upon "the fatted calf."

I shall now proceed to quote at length "the law of the sacrifice of peace offering," in which we shall find some additional points of much interest – points which belong peculiarly to itself: "And this is the law of the sacrifice of peace offerings, which he shall offer unto the Lord. If he offer it for a thanksgiving, then he shall offer with the sacrifice of thanksgiving unleavened cakes mingled with oil, and unleavened wafers anointed with oil, and cakes mingled with oil, of fine flour fried. Besides the cakes, he shall offer for his offering leavened bread with the sacrifice of thanksgiving of his peace offerings. And of it he shall offer one out of the whole oblation for an heave offering unto the Lord, and it shall be the priest's that sprinkleth the blood of the peace offerings. And the flesh of the sacrifice of his peace offerings for thanksgiving shall be eaten the same day that it is offered; he shall not leave any of it until the morning. But if the sacrifice of his offering be a vow, or a voluntary offering, it shall be eaten the same day that he offereth his sacrifice: and on the morrow also the remainder of it shall be eaten; but the remainder of the flesh of the sacrifice on the third day shall be burnt with fire. And if any of the flesh of the sacrifice of his peace offerings be eaten at all on the third day, it shall not be accepted, neither shall it be imputed unto him that offereth it: it shall be an abomination, and the soul that eateth of it shall bear his iniquity. And the flesh that toucheth any unclean thing shall not be eaten; it shall be burnt with fire: and as for the flesh all that be clean shall eat thereof. But the soul that eateth of the flesh of the sacrifice of peace offerings that pertain unto the Lord, having his uncleanness upon him, even that soul shall be cut off from his people. Moreover, the soul that shall touch any unclean thing, as the uncleanness of man, or any unclean beast, or any abominable unclean thing, and eat of the flesh of the sacrifice of peace offerings, which pertain unto the Lord, even that soul shall be cut off from his people." (Lev. 7:11-21)

The sin in us and the sin on us

It is of the utmost importance that we accurately distinguish between sin *in the flesh,* and sin *on the conscience.* If we confound these two, our souls must, necessarily, be unhinged, and our worship marred. An attentive consideration of 1 John 1:8-10 will throw much light upon this subject, the understanding of which is so essential to a due appreciation of the entire doctrine of the peace offering, and more especially of that point therein at which we have now arrived. There is no one who will be so conscious of indwelling sin as the man who walks in the light. "If we say that we have *no sin*, we deceive ourselves and the truth is not in us." In the verse immediately preceding, we read, "the blood of Jesus Christ his Son cleanseth us from *all sin*." Here the distinction between sin *in* us, and sin *on* us, is fully brought out and established. To say that there is sin on the believer, in the presence of God, is to call in question the purging efficacy of the blood of Jesus, and to deny the truth of the divine record. If the blood of Jesus can perfectly purge, then the believer's conscience is perfectly purged. The word of God thus puts the matter; and we must ever remember that it is from God Himself we are to learn what the true condition of the believer is, in His sight. We are more disposed to be occupied in telling God what we are in ourselves, than to allow Him to tell us what we are in Christ. In other words, we are more taken up with our own self-consciousness, than with God's revelation of Himself. God speaks to us on the ground of what He is in Himself and of what He has accomplished, in Christ. Such is the nature and character of His revelation of which faith takes hold, and thus fills the soul with perfect peace. God's revelation is one thing; my consciousness is quite another.

But the same word which tells us we have no sin *on* us, tells us, with equal force and clearness, that we have sin *in* us. "If we say that we have no sin, we deceive ourselves, and the truth is not in us." Every one who has "truth "in him, will know that he has "*sin*" in him, likewise; for truth reveals every thing as it is. What, then, are we to do? It is our privilege so to walk in the power of the new nature, that the "*sin*" which dwells in us may not manifest itself in the form of "*sins*." The Christian's position is one of victory and liberty. He is not only delivered from the guilt of sin, but also from sin as a ruling principle in his life. "Knowing this, that our old man is crucified with him, that the body of sin might be destroyed, that henceforth we should not serve sin. For he that is dead is freed from sin . . . let not sin therefore *reign* in your mortal body, that ye should *obey it* in the lusts thereof...For sin shall not have dominion over you: for we are not under the law, but under grace" (Rom. 6:6-14). Sin is there in all its native vileness; but the believer is "dead to it." How? He died in Christ. By nature he was dead *in* sin. By grace he is dead *to* it. What claim can anything or any one have upon a dead man? None whatever. Christ "died unto sin once," and the believer died in Him. "Now if we be dead with Christ, we believe that we shall also live with him: knowing that Christ being raised from the dead, dieth no more, death hath no more dominion over him. For in that he died, he died unto sin once: but in that he liveth, he liveth unto God." What is the result of this, in reference to believers? "*Likewise* reckon ye also yourselves to be *dead indeed unto sin,* but alive unto God through Jesus Christ our Lord." Such is the believer's unalterable position, before God! So that it is his holy privilege to enjoy freedom from sin as a *ruler* over him, though it be a *dweller* in him.

Confessing sins

But, then, "if any man sin," what is to be done? The inspired apostle furnishes a full and most blessed answer: "If we confess our sins, he is faithful and just to forgive us our sins, and to cleanse us from all unrighteousness" (1 John 1:9). Confession is the mode in which the conscience is to be kept free. The apostle does not say, "If we pray for pardon, he is gracious and merciful to forgive us." No doubt, it is ever happy for a child to breathe the sense of need into his father's ear – to tell him of feebleness, to confess folly, infirmity, and failure. All this is most true; and, moreover, it is equally true that our Father is most gracious and merciful to meet His children in all their weakness and ignorance; but, while all this is true, the Holy Ghost declares, by the apostle, that, "if we *confess,*" God is "*faithful* and *just* to forgive." Confession, therefore, is the divine mode. A Christian, having erred, in thought, word, or deed, might pray for pardon, for days and months together, and not have any assurance, from 1 John 1:9, that he was forgiven; whereas the moment he truly confesses his sin, before God, it is a simple matter of faith to know that he is perfectly forgiven and perfectly cleansed.

There is an immense moral difference between praying for forgiveness, and confessing our sins, whether we look at it in reference to the character of God, the sacrifice of Christ, or the condition of the soul. It is quite possible that a person's prayer may involve the confession of his sin, whatever it may happen to be, and thus come to the same thing. But, then, it is always well to keep close to scripture, in what we think, and say, and do. It must be evident that when the Holy Ghost speaks of *confession*, He does not mean *praying*. And, it is equally evident that He knows there are moral elements in, and practical results flowing out of, confession, which do not belong to prayer. In point of fact, one has often found that a habit of importuning God for the forgiveness of sins, displayed ignorance as to the way in which God has revealed Himself in the Person and work of Christ; as to the relation in which the sacrifice of Christ has set the believer; and as to the divine mode of getting the conscience relieved from the burden, and purified from the soil, of sin.

God has been perfectly satisfied, as to all the believer's sins, in the cross of Christ. On that cross, a full atonement was presented for every jot and tittle of sin, in the believer's nature, and on his conscience. Hence, therefore, God does not need any further propitiation. He does not need anything to draw His heart toward the believer. We do not require to supplicate Him to be "faithful and just," when His faithfulness and justice have been so gloriously displayed, vindicated, and answered, in the death of Christ. Our sins can never come into God's presence, inasmuch as Christ who bore them all, and put them away, is there instead. But, if we sin, conscience will feel it, must feel it; yes, the Holy Ghost will make us feel it. He cannot allow so much as a single light thought to pass unjudged. What then? Has our sin made its way into the presence of God? Has it found its place in the unsullied light of the inner sanctuary? God forbid! The "Advocate" is there – "Jesus Christ the righteous," to maintain, in unbroken integrity, the relationship in which we stand. But, though sin cannot affect God's thoughts in reference to us, it can and does affect our thoughts in reference to Him.[7] Though it cannot make its way into His presence, it can make its way into ours, in a most distressing and humiliating manner. Though it cannot hide the Advocate from God's view, it can hide Him from ours. It gathers, like a thick, dark cloud, on our spiritual horizon, so that our souls cannot bask in the blessed beams of our Father's countenance, It cannot affect our relationship with God, but it can very seriously affect our enjoyment thereof. What, therefore, are we to do? The word answers, "if we confess our sins, he is faithful and just to forgive us our sins, and to cleanse us from all unrighteousness." By confession, we get our conscience cleared; the sweet sense of our relationship restored; the dark cloud dispersed; the chilling, withering influence removed; our thoughts of God set straight. Such is the divine method; and we may truly say that the heart that knows what it is to have ever been in the place of confession, will feel the divine power of the apostle's words, "My little children, these things write I unto you, THAT YE SIN NOT" (1 John 2:1).

Then, again, there is a style of praying for forgiveness, which involves a losing sight of the perfect ground of forgiveness, which has been laid in the sacrifice of the cross. If God forgives sins, He must be "faithful and just," in so doing. But it is quite clear that our prayers, be they ever so sincere and earnest, could not form the basis of God's faithfulness and justice, in forgiving us our sins. Nought save the work of the cross could do this. There the faithfulness and justice of God have had their fullest establishment, and that, too, in immediate reference to our actual sins, as well as to the root thereof, in our nature. God has already judged our sins in the Person of our Substitute, "on the tree;" and, in the act of confession, we judge ourselves. This is essential to divine forgiveness and restoration. The very smallest unconfessed, unjudged sin, on the conscience, will entirely mar our communion with God. Sin *in* us need not do this; but if we suffer sin to remain *on* us, we cannot have fellowship with God. He has put away our sins in such a manner, as that He can have us in His presence; and, so long as we abide in His presence, sin does not trouble us. But, if we get out of His presence, and commit sin, even in thought, our communion must, of necessity, be suspended, until, by confession, we have got rid of the sin. All this, I need hardly add, is founded, exclusively, upon the perfect sacrifice and righteous advocacy of the Lord Jesus Christ.

Finally, as to the difference between prayer and confession, as respects the condition of the heart before God, and its moral sense of the hatefulness of sin, it cannot, possibly, be over-estimated. It is a much easier thing to ask, in a general way, for the forgiveness of our sins than to confess those sins. Confession involves *self-judgment*; asking for forgiveness may not, and, in itself, does not. This alone would be sufficient to point out the difference. Self-judgment is one of the most valuable and healthful exercises of the Christian life; and, therefore, anything which produces it, must be highly esteemed by every earnest Christian.

The difference between asking for pardon, and confessing the sin, is continually exemplified in dealing with children. If a child has done anything wrong, he finds much less difficulty in asking his father to forgive him, than in openly and unreservedly confessing the wrong. In asking for forgiveness, the child may have in his mind a number of things which tend to lessen the sense of the evil; he may be secretly thinking that he was not so much to blame, after all, though, to be sure, it is only proper to ask his father to forgive him; whereas, in confessing the wrong, there is just the one thing, and that is self-judgment. Further, in asking for forgiveness the child may be influenced, mainly, by a desire to escape the consequences of his wrong; whereas, a judicious parent will seek to produce a just sense of its moral evil, which can only exist in connexion with the full confession of the fault – in connexion with self-judgment.

Thus it is, in reference to God's dealings with His children, when they do wrong. He must have the whole thing brought out and thoroughly judged. He will make us not only dread the consequences of sin which are unutterable – but hate the thing itself, because of its hatefulness, in his sight. Were it possible for us, when we commit sin, to be forgiven, merely for the asking, our sense of sin, and our shrinking from it, would not be nearly so intense; and, as a consequence, our estimate of the fellowship with which we are blessed, would not be nearly so high. The moral effect of all this upon the general tone of our spiritual constitution, and also upon our whole character and practical career, must be obvious to every experienced Christian.[8]

Leavened bread with the sacrifice

This entire train of thought is intimately connected with, and fully borne out by, two leading principles laid down in "the law of the peace offering."

In verse 13, of the seventh of Leviticus, we read, "he shall offer for his offering *leavened* bread." And, yet, at verse 20, we read, "But the soul that eateth of the flesh of the sacrifice of peace offerings, that pertain unto the Lord, having his uncleanness *upon* him, even that soul shall be cut off from his people." Here, we have the two things clearly set before us, namely, sin *in* us, and sin *on* us. "Leaven" was permitted, because there was sin in the worshipper's nature. "Uncleanness" was forbidden, because there should be no sin on the worshipper's conscience. If sin be in question, communion must be out of the question. God has met and provided for the sin, which He knows to be in us, by the blood of atonement; and, hence, of the leavened bread in the peace offering, we read, "of it he shall offer one out of the whole oblation for an heave offering unto the Lord, and it shall be *the priest's that sprinkleth the blood of the peace offerings"* (ver. 14). In other words, the "leaven," in the worshipper's nature, was perfectly met by the "blood" of the sacrifice. The priest who eats the leavened bread, must be the sprinkler of the blood. God has put our sin out of His sight for ever. Though it be in us, it is not the object on which His eye rests. He sees only the blood; and, therefore, He can go on with us, and allow us the most unhindered fellowship with Him. But if we allow the *"sin"* which is in us to develop itself in the shape of *"sins,"* there must be confession, forgiveness, and cleansing, ere we can again eat of the flesh of the peace offering. The cutting off of the worshipper, because of ceremonial uncleanness, answers to the suspension of the believer's communion now, because of unconfessed sin. To attempt to have fellowship with God in our sins, would involve the blasphemous insinuation that He could walk in companionship with sin. "If we say that we have fellowship with him, and walk in darkness, we lie, and do not the truth" (1 John 1:6).

In the light of the foregoing line of truth, we may easily see how much we err, when we imagine it to be a mark of spirituality to be occupied with our sins. Could sin or sins ever be the ground or material of our communion with God? Assuredly not. We have just seen that, so long as sin is the object before us, communion must be interrupted. Fellowship can only be "in the light;" and, undoubtedly, there is no sin in the light. There is nought to be seen there, save the blood which has put our sins away, and brought us nigh, and the Advocate which keeps us nigh. Sin has been for ever obliterated from that platform on which God and the worshipper stand in hallowed fellowship. What was it which constituted the material of communion between the Father and the prodigal? Was it the rags of the latter? Was it the husks of "the far country?" By no means. It was not anything that the prodigal brought with him. It was the rich provision of the Father's love – "the fatted calf." Thus it is with God and every true worshipper. They feed together, in holy and elevated communion, upon Him whose precious blood has brought them into everlasting association, in that light to which no sin can ever approach.

Nor need we, for an instant, suppose that true humility is either evidenced or promoted by looking at, or dwelling upon, our sins. An unhallowed and melancholy mopishness may, thus, be superinduced; but the deepest humility springs from a totally different source. Whether was the prodigal an humbler man, "when he came to himself" in the far country, or when he came to the Father's bosom and the Father's house? Is it not evident that the grace which elevates us to the loftiest heights of fellowship with God, is that alone which leads us into the most profound depths of a genuine humility? Unquestionably. The humility which springs from the removal of our sins, must ever be deeper than that which springs from the discovery of them. The former connects us with God; the latter has to do with self. The way to be truly humble is to walk with God in the intelligence and power of the relationship in which He has set us. He has made us His children; and if only we walk as such, we shall be humble.

The Lord's Supper

Ere leaving this part of our subject, I would offer a remark as to the Lord's Supper, which, as being a prominent act of the Church's communion, may, with strict propriety, be looked at in connexion with the doctrine of the peace offering. The intelligent celebration of the Lord's Supper must ever depend upon the recognition of its purely eucharistic or thanksgiving character. It is, very especially, a feast of thanksgiving – thanksgiving for an accomplished redemption. "The cup of blessing which we bless, is it not the communion of the blood of Christ? The bread which we break, is it not the communion of the body of Christ?" (1 Cor. 10:16). Hence, a soul, bowed down under the heavy burden of sin, cannot, with spiritual intelligence, eat the Lord's Supper, inasmuch as that feast is expressive of the complete removal of sin by the death of Christ. "Ye do show the Lord's death till he come" (1 Cor. 11).

In the death of Christ, faith sees the end of everything that pertained to our old-creation standing; and, seeing that the Lord's Supper "shows forth" that death, it is to be viewed as the memento of the glorious fact that the believer's burden of sin was borne by One who put it away for ever. It declares that the chain of our sins, which once tied and bound us, has been eternally snapped by the death of Christ, and can never tie and bind us again. We gather round the Lord's table in all the joy of conquerors. We look back to the cross where the battle was fought and won; and we look forward to the glory where we shall enter into the full and eternal results of the victory.

True, we have "leaven" *in* us; but we have no "uncleanness" *on* us. We are not to gaze upon our sins; but upon Him who bore them on the cross, and put them away for ever. We are not to "deceive ourselves" by the vain notion "that we have no sin" in us; nor are we to deny the truth of God's word, and the efficacy of Christ's blood, by refusing to rejoice in the precious truth that we have no sin on us, for "the blood of Jesus Christ his Son cleanseth us from all sin." It is truly deplorable to observe the heavy cloud that gathers round the Supper of the Lord, in the judgment of so many professing Christians. It tends, as much as anything else, to reveal the immense amount of misapprehension which obtains, in reference to the very elementary truths of the gospel. In fact, we know that when the Lord's Supper is resorted to on any ground save that of known salvation – enjoyed forgiveness – conscious deliverance, the soul becomes wrapped up in thicker and darker clouds than ever. That which is only a memorial of Christ is used to displace Him. That which celebrates an accomplished redemption is used as a stepping-stone thereto. It is thus that the ordinances are abused, and souls plunged in darkness, confusion, and error.

How different from this is the beautiful ordinance of the peace offering! In this latter, looked at in its typical import, we see that the moment the blood was shed, God and the worshipper could feed in happy, peaceful fellowship. Nothing more was needed. Peace was established by the blood; and, on that ground, the communion proceeded. A single question as to the establishment of peace must be the death-blow to communion. If we are to be occupied with the vain attempt to make peace with God, we must be total strangers to either communion or worship. If the blood of the peace offering has not been shed, it is impossible that we can feed upon "the wave breast" or "the heave shoulder." But if, on the other hand, the blood has been shed, then peace is made already. God Himself has made it, and this is enough for faith; and, therefore, by faith, we have fellowship with God, in the intelligence and joy of accomplished redemption. We taste the freshness of God's own joy in that which He has wrought. We feed upon Christ, in all the fullness and blessedness of God's presence.

Worship

This latter point is connected with, and based upon, another leading truth laid down in "the law of the peace offering." "And the flesh of the sacrifice of his peace offerings for thanksgiving shall be eaten the same day that it is offered: he shall not leave any of it until the morning." That is to say, the communion of the worshipper must never be separated from the sacrifice on which that communion is founded. So long as one has spiritual energy to maintain the connexion, the worship and communion are also maintained, in freshness and acceptableness; but no longer. *We must keep close to the sacrifice*, in the spirit of our minds, the affections of our hearts, and the experience of our souls. This will impart power and permanency to our worship. We may commence some act or expression of worship, with our hearts in immediate occupation with Christ; and, ere we reach the close, we may become occupied with what we are doing or saying, or with the persons who are listening to us; and, in this way, fall into what may be termed "iniquity in our holy things." This is deeply solemn, and should make us very watchful. We may begin our worship in the Spirit and end in the flesh. Our care should ever be, not to suffer ourselves to proceed for a single moment beyond the energy of the Spirit, at the time, for the Spirit will always keep us occupied directly with Christ. If the Holy Ghost produces "five words" of worship or thanksgiving, let us utter the five and have done. If we proceed further, we are eating the flesh of our sacrifice beyond the time; and, so far from its being "accepted," it is, really, "an abomination." Let us remember this, and be watchful. It need not alarm us. God would have us led by the Spirit, and so filled with Christ in all our worship. He can only accept of that which is divine; and, therefore, He would have us presenting that only which is divine.

"But if the sacrifice of his offering be a vow or a voluntary offering, it shall be eaten the same day that he offereth his sacrifice: *and on the morrow also the remainder of it shall be eaten"* (Lev. 7:16). When the soul goes forth to God in a voluntary act of worship, such worship will be the result of a larger measure of spiritual energy than where it merely springs from some special mercy experienced at the time. If one has been visited with some marked favour from the Lord's own hand, the soul, at once, ascends in thanksgiving. In this case, the worship is awakened by, and connected with, that favour or mercy, whatever it may happen to be, and there it ends. But, where the heart is led forth by the Holy Ghost in some voluntary or deliberate expression of praise, it will be of a more enduring character. But spiritual worship will always connect itself with the precious sacrifice of Christ.

"The remainder of the flesh of the sacrifice, on the third day, shall be burnt with fire. And if any of the flesh of the sacrifice of his peace offerings be eaten at all on the third day, it shall not be accepted, neither shall it be imputed unto him that offereth it: it shall be an abomination, and the soul that eateth of it shall bear his iniquity." Nothing is of any value, in the judgment of God, which is not immediately connected with Christ. There may be a great deal of what looks like worship, which is, after all, the mere excitement and outgoing of natural feeling. There may be much apparent devotion, which is, merely, fleshly pietism. Nature may be acted upon, in a religious way, by a variety of things, such as pomp, ceremony, and parade, tones and attitudes, robes and vestments, an eloquent liturgy, all the varied attractions of a splendid ritualism, while there may be a total absence of spiritual worship. Yea, it not infrequently happens that the very same tastes and tendencies which are called forth and gratified by the splendid appliances of so-called religious worship, would find most suited aliment at the opera or in the concert room.

All this has to be watched against by those who desire to remember that "God is a spirit, and they that worship him must worship him in spirit and in truth" (John 4). Religion, so called, is, at this moment, decking herself with her most powerful charms. Casting off the grossness of the middle ages, she is calling to her aid all the resources of refined taste, and of a cultivated and enlightened age. Sculpture, music, and painting, are pouring their rich treasures into her lap, in order that she may, therewith, prepare a powerful opiate to lull the thoughtless multitude into a slumber, which shall only be broken in upon by the unutterable horrors of death, judgment, and the lake of fire. She, too, can say, "I have *peace offerings* with me; this day have I paid my *vows* . . . I have decked my bed with coverings of tapestry, with carved works, with fine linen of Egypt. I have perfumed my bed with myrrh, aloes, and cinnamon" (Prov. 7). Thus does corrupt religion allure, by her powerful influence, those who will not hearken to wisdom's heavenly voice.

Reader, beware of all this. See that your worship stands inseparably connected with the work of the cross. See that Christ is the ground, Christ the material, and the Holy Ghost the power of your worship. Take care that your outward act of worship does not stretch itself beyond the inward power. It demands much watchfulness to keep clear of this evil. Its incipient workings are most difficult to be detected and counteracted. We may commence a hymn in the true spirit of worship, and, through lack of spiritual power, we may, ere we reach the close, fall into the evil which answers to the ceremonial act of eating the flesh of the peace offering on the third day. Our only security is in keeping close to Jesus. If we lift up our hearts in "thanksgiving," for some special mercy, let us do so in the power of the name and sacrifice of Christ. If our souls go forth in "voluntary" worship, let it be in the energy of the Holy Ghost. In this way shall our worship exhibit that freshness, that fragrance, that depth of tone, that moral elevation, which must result from having the Father as the object, the Son as the ground, and the Holy Ghost as the power of our worship.

Thus may it be, O Lord, with all thy worshipping people, until we find ourselves, body, soul, and spirit, in the security of thine own eternal presence, beyond the reach of all the unhallowed influences of false worship and corrupt religion, and also beyond the reach of the various hindrances which arise from these bodies of sin and death which we carry about with us!

NOTE. – It is interesting to observe that, although the peace offering itself stands third in order, yet "the law" thereof is given us last of all. This circumstance is not without its import. There is none of the offerings in which the communion of the worshipper is so fully unfolded as in the peace offering. In the burnt offering, it is Christ offering Himself to God. In the meat offering, we have Christ's perfect humanity. Then, passing on to the sin offering, we learn that *sin*, in its root, is fully met. In the trespass offering, there is a full answer to the actual *sins* in the life. But, in none is the doctrine of the communion of the worshipper unfolded. This latter belongs to "the peace offering;" and, hence, I believe, the position which the law of that offering occupies. It comes in, at the close of all, thereby teaching us that, when it becomes a question of the soul's feeding upon Christ, it must be a full Christ, looked at in every possible phase of His life, His character, His Person, His work, His offices. And, furthermore, that, when we shall have done, for ever, with sin and sins, we shall delight in Christ, and feed upon Him, throughout the everlasting ages. It would, I believe, be a serious defect in our study of the offerings, were we to pass over a circumstance so worthy of notice as the above. If "the law of the peace offering" were given in the order in which the offering itself occurs, it would come in immediately after the law of the meat offering; but, instead of that, "the law of the sin offering, and "the law of the trespass offering" are given, and, then, "the law of the peace offering" closes the entire.

---

[5] The "breast" and the "shoulder" are emblematical of love and power – strength and affection.

[6] There is much force and beauty in verse 31: "The breast shall be Aaron's and his sons." It is the privilege of all true believers to feed upon the affections of Christ – the changeless love of that heart which beats with a deathless and changeless love for them.

[7] The reader will bear in mind that the subject treated of in the text, leaves wholly untouched the important and most practical truth taught in John 14:21-23, namely, the peculiar love of the Father for an obedient child, and the special communion of such a child with the Father and the Son. May this truth be written on all our hearts, by the pen of God the Holy Ghost!

[8] The case of Simon Magus, in Acts 8, may present a difficulty to the reader. But of him, it is sufficient to say that one "in the gall of bitterness and in the bond of iniquity," could never be set forth as a model for God's dear children. His case in nowise interferes with the doctrine of 1 John 1:9. He was not in the relationship of a child, and, as a consequence, not a subject of the advocacy. I would further add, that the subject of the Lord's prayer is by no means involved in what is stated above. I wish to confine myself to the immediate passage under consideration. We must ever avoid laying down iron rules. A soul may cry to God, under any circumstances, and ask for what it needs. He is ever ready to hear and answer.

THE SIN OFFERING

The relation of the people to God and the individual conscience

Having considered the "sweet savour" offerings, we now approach the "sacrifices for sin." These were divided into two classes, namely, sin offerings and trespass offerings. Of the former, there were three grades; first, the offering for "the priest that is anointed," and for "the whole congregation." These two were the same in their rites and ceremonies (compare. ver. 3-12, with ver. 13-21). It was the same in result, whether it were the representative of the assembly, or the assembly itself, that sinned. In either case there were three things involved: God's dwelling-place in the assembly, the worship of the assembly, and individual conscience. Now, inasmuch as all three depended upon the blood, we find, in the first grade of sin offering, there were three things done with the blood. It was sprinkled "seven times before the Lord, *before the vail of the sanctuary.*" This secured Jehovah's relationship with the people, and His dwelling in their midst. Again, we read, "The priest shall put some of the blood upon the horns of the altar of sweet incense before the Lord, which is in the tabernacle of the congregation." This secured the worship of the assembly. By putting the blood upon "the golden altar," the true basis of worship was preserved; so that the flame of the incense and the fragrance thereof might continually ascend. Finally, "He shall pour all the blood of the bullock at the bottom of the altar of the burnt offering, which is at the door of the tabernacle of the congregation." Here we have the claims of individual conscience fully answered; for the brazen altar was the place of individual approach. It was the place where God met the sinner.

In the two remaining grades, for "a ruler" or "one of the common people," it was merely a question of individual conscience; and, therefore, there was only one thing done with the blood. It was all poured "at the bottom of the altar of burnt offering" (comp. ver. 7 with ver. 25, 30). There is divine precision in all this, which demands the close attention of my reader, if only he desires to enter into the marvellous detail of this type.[9]

The effect of individual sin could not extend beyond individual conscience. The sin of "a ruler," or of "one of the common people," could not, in its influence, reach "the altar of incense" – the place of priestly worship. Neither could it reach to "the vail of the sanctuary" – the sacred boundary of God's dwelling place in the midst of His people. It is well to ponder this. We must never raise a question of personal sin or failure, in the place of priestly worship, or in the assembly. It must be settled in the place of personal approach. Many err as to this. They come into the assembly, or into the ostensible place of priestly worship, with their conscience defiled, and thus drag down the whole assembly and mar its worship. This should be closely looked into, and carefully guarded against. We need to walk more watchfully, in order that our conscience may ever be in the light. And when we fail, as, alas! we do in many things, let us have to do with God, in secret, about our failure, in order that true worship, and the true position of the assembly may always be kept, with fullness and clearness, before the soul.

Sinning through ignorance or error

Having said thus much as to the three grades of sin offering, we shall proceed to examine, in detail, the principles unfolded in the first of these. In so doing, we shall be able to form, in some measure, a just conception of the principles of all. Before, however, entering upon the direct comparison already proposed, I would call my reader's attention to a very prominent point set forth in the second verse of this fourth chapter. It is contained in the expression, "If a soul shall sin through *ignorance*." This presents a truth of the deepest blessedness, in connexion with the atonement of the Lord Jesus Christ. In contemplating that atonement, we see infinitely more than the mere satisfaction of the claims of conscience, even though that conscience had reached the highest point of refined sensibility. It is our privilege to see, therein, that which has fully satisfied all the claims of divine holiness, divine justice, and divine majesty. The holiness of God's dwelling-place, and the ground of His association with His people, could never be regulated by the standard of man's conscience, no matter how high the standard might be. There are many things which man's conscience would pass over – many things which might escape man's cognizance – many things which his heart might deem all right, which God could not tolerate; and which, as a consequence, would interfere with man's approach to, his worship of, and his relationship with, God. Wherefore, if the atonement of Christ merely made provision for such sins as come within the compass of man's apprehension, we should find ourselves very far short of the true ground of peace. We need to understand that sin has been atoned for, according to God's measurement thereof – that the claims of His throne have been perfectly answered – that sin, as seen in the light of His inflexible holiness, has been divinely judged. This is what gives settled peace to the soul. A full atonement has been made for the believer's sins of ignorance, as well as for his known sins. The sacrifice of Christ lays the foundation of his relationship and fellowship with God, according to the divine estimate of the claims thereof.

    A clear sense of this is of unspeakable value. Unless this feature of the atonement be laid hold of, there cannot be settled peace; nor will there be any just moral sense of the extent and fullness of the work of Christ, or of the true nature of the relationship founded thereon. God knew what was needed in order that man might be in His presence without a single misgiving; and He has made ample provision for it in the cross. Fellowship between God and man were utterly impossible if sin had not been disposed of, according to God's thoughts about it: for, albeit man's conscience were satisfied, the question would ever be suggesting itself, Has God been satisfied? If this question could not be answered in the affirmative, fellowship could never subsist.[10] The thought would be continually intruding itself upon the heart, that things were manifesting themselves in the details of life, which divine holiness could not tolerate. True, we might be doing such things "through ignorance" but this could not alter the matter before God, inasmuch as all is known to Him. Hence, there would be continual apprehension, doubt, and misgiving. All these things are divinely met by the fact that sin has been atoned for, not according to our "ignorance," but according to God's knowledge. The assurance of this gives great rest to the heart and conscience. All God's claims have been answered by His own work. He Himself has made the provision; and, therefore, the more refined the believer's conscience becomes, under the combined action of the word and Spirit of God – the more he grows in a divinely-adjusted sense of all that morally befits the sanctuary – the more keenly alive he becomes to every thing which is unsuited to the divine presence, the fuller, clearer, deeper, and more vigorous will be his apprehension of the infinite value of that sin offering which has not only travelled beyond the utmost bounds of human conscience, but also met, in absolute perfection, all the requirements of divine holiness.

Nothing can more forcibly express man's incompetence to deal with sin, than the fact of there being such a thing as a "sin of ignorance." How could he deal with that which he knows not? How could he dispose of that which has never even come within the range of his conscience? Impossible. Man's ignorance of sin proves his total inability to put it away. If he does not know of it, what can he do about it? Nothing. He is as powerless as he is ignorant. Nor is this all. The fact of a "sin of ignorance" demonstrates, most clearly, the uncertainty which must attend upon every settlement of the question of sin, in which no higher claims have been responded to than those put forth by the most refined human conscience. There can never be settled peace upon this ground. There will always be the painful apprehension that there is something wrong underneath. If the heart be not led into settled repose by the scripture testimony that the inflexible claims of divine Justice have been answered, there must, of necessity, be a sensation of uneasiness, and every such sensation presents a barrier to our worship, our communion, and our testimony. If I am uneasy in reference to the settlement of the question of sin, I cannot worship; I cannot enjoy communion, either with God or His people; nor can I be an intelligent or effective witness for Christ. The heart must be at rest, before God, as to the perfect remission of sin, ere we can "worship him in spirit and in truth." If there be guilt on the conscience, there must be terror in the heart; and, assuredly, a heart filled with terror cannot be a happy or a worshipping heart. It is only from a heart filled with that sweet and sacred repose which the blood of Christ imparts, that true and acceptable worship can ascend to the Father. The same principle holds good with respect to our fellowship with the people of God, and our service and testimony amongst men. All must rest upon the foundation of settled peace; and this peace rests upon the foundation of a perfectly purged conscience; and this purged conscience rests upon the foundation of the perfect remission of all our sins, whether they be sins of knowledge or sins of ignorance.

The sin offering and the burnt offering

We shall now proceed to compare the sin offering with the burnt offering, in doing which, we shall find two very different aspects of Christ. But, although the aspects are different, it is one and the same Christ; and, hence, the sacrifice, in each case, was "without blemish." This is easily understood. It matters not in what aspect we contemplate the Lord Jesus Christ, He must ever be seen as the same pure, spotless, holy, perfect One. True, He did, in His abounding grace, stoop to be the sin-bearer of His people; but it was a perfect, spotless Christ who did so; and it would be nothing short of diabolical wickedness to take occasion, from the depth of His humiliation, to tarnish the personal glory of the humbled One. The intrinsic excellence, the unsullied purity, and the divine glory of our blessed Lord appear in the sin offering, as fully as in the burnt offering. It matters not in what relationship He stands, what office He fills, what work He performs, what position He occupies, His personal glories shine out, in all their divine effulgence.

This truth of one and the same Christ, whether in the burnt offering, or in the sin offering, is seen, not only in the fact that, in each case, the offering was "without blemish," but, also, in "the law of the sin offering," where we read, "this is the law of the sin offering: in the place where the burnt offering is killed shall the sin offering be killed before the Lord: it is most holy" (Lev. 6:25). Both types point to one and the same great Antitype, though they present Him in such contrasted aspects of His work. In the burnt offering, Christ is seen meeting the divine affections; in the sin offering, He is seen meeting the depths of human need. That presents Him to us as the Accomplisher of the will of God; this, as the Bearer of the sin of man. In the former, we are taught the preciousness of the sacrifice; in the latter, the hatefulness of sin. Thus much, as to the two offerings, in the main. The most minute examination of the details will only tend to establish the mind in the truth of this general statement.

In the first place, when considering the burnt offering, we observed that it was a voluntary offering. "He shall offer it of his own voluntary will."[11] Now, the word "voluntary" does not occur in the sin offering. This is precisely what we might expect. It is in full keeping with the specific object of the Holy Ghost, in the burnt offering, to set it forth as a free-will offering. It was Christ's meat and drink to do the will of God, whatever that will might be. He never thought of inquiring what ingredients were in the cup which the Father was putting into His hand. It was quite sufficient for Him that the Father had mingled it. Thus it was with the Lord Jesus as foreshadowed by the burnt offering. But, in the sin offering, we have quite a different line of truth unfolded. This type introduces Christ to our thoughts, not as the "voluntary" Accomplisher of the will of God, but as the Bearer of that terrible thing called "sin," and the Endurer of all its appalling consequences, of which the most appalling, to Him, was the hiding of God's countenance. Hence, the word "voluntary" would not harmonise with the object of the Spirit, in the sin offering. It would be as completely out of place, in that type, as it is divinely in place, in the burnt offering. Its presence and its absence are alike divine; and both alike exhibit the perfect, the divine precision of the types of Leviticus.

Now, the point of contrast which we have been considering, explains, or rather harmonises, two expressions used by our Lord. He says, on one occasion, "the cup which my Father hath given me, shall I not drink it?" And, again, "Father, if it be possible, let this cup pass from me." The former of these expressions was the full carrying out of the words with which He entered upon His course, namely, "Lo, I come to do thy will, O God;" and, moreover, it is the utterance of Christ, as the burnt offering. The latter, on the other hand, is the utterance of Christ, when contemplating the place which He was about to occupy, as the sin offering. What that place was, and what was involved to Him, in taking it, we shall see, as we proceed; but it is interesting and instructive to find the entire doctrine of the two offerings involved, as it were, in the fact that a single word introduced in the one is omitted in the other. If, in the burnt offering, we find the perfect readiness of heart with which Christ offered Himself for the accomplishment of the will of God; then, in the sin offering, we find how perfectly He entered into all the consequences of man's sin, and how He travelled into the most remote distance of man's position as regards God. He delighted to do the will of God;

He shrank from losing, for a moment, the light of His blessed countenance. No one offering could have foreshadowed Him in both these phases. We needed a type to present Him to us as One delighting to do the will of God; and we needed a type to present Him to us as One whose holy nature shrank from the consequences of imputed sin. Blessed be God, we have both. The burnt offering furnishes the one, the sin offering the other. Wherefore, the more fully we enter into the devotion of Christ's heart to God, the more fully we shall apprehend His abhorrence of sin; and *vice versa*. Each throws the other into relief; and the use of the word "voluntary" in the one, and not in the other, fixes the leading import of each.

But, it may be said, "Was it not the will of God that Christ should offer Himself as an atonement for sin? And, if so, how could there be anything of shrinking from the accomplishment of that will?" Assuredly, it was "the determinate counsel" of God that Christ should suffer; and, moreover, it was Christ's joy to do the will of God. But how are we to understand the expression, "If it be possible, let this cup pass from me?" Is it not the utterance of Christ? And is there no express type of the Utterer thereof? Unquestionably. There would be a serious blank among the types of the Mosaic economy, were there not one to reflect the Lord Jesus in the exact attitude in which the above expression presents Him. But the burnt offering does not thus reflect Him. There is not a single circumstance connected with that offering which would correspond with such language. The sin offering alone furnishes the fitting type of the Lord Jesus as the One who poured forth those accents of intense agony, for in it alone do we find the circumstances which evoked such accents from the depths of His spotless soul. The awful shadow of the cross, with its shame, its curse, and its exclusion from the light of God's countenance, was passing across His spirit, and He could not even contemplate it without an "If it be possible let this cup pass from me." But, no sooner had He uttered these words, than His profound subjection manifests itself in, "thy will be done." What a bitter "cup" it must have been to elicit, from a perfectly subject heart, the words," let it pass from me!" What perfect subjection there must have been when, in the presence of so bitter a cup, the heart could breathe forth," thy will be done!"

The laying on of hands

We shall now consider the, typical act of "laying on of hands." This act was common both to the burnt offering and the sin offering; but, in the case of the former, it identified the offerer with an unblemished offering; in the case of the latter, it involved the transfer of the sin of the offerer to the head of the offering. Thus it was in the type; and, when we look at the Antitype, we learn a truth of the most comforting and edifying nature – a truth which, were it more clearly understood, and fully experienced, would impart a far more settled peace than is ordinarily possessed.

What, then, is the doctrine set forth in the laying on of hands? It is this: Christ was "made sin for us, that we might be made the righteousness of God in him" (2 Cor. 5). He took our position with all its consequences, in order that we might get His position with all its consequences. He was treated as sin, upon the cross, that we might be treated as righteousness, in the presence of infinite Holiness. He was cast out of God's presence because He had sin upon Him, by imputation, that we might be received into God's house and into His bosom, because we have a perfect righteousness by imputation. He had to endure the hiding of God's countenance, that we might bask in the light of that countenance. He had to pass through three hours' darkness, that we might walk in everlasting light. He was forsaken of God, for a time, that we might enjoy His presence for ever. All that was due to us, as ruined sinners, was laid upon Him, in order that all that was due to Him, as the Accomplisher of redemption, might be ours. There was everything against Him When He hung upon the cursed tree, in order that there might be nothing against us. He was identified with us, in the reality of death and judgment, in order that we might be identified with Him, in the reality of life and righteousness. He drank the cup of wrath – the cup of trembling, that we might drink the cup of salvation – the cup of infinite favour. He was treated according to our deserts, that we might be treated according to His.

Such is the wondrous truth illustrated by the ceremonial act of imposition of hands. When the worshipper had laid his hand upon the head of the burnt offering, it ceased to be a question as to what he was, or what he deserved, and became entirely a question of what the offering was in the judgment of Jehovah. If the offering was without blemish, so was the offerer; if the offering was accepted, so was the offerer. They were perfectly identified. The act of laying on of hands constituted them one, in God's view. He looked at the offerer through the medium of the offering. Thus it was, in the case of the burnt offering. But, in the sin offering, when the offerer had laid his hand upon the head of the offering, it became a question of what the offerer was, and what he deserved. The offering was treated according to the deserts of the offerer. They were perfectly identified. The act of laying on of hands constituted them one, in the judgment of God. The sin of the offerer was dealt with in the sin offering; the person of the offerer was accepted in the burnt offering. This made a vast difference. Hence, though the act of laying on of hands was common to both types, and, moreover, though it was expressive, in the case of each, of identification, yet here the consequences as different as possible. The just treated as the unjust; the unjust accepted in the just. "Christ hath once suffered for sins, the just for the unjust, that he might bring us to God." This is the doctrine. Our sins brought Christ to the cross; but He brings us to God. And, if He brings us to God, it is in His own acceptableness, as risen from the dead, having put away our sins, according to the perfectness of His own work. He bore away our sins far from the sanctuary of God, in order that He might bring us nigh, even into the holiest of all, in full confidence of heart, having the conscience purged by His precious blood from every stain of sin.

Now, the more minutely we compare all the details of the burnt offering and the sin offering, the more clearly shall we apprehend the truth of what has been above stated, in reference to the laying on of hands, and the results thereof, in each case.

Differences between the burnt offering and the sin offering

In the first chapter of this volume, we noticed the fact that "the sons of Aaron" are introduced in the burnt offering, but not in the sin offering. As priests they were privileged to stand around the altar, and behold the flame of an acceptable sacrifice ascending to the Lord. But in the sin offering, in its primary aspect, it was a question of the solemn judgment of sin, and not of priestly worship or admiration; and, therefore, the sons of Aaron do not appear. It is as convicted sinners that we have to do with Christ, as the Antitype of the sin offering. It is as worshipping priests, clothed in garments of salvation, that we contemplate Christ, as the Antitype of the burnt offering.

But, further, my reader may observe that the burnt offering was "flayed," the sin offering was not. The burnt offering was "cut into his pieces," the sin offering was not. "The inwards and the legs" of the burnt offering were "washed in water," which act was entirely omitted in the sin offering. Lastly, the burnt offering was burnt upon the altar, the sin offering was burnt without the camp. These are weighty points of difference arising simply out of the distinctive character of the offerings. We know there is nothing in the word of God without its own specific meaning; and every intelligent and careful student of Scripture will notice the above points of difference; and, when he notices them, he will, naturally, seek to ascertain their real import. *Ignorance* of this import there may be; but *indifference* to it there should not. In any section of inspiration, but especially one so rich as that which lies before us, to pass over a single point, would be to offer dishonour to the Divine Author, and to deprive our own souls of much profit. We should hang over the most minute details, either to adore God's wisdom in them, or to confess our own ignorance of them. To pass them by, in a spirit of indifference, is to imply that the Holy Ghost has taken the trouble to write what we do not deem worthy of the desire to understand. This is what no right-minded Christian would presume to think. If the Spirit, in writing upon the ordinance of the sin offering, has omitted the various rites above alluded to – rites which get a prominent place in the ordinance of the burnt offering, there must, assuredly, be some good reason for, and some important meaning in, His doing so. These we would seek to apprehend; and, no doubt, they arise out of the special design of the divine mind in each offering. The sin offering sets forth that aspect of Christ's work in which He is seen taking, judicially, the place which belonged to us morally. For this reason we could not look for that intense expression of what He was, in all His secret springs of action, as unfolded in the typical act of "flaying." Neither could there be that enlarged exhibition of what He was, not merely as a whole, but in the most minute features of His character, as seen in the act of "cutting it into his pieces." Nor, yet, could there be that manifestation of what He was, personally, practically, and intrinsically, as set forth in the significant act of "washing the inwards and legs in water."

All these things belonged to the burnt-offering phase of our blessed Lord, and to that alone, because, in it, we see Him offering Himself to the eye, to the heart, and to the altar of Jehovah, without any question of imputed sin, of wrath, or of judgment. In the sin offering, on the contrary, instead of having, as the great prominent idea, what Christ is, we have what sin is. Instead of the preciousness of Jesus, we have the odiousness of sin. In the burnt offering, inasmuch as it is Christ Himself offered to, and accepted by, God, we have every thing done that could possibly make manifest what He was, in every respect. In the sin offering, because it is sin, as judged by God, the very reverse is the case. All this is so plain as to need no effort of the mind to understand it. It naturally flows out of the distinctive character of the type.

The fat offered upon the altar

However, although the leading object in the sin offering, is to shadow forth what Christ became for us, and not what He was in Himself; there is, nevertheless, one rite connected with this type, which most fully expresses His personal acceptableness to Jehovah. This rite is laid down in the following words, "And he shall take off from it all the fat of the bullock for the sin offering; the fat that covereth the inwards, and all the fat that is upon the inwards, and the two kidneys, and the fat that is upon them, which is by the flanks, and the caul above the liver, with the kidneys, it shall he take away, as it was taken off from the bullock of the sacrifice of peace offering; and the priest shall burn them upon the altar of the burnt offering" (Lev. 4:8-10). Thus, the intrinsic excellency of Christ is not omitted, even in the sin-offering. The fat burnt upon the altar is the apt expression of the divine appreciation of the preciousness of Christ's Person, no matter what place He might, in perfect grace, take, on our behalf or in our stead; He was made sin for us, and the sin offering is the divinely-appointed shadow of Him, in this respect. But, inasmuch as it was the Lord Jesus Christ, God's elect, His Holy One, His pure, His spotless, His eternal Son that was made sin, therefore the fat of the sin offering was burnt upon the altar, as a proper material for that fire which was the impressive exhibition of divine holiness.

But, even in this very point, we see what a contrast there is between the sin offering and the burnt offering. In the case of the latter, it was not merely the fat, but the whole sacrifice that was burnt upon the altar, because it was Christ, without any question of sin-bearing whatever. In the case of the former, there was nothing but the fat to be burnt upon the altar, because it was a question of sin-bearing, though Christ was the sin bearer. The divine glories of Christ's

Person shine out, even from amid the darkest shades of that cursed tree to which He consented to be nailed as a curse for us. The hatefulness of that with which, in the exercise of divine love, He connected His blessed Person, on the cross, could not prevent the sweet odour of His preciousness from ascending to the throne of God. Thus, have we unfolded to us the profound mystery of God's face hidden from that which Christ *became*, and God's heart refreshed by what Christ *was*. This imparts a peculiar charm to the sin offering. The bright beams of Christ's Personal glory shining out from amid the awful gloom of Calvary – His Personal worth set forth, in the very deepest depths of His humiliation – God's delight in the One from whom He had, in vindication of His inflexible justice and holiness, to hide His face – all this is set forth in the fact that the fat of the sin offering was burnt upon the altar.

The body of the victim burnt outside the camp

Having, thus, endeavoured to point out, in the first place, what was done with "the blood;" and, in the second place, what was done with "the fat;" we have, now, to consider what was done with "the flesh." "And the skin of the bullock, and *all his flesh* . . . even *the whole bullock* shall he carry forth without the camp unto a clean place, where the ashes are poured out, and burn him on the wood with fire: where the ashes are poured out shall he be burnt" (ver. 11, 12). In this act, we have the main feature of the sin offering – that which distinguished it both from the burnt offering and the peace offering. Its flesh was not burnt upon the altar, as in the burnt offering; neither was it eaten by the priest or the worshipper, as in the peace offering. It was wholly burnt without the camp.[12] "No sin offering, whereof any of the blood is brought into the tabernacle of the congregation, to reconcile withal in the holy place, shall be eaten: it shall be burnt in the fire" (Lev. 6:30). "For the bodies of those beasts, whose blood is brought unto the sanctuary by the high priest for sin, are burned without the camp. Wherefore Jesus also, that he might sanctify the people with his own blood, suffered without the gate" (Heb. 13:11, 12).

The value of Christ's blood

Now, in comparing what was done with the "blood" with what was done with the "flesh" or "body" of the sacrifice, two great branches of truth present themselves to our view, namely, worship and discipleship. The blood brought into the sanctuary is the foundation of the former. The body burnt outside the camp is the foundation of the latter. Before ever we can worship, in peace of conscience, and liberty of heart, we must know, on the authority of the word, and by the power of the Spirit, that the entire question of *sin* has been for ever settled by the blood of the divine sin offering – that His blood has been sprinkled, perfectly, before the Lord – that all God's claims, and all our necessities, as ruined and guilty sinners, have been, for ever, answered. This gives perfect peace; and, in the enjoyment of this peace, we worship God. When an Israelite, of old, had offered his sin offering, his conscience was set at rest, in so far as the offering was capable of imparting rest. True, it was but a temporary rest, being the fruit of a temporary sacrifice. But, clearly, whatever kind of rest the offering was fitted to impart, that the offerer might enjoy. Hence, therefore, our Sacrifice being divine and eternal, our rest is divine and eternal also. As is the sacrifice such is the rest which is founded thereon. A Jew never had an eternally purged conscience, simply because he had not an eternally efficacious sacrifice. He might in a certain way, have his conscience purged for a day, a month, or a year; but he could not have it purged for ever. "But Christ being come, an high priest of good things to come, by a greater and more perfect tabernacle, not made with hands, that is to say, not of this building; neither by the blood of goats and calves, but by his own blood, he entered in once into the holy place, having obtained *eternal* redemption. For if the blood of bulls and of goats, and the ashes of an heifer sprinkling the unclean, sanctifieth to the purifying of the flesh; how much more shall the blood of Christ, who, through the eternal Spirit, offered Himself without spot to God, purge your conscience from dead works to serve the living God?" (Heb. 9:11-14).

Here, we have the full, explicit statement of the doctrine. The blood of goats and calves procured a temporary redemption; the blood of Christ procures eternal redemption. The former purified outwardly; the latter, inwardly. That purged the flesh, for a time; this, the conscience, for ever. The whole question hinges, not upon the character or condition of the offerer, but upon the value of the offering. The question is not, by any means, whether a Christian is a better man than a Jew, but whether the blood of Christ is better than the blood of a bullock. Assuredly, it is better. How much better? Infinitely better. The Son of God imparts all the dignity of His own divine Person to the sacrifice which He offered; and, if the blood of a bullock purified the flesh for a year, "how much more" shall the blood of the Son of God purge the conscience for ever? If that took away *some* sin, how much more shall this take away *"all?"*

Now, why was the mind of a Jew set at rest, for the time being, when he had offered his sin offering? How did he know that the special sin for which he had brought his sacrifice was forgiven? Because God had said, "it shall be forgiven him." His peace of heart, in reference to that particular sin, rested upon the testimony of the God of Israel, and the blood of the victim. So, now, the peace of the believer, in reference to "ALL SIN," rests upon the authority of God's word, and "the precious blood of Christ." If a Jew had sinned, and neglected to bring his sin offering, he should have been "cut off from among his people;" but when he took his place as a sinner – when he laid his hand upon the head of a sin offering, then, the offering was "cut off" instead of him, and he was free, so far. The offering was treated as the offerer deserved; and, hence, for him not to know that his sin was forgiven him, would have been to make God a liar, and to treat the blood of the

THE SIN OFFERING

divinely-appointed sin offering as nothing.

And, if this were true, in reference to one who had only the blood of a goat to rest upon, "how much more" powerfully does it apply to one, who has the precious blood of Christ to rest upon? The believer sees in Christ One who has been judged for all his sin – One who, when He hung upon the cross, sustained the entire burden of his sin – One who, having made Himself responsible for that sin, could not be where He now is, if the whole question of sin had not been settled, according to all the claims of infinite justice. So absolutely did Christ take the believer's place on the cross – so entirely was he identified with Him – so completely was all the believer's sin imputed to Him, there and then, that all question of the believer's liability – all thought of his guilt – all idea of his exposure to judgment and wrath, is eternally set aside.[13] It was all settled on the cursed tree, between Divine Justice and the Spotless Victim. And now the believer is as absolutely identified with Christ, on the throne, as Christ was identified with him on the tree. Justice has no charge to bring against the believer, because it has no charge to bring against Christ. Thus it stands for ever. If a charge could be preferred against the believer, it would be calling in question the reality of Christ's identification with him, on the cross, and the perfectness of Christ's work, on his behalf. If, when the worshipper, of old, was on his way back, after having offered his sin offering, any one had charged him with that special sin for which his sacrifice had bled, what would have been his reply? Just this: "the sin has been rolled away, by the blood of the victim, and Jehovah has pronounced the words, 'It shall be forgiven him.' " The victim had died instead of him; and he lived instead of the victim.

Christ dead and resurrected

Such was the type. And, as to the Antitype, when the eye of faith rests on Christ as the sin offering, it beholds Him as One who, having assumed a perfect human life, gave up that life on the cross, because sin was, there and then, attached to it by imputation. But, it beholds Him, also, as One who, having, in Himself, the power of divine and eternal life, rose from the tomb therein, and who now imparts this, His risen, His divine, His eternal life to all who believe in His name. The sin is gone, because the life to which it was attached is gone, and now, instead of the life to which sin was attached, all true believers possess the life to which righteousness attaches. The question of sin can never once be raised, in reference to the risen and victorious life of Christ; but this is the life which believers possess. There is no other life. All beside is death, because all beside is under the power of sin. "He that hath the Son hath life;" and he that hath life, hath righteousness also. The two things are inseparable, because Christ is both the one and the other. If the judgment and death of Christ, upon the cross, were realities, then, the life and righteousness of the believer are realities. If imputed sin was a reality to Christ, imputed righteousness is a reality to the believer. The one is as real as the other; for, if not, Christ would have died in vain. The true and irrefragable ground of peace is this – that the claims of God's nature have been perfectly met, as to sin. The death of Jesus has satisfied them all – satisfied them for ever. What is it that proves this to the satisfaction of the awakened conscience? The great fact of resurrection. A risen Christ declares the full deliverance of the believer – his perfect discharge from every possible demand. "He was delivered for our offences, and raised again for our justification" (Rom. 4:25). For a Christian not to know that his sin is gone, and gone for ever, is to cast a slight upon the blood of his divine sin offering. It is to deny that there has been the perfect presentation – the sevenfold sprinkling of the blood before the Lord.

And now, ere turning from this fundamental point which has been occupying us, I would desire to make an earnest and a most solemn appeal to my reader's heart and conscience Let me ask you, dear friend, have you been led to repose on this holy and happy foundation? Do you know that the question of your sin has been for ever disposed of? Have you laid your hand, by faith, on the head of the sin offering? Have you seen the atoning blood of Jesus rolling away all your guilt, and carrying it into the mighty waters of God's forgetfulness? Has Divine Justice anything against you? Are you free from the unutterable horrors of a guilty conscience? Do not, I pray you, rest satisfied until you can give a joyous answer to these enquiries. Be assured of it, it is the happy privilege of the feeblest babe in Christ to rejoice in a full and everlasting remission of sins, on the ground of finished atonement; and, hence, for any to teach otherwise, is to lower the sacrifice of Christ to the level of "goats and calves." If we cannot know that our sins are forgiven, then, where are the glad tidings of the gospel? Is a Christian in no wise better off in the matter of a sin offering, than a Jew? The latter was privileged to know that his matters were set straight for a year, by the blood of an annual sacrifice. Can the former not have any certainty at all? Unquestionably. Well, then, if there is any certainty, it must be eternal, inasmuch as it rests on an eternal sacrifice.

This, and this alone, is the basis of worship. The full assurance of sin put away, ministers, not to a spirit of self-confidence, but to a spirit of praise, thankfulness, and worship. It produces, not a spirit of self-complacency, but of Christ-complacency, which, blessed be God, is the spirit which shall characterise the redeemed throughout eternity. It does not lead one to think little of sin, but to think much of the grace which has perfectly pardoned it, and of the blood which has perfectly cancelled it. It is impossible that any one can gaze on the cross – can see the place which Christ took – can meditate upon the sufferings which He endured – can ponder on those three terrible hours of darkness, and, at the same time, think lightly of sin. When all these things are entered into, in the power of the Holy Ghost, there are two results which must follow, namely, an abhorrence of sin, in all its forms, and a genuine love to Christ, His people, and His cause.

Let us go forth unto Him without the camp

Let us now consider what was done with the "flesh" or "body" of the sacrifice, in which, as has been stated, we have the true ground of discipleship. "The whole bullock shall he carry forth, *without the camp,* unto a clean place, where the ashes are poured out, and burn him on the wood with fire" (chap. 4:12). This act is to be viewed in a double way; first, as expressing the place which the Lord Jesus took for us, as bearing sin; secondly, as expressing the place into which He was cast, by a world which had rejected Him. It is to this latter point that I would here call my reader's attention.

The use which the apostle, in Heb. 13, makes of Christ's having "suffered without the gate," is deeply practical. "Let us go forth, therefore, *unto him,* without the camp, *bearing his reproach."* If the sufferings of Christ have secured us an entrance into heaven, the place where He suffered expresses our rejection from earth. His death has procured us a city on high; the place where He died divests us of a city below.[14] "He suffered without the gate," and, in so doing, He set aside Jerusalem as the present centre of divine operation. There is no such thing, now, as a consecrated spot on the earth. Christ has taken His place, as a suffering One, outside the range of this world's religion – its politics, and all that pertains to it. The world hated Him, and cast Him out. Wherefore, the word is, *"go forth."* This is the motto, as regards every thing that men would set up here, in the form of a "camp," no matter what that camp may be. If men set up "a holy city," you must look for a rejected Christ "without the gate." If men set up a religious camp, call it by what name you please, you must "go forth" out of it, in order to find a rejected Christ. It is not that blind superstition will not grope amid the ruins of Jerusalem, in search of relics of Christ. It assuredly will do so, and has done so. It will affect to find out, and do honour to, the site of His cross, and to His sepulchre. Nature's covetousness, too, taking advantage of nature's superstition, has carried on, for ages, a lucrative traffic, under the crafty plea of doing honour to the so-called sacred localities of antiquity. But a single ray of light from Revelation's heavenly lamp, is sufficient to enable us to say that you must "go forth" of all these things, in order to find and enjoy communion with a rejected Christ.

However, my reader will need to remember that there is far more involved in the soul-stirring call to "go forth," than a mere escape from the gross absurdities of an ignorant superstition, or the designs of a crafty covetousness. There are many who can, powerfully and eloquently, expose all such things, who are very far indeed from any thought of responding to the apostolic summons. When men set up a "camp," and rally round a standard on which is emblazoned some important dogma of truth, or some valuable institution – when they can appeal to an orthodox creed – an advanced and enlightened scheme of doctrine – a splendid ritual, capable of satisfying the most ardent aspirations of man's devotional nature – when any or all of these things exist, it demands much spiritual intelligence to discern the real force and proper application of the words, "let us go forth," and much spiritual energy and decision to act upon them. They should, however, be discerned and acted upon, for it is perfectly certain that the atmosphere of a camp, let its ground or standard be what it may, is destructive of personal communion with a rejected Christ; and no so-called religious advantage can ever make up for the loss of that communion. It is the tendency of our hearts to drop into cold stereotyped forms. This has ever been the case in the professing church. These forms may have originated in real power. They may have resulted from positive visitations of the Spirit of God. The temptation is to stereotype the form when the spirit and power have all departed. This is, in principle, to set up a camp. The Jewish system could boast a divine origin. A Jew could triumphantly point to the temple, with its splendid system of worship, its priesthood, its sacrifices, its entire furniture, and show that it had all been handed down from the God of Israel. He could give chapter and verse, as we say, for everything connected with the system to which he was attached. Where is the system, ancient, mediaeval, or modern, that could put forth such lofty and powerful pretensions, or come down upon the heart with such an overwhelming weight of authority? And yet, the command was to "GO FORTH."

This is a deeply solemn matter. It concerns us all, because we are all prone to slip away from communion with a living Christ and sink into dead routine. Hence the practical power of the words, "go forth therefore unto *him*." It is not, Go forth from one system to another – from one set of opinions to another – from one company of people to another. No: but go forth from everything that merits the appellation of a camp, "*to him*" who "suffered without the gate." The Lord Jesus is as thoroughly outside the gate now, as He was when He suffered there eighteen centuries ago. What was it that put Him outside? "The religious world" of that day: and the religious world of that day is, in spirit and principle, the religious world of the present moment. The world is the world still. "There is nothing new under the sun." Christ and the world are not one. The world has covered itself with the cloak of Christianity; but it is only in order that its hatred to Christ may work itself up into more deadly forms underneath. Let us not deceive ourselves. If we will walk with a rejected Christ, we must be a rejected people. If our Master "suffered *without* the gate," we cannot expect to reign *within* the gate. If we walk in His footsteps, whither will they lead us? Surely, not to the high places of this Godless, Christless world.

> "His path, uncheered by earthly smiles,
> Led only to the cross."

He is a despised Christ – a rejected Christ – a Christ outside the camp. Oh! then, dear Christian reader, let us go forth to Him, bearing His reproach. Let us not bask in the sunshine of this world's favour, seeing it crucified, and still hates, with an unmitigated hatred, the beloved One to whom we owe our present and eternal all, and who loves us with a love which many waters cannot quench. Let us not, directly or indirectly, accredit that thing which calls itself by His sacred name, but, in reality, hates His Person, hates His ways, hates His truth, hates the bare mention of His advent. Let us be faithful to an absent Lord. Let us live for Him who died for us. While our consciences repose in His blood, let our heart's affections entwine themselves around His Person; so that our separation from "this present evil world" may not be merely a matter of cold principle, but an affectionate separation, because the object of our affections is not here. May the Lord deliver us from the influence of that consecrated, prudential selfishness, so common at the present time, which would not be without religiousness, but is the enemy of the cross of Christ. What we want, in order to make a successful stand against this terrible form of evil, is not peculiar views, or special principles, or curious theories, or cold intellectual accuracy. We want a deep-toned devotedness to the Person of the Son of God; a whole-hearted consecration of ourselves, body, soul, and spirit, to His service; an earnest longing for His glorious advent. These, my reader, are the special wants of the times in which you and I live. Will you not, then, join in uttering, from the very depths of your heart, the cry, "O Lord, revive thy work" – "accomplish the number of thine elect!" – "hasten thy kingdom!" – "Come, Lord Jesus, come quickly!"

---

[9] There is this difference between the offering for "a ruler," and for "one of the common people:" in the former, it was "a *male* without blemish;" in the latter, "a *female* without blemish." The sin of a ruler would, necessarily, exert a wider influence than that of a common person; and, therefore, a more powerful application of the value of the blood was needed. In chapter 5:13, we find cases demanding a still lower application of the sin offering – cases of swearing and of touching any uncleanness, in which "the tenth part of an ephah of fine flour" was admitted as a sin offering (see Lev. 5:11-13). What a contrast between the view of atonement presented by a ruler's bullock, and a poor man's handful of flour! And yet, in the latter, just as truly as in the former, we read, "it shall be forgiven him."

The reader will observe that chapter 5:1-13, forms a part of chapter 4. Both are comprehended under one head, and present the doctrine of sin offering, in all its applications, from the bullock to the handful of flour. Each class of offering is introduced by the words, "And the Lord spake unto Moses." Thus, for example, the sweet savour offerings (chap. 1 – 3) are introduced by the words, "The Lord called unto Moses." These words are not repeated until chap. 4:1, where they introduce the sin offering. They occur again at chap. 5:14, where they introduce the trespass offering for wrongs done "in the holy things of the Lord;" and again at chap. 6:1, where they introduce the trespass offering for wrong done to one's neighbour.

This classification is beautifully simple, and will help the reader to understand the different classes of offering. As to the different grades in each class, whether "a bullock," "a ram," "a female," "a bird," "or "a handful of flour," they would seem to be so many varied applications of the same grand truth.

[10] I would desire it to be particularly remembered, that the point before us in the text is simply atonement. The Christian reader is fully aware, I doubt not, that the possession of "the divine nature" is essential to fellowship with God. I not only need a *title* to approach God: but a *nature* to enjoy Him. The soul that "believes in the name of the only-begotten Son of God" has both the one and the other (see John 1:12, 13; 3:36; 5:24; 20:31; 1 John 5:11-13).

[11] Some may find difficulty in the fact that the word "voluntary" has reference to the worshipper and not to the sacrifice; but this can, in no wise, affect the doctrine put forward in the text, which is founded upon the fact that a special word used in the burnt offering is omitted in the sin offering. The contrast holds good, whether we think of the offerer or the offering.

[12] The statement in the text refers only to the sin offerings of which the blood was brought into the holy place. There were sin offerings of which Aaron and his *sons* partook (see Lev 6:26, 29; Num. 18:9, 10).

[13] We have a singularly-beautiful example of the divine accuracy of Scripture, in 2 Cor. 5:21. "He hath *made* him to be sin (*hamartian epoiēsen*) for us, that we might *become* (*ginōmetha*) the righteousness of God in him." The English reader might suppose that the word which is rendered "made" is the same in each clause of the passage. This is not the case.

[14] The Epistle to the Ephesians furnishes the most elevated view of the Church's place above, and gives it to us, not merely as to the title, but also as to the mode. The title is, assuredly, the blood; but the mode is thus stated: "But God, who is rich in mercy, for his great love, wherewith he loved us, even when we were dead in sins, hath quickened us together with Christ (by grace ye are saved); and hath raised us up together, and made us sit together in heavenly places in Christ Jesus" (Eph. 2:4-6).

THE TRESPASS OFFERING

The holiness of God

These verses contain the doctrine of the trespass offering, of which there were two distinct kinds, namely, trespass against *God*, and trespass against *man*. "If a soul commit a trespass, and sin *through ignorance*, in the holy things of the Lord, then shall he bring for his trespass unto the Lord, a ram without blemish out of the flocks, with thy estimation by shekels of silver, after the shekel of the sanctuary, for a trespass offering." Here we have a case in which a positive wrong was done, in the holy things which pertained unto the Lord; and, albeit this was done "through ignorance," yet could it not be passed over. God can forgive all manner of trespass, but He cannot pass over a single jot or tittle. His grace is perfect, and therefore He can forgive *all*. His holiness is perfect, and therefore He cannot pass over anything. He cannot sanction iniquity, but He can blot it out, and that, moreover, according to the perfection of His grace, and according to the perfect claims of His holiness.

It is a very grave error to suppose that, provided a man acts up to the dictates of his conscience, he is all right and safe. The peace which rests upon such a foundation as this will be eternally destroyed when the light of the judgment-seat shines in upon the conscience. God could never lower His claim to such a level. The balances of the sanctuary are regulated by a very different scale from that afforded by the most sensitive conscience. We have had occasion to dwell upon this point before, in the notes on the sin offering. It cannot be too strongly insisted upon. There are two things involved in it. First, a just perception of what the holiness of God really is; and, secondly, a clear sense of the ground of a believer's peace, in the divine presence.

Whether it be a question of my condition or my conduct, my nature or my acts, God alone can be the Judge of what suits Himself, and of what befits His holy presence. Can human ignorance furnish a plea, when divine requirements are in question? God forbid. A wrong has been done "in the holy things of the Lord;" but man's conscience has not taken cognizance of it. What then? Is there to be nothing more about it? Are the claims of God to be thus lightly disposed of? Assuredly not. This would be subversive of every thing like divine relationship. The righteous are called to give thanks at the remembrance of God's holiness (Psalm 97:12). How can they do this? Because their peace has been secured on the ground of the full vindication and perfect establishment of that holiness. Hence, the higher their sense of what that holiness is, the deeper and more settled must be their peace. This is a truth of the most precious nature. The unregenerate man could never rejoice in the divine holiness. His aim would be to lower that holiness, if he could not ignore it altogether. Such an one will console himself with the thought that God is good, God is gracious, God is merciful; but you will never find him rejoicing in the thought that God is holy. He has unholy thoughts respecting God's goodness, His grace, and His mercy. He would fain find in those blessed attributes, an excuse for his continuing in sin.

On the contrary, the renewed man exults in the holiness of God. He sees the full expression thereof in the cross of the Lord Jesus Christ. It is that holiness which has laid the foundation of his peace; and, not only so, but he is made a partaker of it, and he delights in it, while he hates sin with a perfect hatred. The instincts of the divine nature shrink from it, and long after holiness. It would be impossible to enjoy true peace and liberty of heart, if one did not know that the claims connected with "the holy things of the Lord" had been perfectly met by our divine Trespass Offering;. There would ever be, springing up in the heart, the painful sense that those claims had been slighted, through our manifold infirmities and shortcomings. Our very best services, our holiest seasons, our most hallowed exercises, may present something of trespass "in the holy things of the Lord" – "something that ought not to be done." How often are our seasons of public worship and private devotion infringed upon and marred by barrenness and distraction! Hence it is that we need the assurance that our trespasses have all been divinely met by the precious blood of Christ. Thus, in the ever-blessed Lord Jesus, we find One who has come down to the full measure of our necessities as sinners by nature, and trespassers in act. We find in Him the perfect answer to all the cravings of a guilty conscience, and to all the claims of infinite holiness, in reference to *all* our sins and *all* our trespasses; so that the believer can stand, with an uncondemning conscience and emancipated heart, in the full light of that holiness which is too pure to behold iniquity or look upon sin.

Restitution and a fifth part added

"And he shall make amends for the harm that he hath done in the holy thing, and shall add the fifth part thereto, and give it unto the priest: and the priest shall make an atonement for him with the ram of the trespass offering, and it shall be forgiven him" (chap. 5:16). In the addition of "the fifth part," as here set forth, we have a feature of the true Trespass Offering, which, it is to be feared, is but little appreciated. When we think of all the wrong and all the trespass which we have done against the Lord; and, further, when we remember how God has been wronged of His rights in this wicked world, with what interest can we contemplate the work of the cross as that wherein God has not merely received back what was lost, but whereby He is an actual gainer. He has gained more by redemption than ever He lost by the fall. He reaps a richer harvest of glory, honour, and praise, in the fields of redemption, than ever He could have reaped from those of creation. "The sons of God" could raise a loftier song of praise around the empty tomb of Jesus than ever they raised in view of the Creator's accomplished work. The wrong has not only been perfectly atoned for, but an eternal advantage has been gained, by the work of the cross. This is a stupendous truth. God is a gainer by the work of Calvary. Who could have conceived this? When we behold man, and the creation of which he was lord, laid in ruins at the feet of the enemy, how could we conceive that, from amid those ruins, God should gather richer and nobler spoils than any which our unfallen world could have yielded? Blessed be the name of Jesus for all this! It is to Him we owe it all. It is by His precious cross that ever a truth so amazing, so divine, could be enunciated. Assuredly, that cross involves a mysterious wisdom "which none of the princes of this world knew; for had they known it, they would not have crucified the Lord of glory" (1 Cor. 2:8). No marvel, therefore, that round that cross, and round Him who was crucified thereon, the affections of patriarchs, prophets, apostles, martyrs, and saints, have ever entwined themselves. No marvel that the Holy Ghost should have given forth that solemn but just decree, "If any man love not our Lord Jesus Christ, let him be Anathema Maranatha" (1 Cor. 16:22). Heaven and earth shall echo forth a loud and an eternal amen to this anathema. No marvel that it should be the fixed and immutable purpose of the divine mind, that "at the name of Jesus every knee should bow, of things in heaven, and things on earth, and things under the earth; and that every tongue should confess that Jesus Christ is Lord, to the glory of God the Father" (Phil. 2:10, 11).

The same law in reference to "the fifth part" obtained in the case of a trespass committed against a man, as we read, "If a soul sin, and commit a trespass *against the Lord*,[15] and lie unto his neighbour in that which was delivered him to keep, or in fellowship, or in a thing taken away by violence, or have deceived his neighbour, or have found that which was lost, and lieth concerning it, and sweareth falsely; in any of all these that a man doeth, sinning therein: then it shall be, because he hath sinned, and is guilty, that he shall restore that which he took violently away, or the thing which he hath deceitfully gotten, or that which was delivered him to keep, or the lost thing which he found, or all that about which he hath sworn falsely; he shall even restore it in the principal, and shall *add the fifth part more thereto*, and give it unto him to whom it appertaineth, in the day of his trespass offerings (Lev. 6:2-5).

Man, as well as God, is a positive gainer by the cross. The believer can say, as he gazes upon that cross, "Well, it matters not how I have been wronged, how I have been trespassed against, how I have been deceived, what ills have been done to me, I am a gainer by the cross. I have not merely received back all that was lost, but much more beside."

Thus, whether we think of the injured, or the injurer, in any given case, we are equally struck with the glorious triumphs of redemption, and the mighty practical results which flow from that gospel which fills the soul with the happy assurance, that "all trespasses" are "forgiven," and that the root from whence those trespasses have sprung, has been judged. "The gospel of the glory of the blessed God" is that which alone can send forth a man into the midst of a scene which has been the witness of his sins, his trespasses, and his injurious ways – can send him back to all who, in anywise, have been sufferers by his evil doings, furnished with grace, not only to repair the wrongs, but, far more, to allow the full tide of practical benevolence to flow forth in all his ways, yea, to love his enemies, to do good to them that hate him, and to pray for them that despitefully use him and persecute him. Such is the precious grace of God, that acts in connexion with our great Trespass Offering – such are its rich, rare, and refreshing fruits!

What a triumphant answer to the caviller who could say, "shall we continue in sin, that grace may abound?"

Grace not merely cuts up sin by the roots, but transforms the sinner from a curse into a blessing; from a moral plague, into a channel of divine mercy; from an emissary of Satan, into a messenger of God; from a child of darkness, into a son of the light; from a self-indulgent pleasure-hunter, into a self-denying lover of God; from a slave of vile, selfish lusts, into a willing-hearted servant of Christ; from a cold, narrow-hearted miser, into a benevolent minister to the need of his fellow-man. Away, then, with the oft-repeated taunts, "Are we to do nothing?" – "That is a marvellously easy way to be saved" – "According to this gospel we may live as we list." Let all who utter such language behold yonder thief transformed into a liberal donor, and let them be silent for ever (see Eph. 4:28). They know not what grace means. They have never felt its sanctifying and elevating influences. They forget that, while the blood of the trespass offering cleanses the conscience, the law of that offering sends the trespasser back to the one whom he has wronged, with "the principal" and "the fifth" in his hand. Noble testimony this, both to the grace and righteousness of the God of Israel! Beauteous exhibition of the results of that marvellous scheme of redemption, whereby the injurer is forgiven, and the injured becomes an actual gainer! If the conscience has been set to rights, by the blood of the cross, in reference to the claims of God, the conduct must be set to rights, by the holiness of the cross, in reference to the claims of practical righteousness. These things must never be separated. God has joined them together, and let not man put them asunder. The hallowed union will never be dissolved by any mind which is governed by pure gospel morality. Alas! it is easy to profess the principles of grace, while the practice and power thereof are completely denied. It is easy to talk of resting in the blood of the trespass offering, while "the principal" and "the fifth" are not forthcoming. This is vain, and worse than vain. "He that doeth not righteousness is not of God" (1 John 3:10).

Nothing can be more dishonouring to the pure grace of the gospel than the supposition that a man may belong to God, while his conduct and character exhibit not the fair traces of practical holiness. "Known unto God are all his works," no doubt; but He has given us, in His holy word, those evidences by which we can discern those that belong to Him. "The foundation of God standeth sure, having this seal, The Lord knoweth them that are His: and, Let every one that nameth the name of Christ depart from iniquity" (2 Tim. 2:19). We have no right to suppose that an evildoer belongs to God. The holy instincts of the divine nature are shocked by the mention of such a thing. People sometimes express much difficulty in accounting for such and such evil practices on the part of those whom they cannot help regarding in the light of Christians. The word of God settles the matter so clearly and so authoritatively, as to leave no possible ground for any such difficulty. "In this the children of God are manifest, and the children of the devil: whosoever doeth not righteousness is not of God, neither he that loveth not his brother." It is well to remember this, in this day of laxity and self-indulgence. There is a fearful amount of easy, uninfluential profession abroad, against which the genuine Christian is called upon to make a firm stand, and bear a severe testimony – a testimony resulting from the steady exhibition of "the fruits of righteousness which are by Jesus Christ unto the glory and praise of God." It is most deplorable to see so many going along the beaten path – the well-trodden highway of religious profession, and yet manifesting not a trace of love or holiness in their conduct. Christian reader, let us be faithful. Let us rebuke, by a life of self-denial and genuine benevolence, the self-indulgence and culpable inactivity of evangelical yet worldly profession. May God grant unto all His true-hearted people abundant grace for these things!

Trespasses against God and trespasses against man

Let us now proceed to compare the two classes of trespass offering; namely, the offering on account of trespass "in the holy things of the Lord," and that which had reference to a trespass committed in the common transactions and relations of human life. In so doing, we shall find one or two points which demand our attentive consideration.

And, first, the expression, "if a soul sin through ignorance," which occurs in the former, is omitted in the latter. The reason of this is obvious. The claims which stand connected with the holy things of the Lord, must pass, infinitely, beyond the reach of the most elevated human sensibility. Those claims may be, continually, interfered with – continually trespassed upon, and the trespasser not be aware of the fact. Man's consciousness can never be the regulator in the sanctuary of God. This is an unspeakable mercy. God's holiness alone must fix the standard, when God's rights are in question.

On the other hand, the human conscience can readily grasp the full amount of a human claim, and can readily take cognizance of any interference with such claim. How often may we have wronged God, in His holy things, without ever taking a note of it in the tablet of conscience – yea, without having the competency to detect it (see Mal. 3:8). Not so, however, when man's rights are in question. The wrong which the human eye can see, and the human heart feel, the human conscience can take notice of. A man, "through ignorance" of the laws which governed the sanctuary of old, might commit a trespass against those laws, without being aware of it, until a higher light had shone in upon his conscience. But a man could not, "through ignorance," tell a lie, swear falsely, commit an act of violence, deceive his neighbour, or find a lost thing and deny it. These were all plain and palpable acts, lying within the range of the most sluggish sensibility. Hence it is that the expression, "through ignorance" is introduced, in reference to "the holy things of the Lord," and omitted, in reference to the common affairs of men. How blessed it is to know that the precious blood of Christ has settled all questions whether with respect to God or man – our sins of ignorance or our known sins! Here lies the deep and settled foundation of the believer's peace. The cross has divinely met ALL.

Again, when it was a question of trespass "in the holy things of the Lord," the unblemished sacrifice was first introduced; and, afterward "the principal" and "the fifth."

This order was reversed when it was a question of the common affairs of life (comp. chap. 5:15, 16 with chap. 6:4-7) The reason of this is equally obvious. When the divine rights were infringed, the blood of atonement was made the great prominent matter. Whereas, when human rights were interfered with, restitution would naturally assume the leading place in the mind. But, inasmuch as the latter involved the question of the soul's relation with God, as well as the former, therefore the sacrifice is introduced, though it be last in order. If I wrong my fellow man, that wrong will, undoubtedly, interfere with my communion with God; and that communion can only be restored on the ground of atonement. Mere restitution would not avail. It might satisfy the injured man, but it could not form the basis of restored communion with God. I might restore "the principal" and add "the fifth," ten thousand times over, and yet my sin remain, for "Without shedding of blood is no remission." (Heb. 9:22) Still, if it be a question of injury done to my neighbour, then restitution must first be made. "If thou bring thy gift to the altar, and there rememberest that thy brother hath anything against thee, leave there thy gift before the altar, and go thy way; first be reconciled to thy brother, and then come and offer thy gift" (Matt. 5:23, 24).[16]

There is far more involved in the divine order prescribed in the trespass offering, than might, at first sight, appear. The claims which arise out of our human relations must not be disregarded. They must ever get their proper place in the heart. This is distinctly taught in the trespass offering. When an Israelite had, by an act of trespass, deranged his relation with Jehovah, the order was, sacrifice and restitution. When he had, by an act of trespass, deranged his relation with his neighbour, the order was, restitution and sacrifice. Will any one undertake to say this is a distinction without a difference? Does the change of the order not convey its own appropriate, because divinely appointed, lesson? Unquestionably. Every point is pregnant with meaning, if we will but allow the Holy Ghost to convey that meaning to our hearts, and not seek to grasp it by the aid of our poor vain imaginings. Each offering conveys its own characteristic view of the Lord Jesus, and His work; and each is presented in its own characteristic order; and we may safely say, it is, at once, the business and the delight of the spiritual mind to apprehend both the one and the other. The very same character of mind which would seek to make nothing of the peculiar order of each offering, would also set aside the idea of a peculiar phase of Christ in each. It would deny the existence of any difference between the burnt offering and the sin offering; and between the sin offering and the trespass offering; and between any or all of these and the meat offering or the peace offering. Hence, it would follow that the first seven chapters of the Book of Leviticus are all a vain repetition, each successive chapter going over the same thing. Who could cede anything so monstrous as this? What Christian mind could suffer such an insult to be offered to the sacred page? A German rationalist or neologian may put forth such vain and detestable notions; but those who have been divinely taught that "all scripture is given by inspiration of God," will be led to regard the various types, in their specific order, as so many variously-shaped caskets, in which the Holy Ghost has treasured up, for the people of God, "the unsearchable riches of Christ." There is no tedious repetition, no redundancy. All is rich, divine, heavenly variety; and all we need is to be personally acquainted with the great Antitype, in order to enter into the beauties and seize the delicate touches of each type. Directly the heart lays hold of the fact that it is Christ we have, in each type, it can hang, with spiritual interest, over the most minute details. It sees meaning and beauty in everything – it finds Christ in all. As, in the kingdom of nature, the telescope and the microscope present to the eye their own special wonders, so with the word of God. Whether we look at it as a whole, or scrutinise each clause, we find that which elicits the worship and thanksgiving of our hearts.

Christian reader, may the name of the Lord Jesus ever

be more precious to our hearts! Then shall we value everything that speaks of Him – everything that sets Him forth – everything according a fresh insight into His peculiar excellency and matchless beauty.

---

[15] There is a fine principle invoked in the expression, "against the Lord." Although the matter in question was a wrong done to one's neighbour, yet the Lord looked upon it as a trespass against Himself. Everything must be viewed in reference to the Lord. It matters not who may be affected, Jehovah must get the first place. Thus, when David's conscience was pierced by the arrow of conviction, in reference to his treatment of Uriah, he exclaims, "I have sinned *against the Lord*" (2 Sam. 12:13). This principle does not, in the least, interfere with the injured man's claim.

[16] From a comparison of Matt. 5:23, 24 with Matt. 18:21, 22, we may learn a fine principle, as to the way in which wrongs and injuries are to be settled between two brothers. The injurer is sent back from the altar, in order to have his matters set straight with the injured one; for there can be no communion with the Father so long as my brother "hath anything against me." But, then, mark the beauteous way in which the injured one is taught to receive the injurer. "Lord, how oft shall my brother sin against me, and I forgive him? till seven times? Jesus saith unto him, I say not unto thee, until seven times; but, *until seventy times seven*." Such is the divine mode of settling all questions between brethren. "Forbearing one another, and forgiving one another, if any man have a quarrel against any: even as Christ forgave you, so also do ye" (Col 3:13).

Chapter 6:8-30 & Chapter 7

THE LAW OF VARIOUS OFFERINGS

The remainder of chap. 6, together with the whole of chap. 7, is occupied with the law of the various offerings to which reference has already been made. There are, however, some points presented in the law of the sin offering and the trespass offering which may be noticed ere we leave this copious section of our book.

In none of the offerings is Christ's personal holiness more strikingly presented than in the sin offering. "Speak unto Aaron and to his sons, saying, This is the law of the sin offering. In the place where the burnt offering is killed shall the sin offering be killed before the Lord: *it is most holy* . . . Whatsoever shall touch the flesh thereof *shall be holy* . . . All the males among the priests shall eat thereof: *it is most holy*" (chap. 6:25- 29). So also in speaking of the meat offering, "it is most holy, *as is the sin offering,* and as the trespass offering." This is most marked and striking. The Holy Ghost did not need to guard with such jealousy, the personal holiness of Christ in the burnt offering; but lest the soul should, by any means, lose sight of that holiness, while contemplating the place which the Blessed One took in the sin offering, we are, again and again, reminded of it by the words, "it is most holy." Truly edifying and refreshing it is to behold the divine and essential holiness of the Person of Christ shining forth in the midst of Calvary's profound and awful gloom. The same point is observable in "the law of the trespass offering" (see chap. 7:1, 6). Never was the Lord Jesus more fully seen to be "the Holy One of God" than when He was "made sin" upon the cursed tree. The vileness and blackness of that with which He stood identified on the cross, only served to show out more clearly that He was "most holy." Though a sin-bearer, He was sinless. Though enduring the wrath of *God,* He was the *Father's* delight. Though deprived of the light of *God's* countenance, He dwelt in the *Father's* bosom. Precious mystery! Who can sound its mighty depths? How wonderful to find it so accurately shadowed forth in "the law of the sin offering!"

Again, my reader should seek to apprehend the meaning of the expression, "all the *males* among the priests shall eat thereof." The ceremonial act of eating the sin offering, or the trespass offering, was expressive of full identification. But, to eat the sin offering – to make another's sin one's own, demanded a higher degree of priestly energy, such as was expressed in "the *males* among the priests." "And the Lord spake unto Aaron, Behold, I also have given thee the charge of mine heave offerings, of all the hallowed things of the children of Israel; unto thee have I given them by reason of the anointing, and *to thy sons,* by an ordinance for ever. This shall be thine of the most holy things, reserved from the fire: every oblation of theirs, every meat offering of theirs, and every sin offering of theirs, and every trespass offering of theirs, which they shall render unto me, shall be most holy for thee and for *thy sons.* In the most holy place shalt thou eat it; *every male* shall eat it: it shall be holy unto thee. And this is thine; the heave offering of their gift, with all the wave offerings of the children of Israel: I have given them unto thee, and to thy sons, and to *thy daughters* with thee, by a statute for ever: *every one that is clean* in thy house shall eat of it" (Num. 18:8-11).

It demanded a larger measure of priestly energy to eat of the sin or trespass offering, than merely to partake of the heave and wave offerings of gift. The "daughters" of Aaron could eat of the latter. None but the "sons" could eat of the former. In general, "the male," expresses a thing according to the divine idea: "the female," according to human development. The former gives you the thing in full energy; the latter, in its imperfection. How few of us have sufficient priestly energy to enable us to make another's sin or trespass our own! The blessed Lord Jesus did this perfectly. He made His people's sins His own, and bore the judgment thereof, on the cross. He fully identified Himself with us, so that we may know, in full and blessed certainty, that the whole question of sin and trespass has been divinely settled. If Christ's identification was perfect, then, the settlement was perfect, likewise; and that it was perfect, the scene enacted at Calvary declares. All is accomplished. The sin, the trespasses, the claims of God, the claims of man – all have been eternally settled; and, now, perfect peace is the portion of all who, by grace, accept as true the record of God. It is as simple as God could make it, and the soul that believes it is made happy. The peace and happiness of the believer depend wholly upon the perfection of Christ's sacrifice. It is not a question of his mode of receiving it, his thoughts about it, or his feelings respecting it. It is simply a question of his crediting, by faith, the testimony of God, as to the value of the sacrifice. The Lord be praised for His own simple and perfect way of peace! May many troubled souls be led by the Holy Spirit into an understanding thereof!

We shall here close our meditations upon one of the richest sections in the whole canon of inspiration. It is but little we have been enabled to glean from it. We have hardly penetrated below the surface of an exhaustless mine. If, however, the reader has, for the first time, been led to view the offerings as so many varied exhibitions of the great Sacrifice, and if he is led to cast himself at the feet of the great Teacher, to learn more of the living depths of these things, I cannot but feel that an end has been gained for which we may well feel deeply thankful.

THE PRIESTHOOD

Christ, sacrifice and priest

Having considered the doctrine of sacrifice, as unfolded in the first seven chapters of this book, we now approach the subject of priesthood. The two subjects are intimately connected. The sinner needs a *sacrifice*; the believer needs a *priest*. We have both the one and the other in Christ, who, having offered Himself, without spot, to God, entered upon the sphere of His priestly ministry, in the sanctuary above. We need no other sacrifice, no other priest. Jesus is divinely sufficient. He imparts the dignity and worth of His own Person to every office He sustains, and to every work He performs. When we see Him as a sacrifice, we know that we have in Him all that a perfect sacrifice could be; and, when we see Him as a priest, we know that every function of the priesthood is perfectly discharged by Him. As a sacrifice, He introduces His people into a settled relationship with God; and, as a priest, He maintains them therein, according to the perfectness of what He is. Priesthood is designed for those who already stand in a certain relationship with God. As sinners, by nature and by practice, we are "brought nigh to God by the blood of the cross." We are brought into an established relationship with Him. We stand before Him as the fruit of His own work. He has put away our sins, in such a manner as suits Himself, so that we might be before Him, to the praise of His name, as the exhibition of what He can accomplish through the power of death and resurrection.

A high priest in the heavens

But, though so fully delivered from every thing that could be against us; though so perfectly accepted in the Beloved; though so complete in Christ; though so highly exalted, yet are we, in ourselves, while down here, poor feeble creatures, ever prone to wander, ready to stumble, exposed to manifold temptations, trials, and snares. As such, we need the ceaseless ministry of our "Great High Priest," whose very presence, in the sanctuary above, maintains us, in the full integrity of that place and relationship in which, through grace, we stand. "He ever liveth to make intercession for us" (Heb. 7:25). We could not stand, for a moment, down here, if He were not living for us, up there. "Because I live, ye shall live also" (John 14:19). "For if, when we were enemies, we were reconciled to God by the death of his Son, much more, being reconciled, we shall be saved by his life" (Rom. 5:10). The "death" and the "life" are inseparably connected, in the economy of grace. But, be it observed, the life comes after the death. It is Christ's life as risen from the dead, and not His life down here, that the apostle refers to, in the last-quoted passage. This distinction is eminently worthy of my reader's attention. The life of our blessed Lord Jesus, while down here, was, I need hardly remark, infinitely precious; but He did not enter upon His sphere of priestly service until He had accomplished the work of redemption. Nor could He have done so, inasmuch as "it is evident that our Lord sprang out of Judah; of which tribe Moses spake nothing concerning priesthood" (Heb. 7:14). "For every high priest is ordained to offer gifts and sacrifices: wherefore it is of necessity that this man have somewhat also to offer. For if he were on earth, he should not be a priest, seeing that there are priests that offer gifts according to the law" (Heb. 8:3, 4). "But Christ being come an high priest of good things to come, by a greater and more perfect tabernacle, not made with hands, that is to say, not of this building; neither by the blood of goats and calves, but by his own blood he entered in once into the holy place, having obtained eternal redemption

". . . For Christ is not entered into the holy places made with hands, which are the figures of the true; but into heaven itself, now to appear in the presence of God for us" (Heb. 9:11, 12, 24).

Heaven, not earth, is the sphere of Christ's priestly ministry; and on that sphere He entered when He had offered Himself without spot to God. He never appeared as a priest in the temple below. He ofttimes went up to the temple to teach, but never to sacrifice or burn incense. There never was any one ordained of God to discharge the functions of the priestly office on earth, save Aaron and his sons. "If he were on earth, he should not be a priest." This is a point of much interest and value, in connexion with the doctrine of priesthood. Heaven is the sphere, and accomplished redemption the basis, of Christ's priesthood.

Priests on earth?

Save in the sense that all believers are priests (1 Peter 2:5), there is no such thing as a priest upon earth. Unless a man can show his descent from Aaron, unless he can trace his pedigree up to that ancient source, he has no right to exercise the priestly office. Apostolic succession itself, could it be proved, would be of no possible value here, inasmuch as the Apostles themselves were not priests, save in the sense above referred to. The feeblest member of the household of faith is as much a priest as the Apostle Peter himself. He is a spiritual priest; he worships in a spiritual temple; he stands at a spiritual altar; he offers a spiritual sacrifice; he is clad in spiritual vestments. "Ye also, as lively stones, are built up a spiritual house, an holy priesthood, to offer up spiritual sacrifices, acceptable to God by Jesus Christ" (1 Peter 2:5). "By him, therefore, let us offer the sacrifice of praise to God continually, that is, the fruit of our lips, giving thanks to his name. But to do good and to communicate forget not, for with such sacrifices God is well pleased" (Heb. 13:15, 16).

If one of the direct descendants of the house of Aaron were

converted to Christ, he would enter upon an entirely new character and ground of priestly service. And be it observed, that the passages just quoted present the two great classes of spiritual sacrifice which the spiritual priest is privileged to offer. There is the sacrifice of praise to God, and the sacrifice of benevolence to man. There is a double stream continually going forth from the believer who is living in the realization of his priestly place – a stream of grateful praise ascending to the throne of God, and a stream of active benevolence flowing forth to a needy world. The spiritual priest stands with one hand lifted up to God, in the presentation of the incense of grateful praise; and the other opened wide to minister, in genuine beneficence, to every form of human need. Were these things more distinctly apprehended, what hallowed elevation, and what moral grace, would they not impart to the Christian character! Elevation, inasmuch as the heart would ever be lifted up to the infinite Source of all that is capable of elevating – moral grace, inasmuch as the heart would ever be kept open to all demands upon its sympathies. The two things are inseparable. Immediate occupation of heart with God must, of necessity, elevate and enlarge. But, on the other hand, if one walks at a distance from God, the heart will become grovelling and contracted. Intimacy of communion with God – the habitual realisation of our priestly dignity, is the only effectual remedy for the downward and selfish tendencies of the old nature.

The consecration of Aaron before all the assembly

Having said thus much on the subject of priesthood in general, both as to its primary and secondary aspects, we shall proceed to examine the contents of the eighth and ninth chapters of the Book of Leviticus.

"And the Lord spake unto Moses, saying, take Aaron and his sons with him, and the garments, and the anointing oil, and a bullock for the sin offering, and two rams, and a basket of unleavened bread; and gather thou all the congregation together unto the door of the tabernacle of the congregation. And Moses did as the Lord commanded him; and the assembly was gathered together unto the door of the tabernacle of the congregation." There is special grace unfolded here. The whole assembly is convened at the door of the tabernacle of the congregation, in order that all might have the privilege of beholding the one who was about to be entrusted with the charge of their most important interests. In the 28th and 29th of Exodus we are taught the same general truth with respect to the vestments and sacrifices connected with the priestly office; but, in Leviticus, the congregation is introduced, and allowed to look on at every movement in the solemn and impressive service of consecration. The humblest member of the assembly had his own place. Each one, the lowest as well as the highest, was permitted to gaze upon the person of the high priest, upon the sacrifice which he offered, and upon the robes which he wore. Each one had his own peculiar need, and the God of Israel would have each to see and know that his need was fully provided for by the varied qualifications of the high priest who stood before him. Of these qualifications the priestly robes were the apt typical expression. Each portion of the dress was designed and adapted to set forth some special qualification in which the assembly as a whole, and each individual member, would, of necessity, be deeply interested. The coat, the girdle, the robe, the ephod, the breastplate, the Urim and the Thummim, the mitre, the holy crown – all told out the varied virtues, qualifications, and functions of the one who was to represent the congregation and maintain the interests thereof in the divine presence.

Christ, our great high Priest

Thus it is the believer can, with the eye of faith, behold his great High Priest, in the heavens, and see in Him the divine realities of which the Aaronic vestments were but the shadows. The Lord Jesus Christ is the holy One, the anointed One, the mitred One, the girded One. He is all these, not in virtue of outward garments to be put on or off, but in virtue of the divine and eternal graces of His Person, the changeless efficacy of His work, and the imperishable virtue of His sacred offices. This is the special value of studying the types of the Mosaic economy. The enlightened eye sees Christ in all. The blood of the sacrifice and the robe of the high priest both point to Him – both were designed of God to set Him forth. If it be a question of conscience, the blood of the sacrifice meets it, according to the just claims of the sanctuary. Grace has met the demand of holiness. And, then, if it be a question of the need connected with the believer's position down here, he can see it all divinely answered in the official robes of the high priest.

And, here, let me say, there are two ways in which to contemplate the believer's position – two ways in which that position is presented in the word, which must be taken into account ere the true idea of priesthood can be intelligently laid hold of. The believer is represented as being part of a body of which Christ is the Head. This body, with Christ its Head, is spoken of as forming one man, complete, in every respect. It was quickened with Christ, raised with Christ, and seated with Christ, in the heavens. It is one with Him, complete in Him, accepted in Him, possessing His life, and standing in His favour, before God. All trespasses are blotted out. There is no spot. All is fair and lovely beneath the eye of God (see 1 Cor. 12:12, 13; Eph. 2:5-10; Col. 2:6-15; 1 John 4:17).

Then, again, the believer is contemplated as in the place of need, weakness, and dependence, down here, in this world. He is ever exposed to temptation, prone to wander, liable to stumble and fall. As such, he, continually, stands in need of the perfect sympathy and powerful ministrations of the High Priest, who ever appears in the presence of God, in the full value of His Person and work, and who represents the believer and maintains His cause before the throne.

Now my reader should ponder both these aspects of the believer, in order that he may see, not only what a highly exalted and privileged place he occupies with Christ on high, but also what ample provision there is for him, in reference to his every need and weakness, here below. This distinction might, further, be developed, in this way. The believer is represented as being *of the Church,* and in the *kingdom.* As the former, heaven is his place, his home, his portion, the seat of his affections. As the latter, he is on earth, in the place of trial, responsibility, and conflict. Hence, therefore, priesthood is a divine provision for those who, though being of the Church, and belonging to heaven, are, nevertheless, in the kingdom, and walking on the earth. This distinction is a very simple one, and, when apprehended, explains a vast number of passages of Scripture in which many minds encounter considerable difficulty.[17]

In looking into the contents of the chapters which lie open before us, we may remark three things put prominently forward, namely, the authority of the word, the value of the blood, the power of the Spirit. These are weighty matters – matters of unspeakable importance – matters which must be regarded, by every Christian, as, unquestionably, vital and fundamental.

This is the thing which the LORD has commanded

And, first, as to the authority of the word, it is of the deepest interest to see that, in the consecration of the priests, as well as in the entire range of the sacrifices, we are brought immediately under the authority of the word of God. "And Moses said unto the congregation, *This is the thing which the Lord* commanded to be done" (chap. 8:5). And, again, "Moses said, *This is the thing which the Lord* commanded that ye should do: *and the glory of the Lord shall appear unto you*" (chap. 9:6). Let these words sink down into our ears. Let them be carefully and prayerfully pondered. They are priceless words. "*This* is *the* thing which *the Lord* commanded." He did not say, "This is the thing which is expedient, agreeable, or suitable." Neither did He say, "This is the thing which has been arranged by the voice of the fathers, the decree of the elders, or the opinion of the doctors." Moses knew nothing of such sources of authority. To him there was one holy, elevated, paramount source of authority, and that was, the word of Jehovah, and he would bring every member of the assembly into direct contact with that blessed source. This gave assurance to the heart, and fixedness to all the thoughts. There was no room left for tradition, with its uncertain sound, or for man, with his doubtful disputations. All was clear, conclusive, and authoritative. Jehovah had spoken; and all that was needed was to hear what He had said, and obey. Neither tradition nor expediency has any place in the heart that has learnt to prize, to reverence, and to obey the word of God.

And what was to be the result of this strict adherence to the word of God? A truly blessed result, indeed. "The glory of the Lord shall appear unto you." Had the word been disregarded, the glory would not have appeared. The two things were intimately connected. The slightest deviation from "thus saith Jehovah" would have prevented the beams of the divine glory from appearing to the congregation of Israel. Had there been the introduction of a single rite or ceremony not enjoined by the word, or had there been the omission of anything which that word commanded, Jehovah would not have manifested His glory. He could not sanction by the glory of His presence the neglect or rejection of His word. He can bear with ignorance and infirmity, but He cannot sanction neglect or disobedience.

Oh! that all this were more solemnly considered, in this day of tradition and expediency. I would, in earnest affection, and in the deep sense of personal responsibility to my reader, exhort him to give diligent heed to the importance of close – I had almost said severe – adherence and reverent subjection to the word of God. Let him try everything by that standard, and reject all that comes not up to it; let him weigh everything in that balance, and cast aside all that is not full weight; let him measure everything by that rule, and refuse all deviation. If

I could only be the means of awakening one soul to a proper sense of the place which belongs to the word of God, I should feel I had not written my book for nought or in vain.

Reader, pause, and, in the presence of the Searcher of hearts, ask yourself this plain, pointed question, "Am I sanctioning by my presence, or adopting in my practice, any departure from, or neglect of, the word of God?" Make this a solemn, personal matter before the Lord. Be assured of it, it is of the very deepest moment, the very last importance. If you find that you have been, in any wise, connected with, or involved in, anything that wears not the distinct stamp of divine sanction, reject it at once and for ever. Yes, reject it, though arrayed in the imposing vestments of antiquity, accredited by the voice of tradition, and putting forward the almost irresistible plea of expediency. If you cannot say, in reference to everything with which you stand connected, "this is the thing which the Lord hath commanded," then away with it unhesitatingly, away with it for ever. Remember these words, "*As* he hath done this day, *so* the Lord hath commanded to do." Yes, remember the "*as*" and the "*so;*" see that you are connecting them in your ways and associations, and let them never be separated.

The eighth day

"So Aaron and his sons did *all* things *which the Lord commanded* by the hand of Moses." (Lev. 8:36) "And Moses and Aaron went into the tabernacle of the congregation, and came out, and blessed the people: and the glory of the Lord appeared unto all the people. And there came a fire out from before the Lord, and consumed upon the altar the burnt offering and the fat: which, when all the people saw, they shouted and fell on their faces" (chap. 9:23, 24). Here we have an "eighth day" scene – a scene of resurrection-glory. Aaron, having offered the sacrifice, lifted up his hands in priestly benediction upon the people; and then Moses and Aaron retire into the tabernacle, and disappear, while the whole assembly is seen in waiting outside. Finally, Moses and Aaron, representing Christ in His double character as Priest and King, come forth, and bless the people; the glory appears in all its splendour, the fire consumes the sacrifice, and the entire congregation falls prostrate in worship before the presence of the Lord of all the earth.

Now, all this was literally enacted at the consecration of Aaron and his sons. And, moreover, all this was the result of strict adherence to the word of Jehovah. But, ere I turn from this branch of the subject, let me remind the reader, that all that these chapters contain is but "a shadow of good things to come." This, indeed, holds good in reference to the entire Mosaic economy (Heb 10:1). Aaron and his sons, together, represent Christ and His priestly house. Aaron alone represents Christ in His sacrificial and intercessory functions. Moses and Aaron, together, represent Christ as King and Priest. "The eighth day" represents the day of resurrection-glory, when the congregation of Israel shall see the Messiah, seated as Royal Priest upon His throne, and when the glory of Jehovah shall fill the whole earth, as the waters cover the sea. These sublime truths are largely unfolded in the word, they glitter like gems of celestial brilliancy, all along the inspired page; but, lest they should, to any reader, wear the suspicious aspect of novelty, I shall refer him to the following direct scripture proofs; viz., Num. 14:21; Isa. 9:6, 7; 11; 25:6-12; 32:1, 2; 35; 37:31, 32; 40:1-5; 54; 59:16-21; 60 – 66; passim. Jer. 23:5-8; 30:10-24; 33:6-22; Ezek. 48:35; Dan. 7:13, 14; Hosea 14:4-9; Zeph. 3:14-20; Zech. 3:8-10; 6:12, 13; 14.

The blood of the victim

Let us, now, consider the second point presented in our section, namely, the efficacy of the blood. This is unfolded with great fullness, and put forward in great prominence. Whether we contemplate the doctrine of sacrifice or the doctrine of priesthood, we find the shedding of blood gets the same important place. "And he brought the bullock for the sin offering; and Aaron and his sons laid their hands upon the head of the bullock for the sin offering. And he slew it; and Moses took the blood, and put it upon the horns of the altar round about with his finger, and purified the altar, and poured the blood at the bottom of the altar, and sanctified it, to make reconciliation upon it" (chap. 8:14, 15). "And he brought the ram for the burnt offering: and Aaron and his sons laid their hands upon the head of the ram. And he killed it; and Moses sprinkled the blood upon the altar round about" (ver. 18, 19). "And he brought the other ram, the ram of consecration; and Aaron and his sons laid their hands upon the head of the ram. And he slew it; and Moses took of the blood of it, and put it upon the tip of Aaron's right ear, and upon the thumb of his right hand, and upon the great toe of his right foot. And he brought Aaron's sons, and Moses put of the blood upon the tip of their right ear, and upon the thumbs of their right hands, and upon the great toes of their right feet: and Moses sprinkled the blood upon the altar round about" (ver. 22-24).

The import of the various sacrifices has been, in some degree, developed in the opening chapters of this volume; but the passages just quoted serve to show the prominent place which the blood occupies in the consecration of the priests. A blood-stained *ear* was needed to hearken to the divine communications; a blood-stained *hand* was needed to execute the services of the sanctuary; and a blood-stained *foot* was needed to tread the courts of the Lord's house. All this is perfect in its way. The shedding of blood was the grand foundation of all sacrifice for sin; and it stood connected with all the vessels of the ministry, and with all the functions of the priesthood. Throughout the entire range of Levitical service, we observe the value, the efficacy, the power, and the wide application of the blood. "Almost all things are by the law purged with blood" (Heb. 9:22). Christ has entered, by His own blood, into heaven itself. He appears on the throne of the majesty in the heavens, in the value of all that He has accomplished on the cross. His presence on the throne attests the worth and acceptableness of His atoning blood. He is there *for us.* Blessed assurance! He ever liveth. He never changeth; and we are in Him, and as He is. He presents us to the Father, in His own eternal perfectness; and the Father delights in us, as thus presented, even as He delights in the One who presents us. This identification is typically set forth in "Aaron and his sons" laying their hands upon the head of each of the sacrifices. They all stood before God, in the value of the same sacrifice. Whether it were the "bullock for the sin offering," "the ram for the burnt offering," or "the ram of consecration," they jointly laid their hands on all. True, Aaron alone was anointed before the blood was shed. He was clad in his robes of office, and anointed with the holy oil, before ever his sons were clothed or anointed. The reason of this is obvious. Aaron, when spoken of by himself, typifies Christ in His own peerless excellency and dignity; and, as we know, Christ appeared in all His own personal worth and was anointed by the Holy Ghost, previous to the accomplishment of His atoning work. In all things He has the pre-eminence (Col. 1). Still, there is the fullest identification, afterwards, between Aaron and his sons, as there is the fullest identification between Christ and His people. "The sanctifier and the sanctified are all of one" (Heb. 2). The personal distinctness enhances the value of the mystic oneness.

Aaron and his sons; Christ and the church

This truth of the distinctness and yet oneness of the Head and members leads us, naturally, to our third and last point, namely, the power of the Spirit. We may remark how much takes place between the anointing of Aaron and the anointing of his sons with him. The blood is shed, the fat consumed on the altar, and the breast waved before the Lord. In other words, the sacrifice is perfected, the sweet odour thereof ascends to God, and the One who offered it ascends in the power of resurrection, and takes His place on high. All this comes in between the anointing of the Head and the anointing of the members. Let us quote and compare the passages. First, as to Aaron alone, we read, "And he put upon him the coat, and girded him with the girdle, and clothed him with the robe, and put the ephod upon him, and he girded him with the curious girdle of the ephod, and bound it unto him therewith. And he put the breastplate upon him: also he put in the breastplate the Urim and the Thummim. And he put the mitre upon his head: and upon the mitre, even upon his forefront, did he put the golden plate, the holy crown; as the Lord commanded Moses. And Moses took the anointing oil, and anointed the tabernacle and all that was therein, and sanctified them. And he sprinkled thereof upon the altar seven times, and anointed the altar and all his vessels, both the laver and his foot, to sanctify them. And he poured of the anointing oil upon Aaron's head, and anointed him, to sanctify him" (chap. 8:7-12).

Here we have Aaron presented alone. The anointing oil is poured upon his head, and that, too, in immediate connexion with the anointing of all the vessels of the tabernacle. The whole assembly was permitted to behold the high priest clothed in his official robes, mitred and anointed; and not only so, but as each garment was put on, as each act was performed, as each ceremony was enacted, it was seen to be immediately founded upon the authority of the word. There was nothing vague, nothing arbitrary, nothing imaginative. All was divinely stable. The need of the congregation was fully met, and met in such a way as that it could be said, "This is the thing which Jehovah commanded to be done."

Now, in Aaron anointed, alone, previous to the shedding of the blood, we have a type of Christ who, until He offered Himself upon the cross, stood entirely alone. There could be no union between Him and His people, save on the ground of death and resurrection. This all-important truth has already been referred to, and, in some measure, developed in connexion with the subject of sacrifice; but it adds force and interest to it to see it so distinctly presented in connexion with the question of priesthood. Without shedding of blood there was no remission – the sacrifice was not completed. So, also, without shedding of blood Aaron and his sons could not be anointed together. Let the reader note this fact. Let him be assured of it, it is worthy of his deepest attention. We must ever beware of passing lightly over any circumstance in the Levitical economy. Everything has its own specific voice and meaning; and the One who designed and developed the order can expound to the heart and understanding what that order means.

"And Moses took of the anointing *oil*, and of the *blood* which was upon the altar, and sprinkled it upon Aaron, and upon his garments, and upon his sons, and upon his sons' garments *with him*"; and sanctified Aaron, and his garments, and his sons, and his sons' garments *with him*' (chap. 8:30). Why were not Aaron's sons anointed with him at verse 12? Simply because the blood had not been shed. When "the blood" and "the oil" could be connected together, then Aaron and his sons could be "anointed" and "sanctified" together; but not until then. "And for their sakes I sanctify myself, that they also might be sanctified through the truth" (John 17:19). The reader who could lightly pass over so marked a circumstance, or say it meant nothing, has yet to learn to value aright the types of the Old Testament Scriptures – "the shadows of good things to come." And, on the other hand, the one who admits that it does mean something, but yet refuses to enquire and understand what that something is, is doing serious damage to his own soul, and manifesting but little interest in the precious oracles of God.

"And Moses said unto Aaron and to his sons, Boil the flesh at the door of the tabernacle of the congregation; and there eat it with the bread that is in the basket of consecrations, as I commanded, saying, Aaron and his sons shall eat it. And that which remaineth of the flesh and of the bread shall ye burn with fire. And ye shall not go out of the door of the tabernacle of the congregation in seven days, until the days of your consecration be at an end: for seven days shall he consecrate you. As he hath done this day, so the Lord hath commanded to do, to make an atonement for you. Therefore shall ye abide at the door of the tabernacle of the congregation day and night seven days, and keep the charge of the Lord, that ye die not: for so I am commanded" (ver. 31-35). These verses furnish a fine type of Christ and His people feeding together upon the results of accomplished atonement. Aaron and his sons, having been anointed together, on the ground of the shed blood, are here presented to our view as shut in within the precincts of the tabernacle during "seven days." A striking figure of the present position of Christ and His members, during the entire of this dispensation, shut in with God, and waiting for the manifestation of the glory. Blessed position! Blessed portion! Blessed hope! To be associated with Christ, shut in with God, waiting for the day of glory, and, while waiting for the glory, feeding upon the riches of divine grace, in the power of holiness, are blessings of the most precious nature, privileges of the very highest order. Oh! for a capacity to take them in, a heart to enjoy them, a deeper sense of their magnitude. May our hearts be withdrawn from all that pertains to this present evil world, so that we may feed upon the contents of "the basket of consecrations," which is our proper food as priests in the sanctuary of God.

The glory of the millennial reign

"And it came to pass *on the eighth day,* that Moses called Aaron, and his sons, and *the elders of Israel.* And he said unto Aaron, Take thee a young calf for a sin offering, and a ram for a burnt offering, without blemish, and offer them before the Lord. And unto *the children of Israel* thou shalt speak, saying, Take ye a kid of the goats for a sin offering; and a calf and a lamb, both of the first year, without blemish, for a burnt offering; also a bullock and a ram for peace offerings, to sacrifice before the Lord; and a meat offering mingled with oil; for TODAY THE LORD WILL APPEAR UNTO YOU" (chap. 9:1-4).

The "seven days" being over, during which Aaron and his sons were shut in in the retirement of the tabernacle, the whole congregation is now introduced, and the glory of

Jehovah unfolds itself. This gives great completeness to the whole scene. The shadows of good things to come are here passing before us, in their divine order. "The eighth day" is a shadow of that bright millennial morning which is about to dawn upon this earth, when the congregation of Israel shall behold the True Priest coming forth from the sanctuary, where He is now, hidden from the eyes of men, and with Him a company of priests, the companions of His retirement, and the happy participators of His manifested glory. In short, nothing, as a type or shadow, could be more complete. In the first place, Aaron and his sons washed with water – a type of Christ and His people, as viewed in God's eternal decree, sanctified together, in purpose (chap. 8:6). Then we have the mode and order in which this purpose was to be carried out. Aaron, in solitude, is robed and anointed – a type of Christ as sanctified and sent into the world, and anointed by the Holy Ghost (ver. 7-12; comp. Luke 3:21, 22; John 10:36; 12:24). Then, we have the presentation and acceptance of the sacrifice, in virtue of which Aaron and his sons were anointed and sanctified *together* (ver. 14 – 29), a type of the cross, in its application to those who now constitute Christ's priestly household, who are united to Him, anointed with Him, hidden with Him, and expecting with Him "the eighth day," when He with them shall be manifested in all the brightness of that glory which belongs to Him in the eternal purpose of God (John 14:19; Acts; 2:33; 19:1-7; Col. 3:1-4). Finally, we have Israel brought into the full enjoyment of the results of accomplished atonement. They are gathered before the Lord: "And Aaron lifted up his hand toward the people, and blessed them, and came down from offering of the sin offering, and the burnt offering, and peace offerings" (see Lev. 9:1-22.).

What, now, we may legitimately enquire, remains to be done? Simply that the topstone should be brought forth with shoutings of victory and hymns of praise. "And Moses and Aaron went into the tabernacle of the congregation, and came out, and blessed the people: *and the glory of the Lord appeared unto all the people.* And there came a fire out from before the

Lord, and consumed upon the altar the burnt offering and the fat: which when all the people saw, THEY SHOUTED, AND FELL ON THEIR FACES" (ver. 23, 24). This was the shout of victory – the prostration of worship. All was complete. The sacrifice – the robed and mitred priest – the priestly family associated with their Head – priestly benediction – the appearance of the King and Priest – in short, nothing was lacking, and therefore the divine glory appeared, and the whole assembly fell prostrate, in adoring worship. It is, altogether, a truly magnificent scene – a marvellously beautiful shadow of good things to come. And, be it remembered, that all which is here shadowed forth will, ere long, be fully actualized. Our great High Priest has passed into the heavens, in the full value and power of accomplished atonement. He is hidden there, now and, with Him, all the members of His priestly family; but when the "seven days" have run their course, and "the eighth day" casts its beams upon the earth, then shall the remnant of Israel – a repentant and an expectant people – hail, with a shout of victory, the manifested presence of the Royal Priest; and, in immediate association with Him, shall be seen a company of worshippers occupying the most exalted position. These are "the good things to come" things, surely, well worth waiting for – things worthy of God to give – things in which He shall be eternally glorified, and His people eternally blessed.

---

[17] A comparison of the Epistle to the Ephesians with the First Epistle of Peter will furnish the reader with much valuable instruction in reference to the double aspect of the believer's position. The former shows him as seated in heaven; the latter, as a pilgrim and a sufferer, on earth.

Chapter 10

NADAB AND ABIHU OFFER STRANGE FIRE

Man corrupts the divine institutions

The page of human history has ever been a sadly blotted one. It is a record of failure, from first to last. Amid all the delights of Eden, man hearkened to the tempter's lie (Gen. 3). When preserved from judgment, by the hand of electing love, and introduced into a restored earth, he was guilty of the sin of intemperance (Gen. 9). When conducted, by Jehovah's outstretched arm, into the land of Canaan, he "forsook the Lord, and served Baal and Ashteroth" (Judges 2:13). When placed at the very summit of earthly power and glory, with untold wealth at his feet, and all the resources of the world at his command, he gave his heart to the uncircumcised stranger (1 Kings 11). No sooner had the blessings of the gospel been promulgated than it became needful for the Holy Ghost to prophesy concerning "grievous wolves," "apostasy," and all manner of failure (Acts 20:29; 1 Tim. 4:1-3; 2 Tim. 3:1-5; 2 Peter 2; Jude). And, to crown all, we have the prophetic record of human apostasy from amid all the splendours of millennial glory (Rev. 20:7-10).

Thus, man spoils everything. Place him in a position of highest dignity, and he will degrade himself. Endow him with the most ample privileges, and he will abuse them. Scatter blessings around him, in richest profusion, and he will prove ungrateful. Place him in the midst of the most impressive institutions, and he will corrupt them. Such is man! Such is nature, in its fairest forms, and under the most favourable circumstances!

Hence, therefore, we are, in a measure, prepared for the words with which our chapter opens. "And Nadab and Abihu, the sons of Aaron, took either of them his censer, and put fire therein, and put incense thereon, and offered strange fire before the Lord which he commanded them not." What a contrast to the scene with which our last section closed! There all was done "as the Lord commanded," and the result was, manifested glory. Here something is done "which the Lord commanded them not," and the result is judgment. Hardly had the echo of the shout of victory died away ere the elements of a spurious worship were prepared. Hardly had the divine position been assured ere it was deliberately abandoned, through neglect of the divine commandment. No sooner were those priests inaugurated, than they grievously failed in the discharge of their priestly functions.

And in what did their failure consist? Were they spurious priests? Were they mere pretenders? By no means. They were genuine sons of Aaron – true members of the priestly family – duly appointed priests. Their vessels of ministry and their priestly garments, too, would seem to have been all right. What, then, was their sin? Did they stain the curtains of the tabernacle with human blood, or pollute the sacred precincts with some crime which shocks the moral sense? We have no proof of their having done so. Their sin was this: "They offered strange fire before the Lord which he commanded them not." Here was their sin. They departed in their worship from the plain word of Jehovah, who had fully and plainly instructed them as to the mode of their worship. We have already alluded to the divine fullness and sufficiency of the word of the Lord, in reference to every branch of priestly service. There was no room left for man to introduce what he might deem desirable or expedient. "This is the thing which the Lord hath commanded" was quite sufficient. It made all very plain and very simple. Nothing was needed, on man's part, save a spirit of implicit obedience to the divine command. But, herein, they failed. Man has always proved himself ill-disposed to walk in the narrow path of strict adherence to the plain word of God. The by-path has ever seemed to present resistless charms to the poor human heart. "Stolen waters are sweet, and bread eaten in secret is pleasant" (Prov. 9:17). Such is the enemy's language; but the lowly, obedient heart knows full well that the path of subjection to the word of God is the only one that leads to "waters" that are really "sweet," or to "bread" that can rightly be called "pleasant." Nadab and Abihu might have deemed one kind of "fire" as good as another; but it was not their province to decide as to that. They should have acted according to the word of the Lord; but, instead of this, they took their own way, and reaped the awful fruits thereof. "He knoweth not that the dead are there; and that her guests are in the depths of hell."

The judgment of God in His house

"And there went out fire from the Lord, and devoured them; and they died before the Lord." How deeply solemn! Jehovah was dwelling in the midst of His people, to govern, to judge, and to act, according to the claims of His nature. At the close of chapter 9 we read, "And there came a fire out from before the Lord, and consumed upon the altar the burnt offering and the fat." This was Jehovah's acceptance of a true sacrifice. But, in chapter 10 it is His judgment upon erring priests. It is a double action of the same fire. The burnt offering went up as a sweet odour; the "strange fire" was rejected as an abomination. The Lord was glorified in the former; but it would have been a dishonour to accept the latter. Divine grace accepted and delighted in that which was a type of Christ's most precious sacrifice; divine holiness rejected that which was the fruit of man's corrupt will – a will never more hideous and abominable than when active in the things of God.

"Then Moses said unto Aaron, This is it that the Lord spake, saying, I will be sanctified in them that come nigh me, and before all the people I will be glorified." The dignity and glory of the entire economy depended upon the strict maintenance of Jehovah's righteous claims. If these were to be trifled with, all was forfeited. If man were permitted to defile the sanctuary of the divine presence by "strange fire," there was an end to everything. Nothing could be permitted to ascend from the priestly censer but the pure fire, kindled from off the altar of God, and fed by the "pure incense beaten small." Beauteous type of true saintly worship, of which the Father is the object, Christ the material, and the Holy Ghost the power. Man must not be allowed to introduce his devices into the worship of God. All his efforts can only issue in the presentation of "strange fire" – unhallowed incense – false worship. His very best attempts are an absolute abomination in the sight of God.

I speak not, here, of the honest struggles of earnest spirits searching after peace with God – of the sincere efforts of upright, though unenlightened, consciences, to attain to a knowledge of the forgiveness of sins, by works of law or the ordinances of systematic religion. All such will, doubtless, issue, through the exceeding goodness of God, in the clear light of a known and an enjoyed salvation. They prove, very clearly, that peace is earnestly sought; though, at the same time, they prove, just as clearly, that peace has not yet been found. There never yet was one, who honestly followed the faintest glimmerings of light which fell upon his understanding, who did not, in due time, receive more. "To him that hath shall more be given." And again, "The path of the just is as the shining light, which shineth more and more unto the perfect day."

All this is as plain as it is encouraging; but it leaves wholly untouched the question of the human will, and its impious workings in connexion with the service and worship of God. All such workings must, inevitably, call down, sooner or later, the solemn judgment of a righteous God who cannot suffer His claims to be trifled with. "I will be sanctified in them that come nigh me, and before all the people I will be glorified." Men will be dealt with according to their profession. If men are honestly seeking, they will, assuredly, find; but, when men approach as worshippers, they are no longer to be regarded as seekers, but as those who profess to have found; and, then, if their priestly censer smokes with unhallowed fire, if they offer unto God the elements of a spurious worship, if they profess to tread His courts, unwashed, unsanctified, unsubdued, if they place on His altar the workings of their own corrupt will, what must be the result? Judgment! Yes, sooner or later, judgment must come. It may linger; but it will come. It could not be otherwise. And not only must judgment come, at last; but there is, in every case, the immediate rejection, on the part of Heaven, of all worship which has not the Father for its object, Christ for its material, and the Holy Ghost for its power. God's holiness is as quick to reject all "strange fire" as His grace is ready to accept the faintest, feeblest breathings of a true heart. He must pour out His righteous judgment upon all false worship, though He will never "quench the smoking flax nor break the bruised reed," The thought of this is most solemnising, when one calls to mind the thousands of censers smoking with strange fire throughout the wide domain of Christendom. May the Lord, in His rich grace, add to the number of true worshippers who worship the Father in spirit and in truth (John 4). It is infinitely happier to think of the true worship ascending, from honest hearts, to the throne of God, than to contemplate, even for a moment, the spurious worship on which the divine judgments must, ere long, be poured out. Every one who knows, through grace, the pardon of his sins, through the atoning blood of Jesus, can worship the Father, in spirit and in truth. He knows the proper ground, the proper object, the proper title, the proper capacity of worship. These things can only be known in a divine way. They do not belong to nature or to earth. They are spiritual and heavenly. Very much of that which passes among men for the worship of God is but "strange fire" after all. There is neither the pure fire nor the pure incense, and, therefore, Heaven accepts it not; and, albeit the divine judgment is not seen to fall upon those who present such worship, as it fell upon Nadab and Abihu, of old, this is only because "God is in Christ reconciling the world unto himself, not imputing their trespasses unto them." It is not because the worship is acceptable to God, but because God is gracious. The time, however, is rapidly approaching when the strange fire will be quenched for ever, when the throne of God shall no longer be insulted by clouds of impure incense ascending from unpurged worshippers; when all that is spurious shall be abolished, and the whole universe shall be as one vast and magnificent temple, in which the one true God, Father, Son, and Holy Ghost, shall be worshipped throughout the everlasting ages.

> Grateful incense this, ascending
> Ever to the Father's throne;
> Every knee to Jesus bending,
> All the mind in heaven is one.
>
> All the Father's counsels claiming
> Equal honours to the Son,
> All the Son's effulgence beaming,
> Makes the Father's glory known.
>
> By the Spirit all pervading,
> Hosts unnumbered round the Lamb,
> Crowned with light and joy unfading,
> Hail Him as the great "I AM."

For this the redeemed are waiting; and, blessed be God, it is but a little while when all their longing desires shall be fully met, and met for ever – yea met, after such a fashion, as to elicit from each and all the touching confession of Sheba's queen, that "the half was not told me." May the Lord hasten the happy time!

The attitude of the priests in the face of this judgment

We must, now, return to our solemn chapter, and, lingering a little longer over it, endeavour to gather up and bear away with us some of its salutary teaching, for truly salutary it is, in an age like the present, when there is so much "strange fire" abroad.

There is something unusually arresting and impressive in the way in which Aaron received the heavy stroke of divine judgment. *"Aaron held his peace."* It was a solemn scene. His two sons struck dead at his side, smitten down by the fire of divine judgment.[18] He had but just seen them clothed in their garments of glory and beauty – washed, robed, and anointed. They had stood with him, before the Lord, to be inaugurated into the priestly office. They had offered, in company with him, the appointed sacrifices. They had seen the beams of the divine glory darting from the Shekinah, they had seen the fire of Jehovah fall upon the sacrifice and consume it. They had heard the shout of triumph issuing from an assembly of adoring worshippers. All this had but recently passed before him; and now, alas! his two sons lie at his side, in the grasp of death. The fire of the Lord which so recently fed upon an acceptable sacrifice, had, now, fallen in judgment upon them, and what could he say? Nothing. "Aaron held his peace." "I was dumb and opened not my mouth, because thou didst it." It was the hand of God; and although it might, in the judgment of flesh and blood, seem to be a very heavy hand, yet he had only to bow his head, in silent awe and reverent acquiescence. "*I was dumb . . . because thou didst it.*" This was the suited attitude, in the presence of the divine visitation. Aaron, doubtless, felt that the very pillars of his house were shaken by the thunder of divine judgment; and he could only stand, in silent amazement, in the midst of the soul-subduing scene. A father bereaved of his two sons, and, in such a manner, and under such circumstances, was no ordinary case. It furnished a deeply-impressive commentary upon the words of the Psalmist, "God is greatly to be feared in the assembly of the saints; and to be had in reverence of all them that are about him" (Psalm 89). "Who would not fear thee, O Lord, and glorify thy name?" May we learn to walk softly in the divine presence – to tread Jehovah's courts with unshod foot and reverent spirit. May our priestly censer ever bear upon it the one material, the beaten incense of Christ's manifold perfections, and may the power of the Spirit kindle up the hallowed flame. All else is not only worthless, but vile. Everything that springs from nature's energy, everything produced by the actings of the human will, the most fragrant incense of man's devising, the most intense ardour of natural devotion, will all issue in "strange fire" and evoke the solemn judgment of the Lord God Almighty. Oh! for a thoroughly truthful heart, and worshipping spirit, in the presence of our God and Father, continually!

But let not any upright, though timid, heart be discouraged or alarmed. It is too often the case that those who really ought to be alarmed take no heed; while those for whom the Spirit of grace would only design a word of comfort and encouragement, apply to themselves, in a wrong way, the startling warnings of Holy Scripture. No doubt, the meek and contrite heart that trembles at the word of the Lord, is in a safe condition; but then we should remember that a father warns his child, not because he does not regard him as his child, but because he does; and one of the happiest proofs of the relationship is the disposition to receive and profit by the warning. The parental voice, even though its tone be that of solemn admonition, will reach the child's heart, but, certainly, not to raise, in that heart, a question as to its relationship with the one who speaks. If a son were to question his sonship whenever his father warns, it would be a poor affair indeed. The judgment which had just fallen upon Aaron's house did not make him doubt that he was really a priest. It merely had the effect of teaching him how to conduct himself in that high and holy position.

"And Moses said unto Aaron, and unto Eleazar and unto Ithamar, his sons, Uncover not your heads, neither rend your clothes; lest ye die, and lest wrath come upon all the people; but let your brethren, the whole house of Israel, bewail the burning which the Lord hath kindled. And ye shall not go out from the door of the tabernacle of the congregation lest ye die: for the anointing oil of the Lord is upon you. And they did according to the word of Moses."

Aaron, Eleazar, and Ithamar, were to remain unmoved in their elevated place – their holy dignity – their position of priestly sanctity. Neither the failure, nor yet the judgment consequent thereon, was to be allowed to interfere with those who wore the priestly robes, and were anointed with "the oil of the Lord." That holy oil had placed them in a sacred enclosure where the influences of sin, of death, and of judgment could not reach them. Those who were outside, who were at a distance from the sanctuary, who were not in the position of priests, they might "bewail the burning;" but as for Aaron and his sons, they were to go on in the discharge of their hallowed functions, as though nothing had happened. Priests in the sanctuary were not to bewail, but to worship. They were not to weep, as in the presence of death, but to bow their anointed heads, in presence of the divine visitation. "The fire of the Lord" might act, and do its solemn work of judgment; but, to a true priest, it mattered not what that "fire" had come to do, whether to express the divine approval, by consuming a sacrifice, or the divine displeasure, by consuming the offerers of "strange fire," he had but to worship. That "fire" was a well-known manifestation of the divine presence, in Israel of old, and whether it acted in "mercy or in judgment," the business of all true priests was to worship. "I will sing of mercy and of judgment; unto thee, O Lord, will I sing."

There is a deep and holy lesson for the soul in all this. Those who are brought nigh to God, in the power of the blood, and by the anointing of the Holy Ghost, must move in a sphere beyond the range of nature's influences. Priestly nearness to God gives the soul such an insight into all His ways, such a sense of the rightness of all His dispensations, that one is enabled to worship in His presence, even though the stroke of His hand has removed from us the object of tender affection. It may be asked, Are we to be stoics? I ask, were Aaron and his sons stoics? Nay, they were priests. Did they not feel as men? Yes; but they worshipped as priests. This is profound. It opens up a region of thought, feeling, and experience, in which nature can never move – a region of which, with all its boasted refinement and sentimentality, nature knows absolutely nothing. We must tread the sanctuary of God, in true priestly energy, in order to enter into the depth, meaning, and power of such holy mysteries.

The Prophet Ezekiel was called, in his duty, to sit down to this difficult lesson. "Also the word of the Lord came unto me, saying, Son of man, behold, I take away from thee the desire of thine eyes with a stroke: yet neither shalt thou mourn nor weep, neither shall thy tears run down. Forbear to cry, make no mourning for the dead, bind the tire of thine head upon thee, and put on thy shoes upon thy feet, and cover not thy lips, and eat not the bread of *men* . . . And I did in the morning as I was commanded" (Ezek. 24:16-18). It will be said that all this was as "a sign" to Israel. True; but it proves that in prophetic testimony, as well as in priestly worship, we must rise superior to all the claims and influences of nature and of earth. Aaron's sons and Ezekiel's wife were cut down with a stroke; and, yet, neither the priest nor the prophet was to uncover his head or shed a tear.

Oh! my reader, how far have you and I progressed in this profound lesson? No doubt, both reader and writer have to make the same humiliating confession. Too often, alas! we "walk as men" and "eat the bread of men." Too often are we robbed of our high priestly privileges by the workings of nature and the influences of earth. These things must be watched against. Nothing save realised priestly nearness to God can ever preserve the heart from the power of evil, or maintain its spiritual tone. All believers are priests unto God, and nothing can possibly deprive them of their position as such. But though they cannot lose their position, they may grievously fail in the discharge of their functions. These things are not sufficiently distinguished. Some there are who, while looking at the precious truth of the believer's security, forget the possibility of his failing in the discharge of his priestly functions. Others, on the contrary, looking at the failure, venture to call in question the security.

Now, I desire that my reader should keep clear of both the above errors. He should be fully established in the divine doctrine of the eternal security of every member of the true priestly house; but he should also bear in mind the possibility of failure, and the constant need of watchfulness and prayer, lest he should fail. May all those who have been brought to know the hallowed elevation of priests unto God be preserved, by His heavenly grace, from every species of failure, whether it be personal defilement, or the presentation of any of the varied forms of "strange fire" which abound so in the professing church.

Neither wine nor strong drink in the presence of God

"And the Lord spake unto Aaron, saying, Do not drink wine nor strong drink, thou nor thy sons with thee, when ye go into the tabernacle of the congregation, lest ye die: it shall be a statute for ever throughout your generations; and that ye may put difference between holy and unholy, and between unclean and clean; and that ye may teach the children of Israel all the statutes which the Lord hath spoken unto them by the hand of Moses" (ver. 8-11).

The effect of wine is to excite nature, and all natural excitement hinders that calm, well-balanced condition of soul which is essential to the proper discharge of the priestly office. So far from using any means to excite nature, we should treat it as a thing having no existence. Thus only shall we be in a moral condition to serve in the sanctuary, to form a dispassionate judgment between clean and unclean, and to expound and communicate the mind of God. It devolves upon each one to judge, for himself, what, in his special case, would act as "wine or strong drink."[19] The things which excite mere nature are manifold indeed – wealth, ambition, politics, the varied objects of emulation around us in the world. All these things act, with exciting power, upon nature, and entirely unfit us for every department of priestly service. If the heart be swollen with feelings of pride, covetousness, or emulation, it is utterly impossible that the pure air of the sanctuary can be enjoyed, or the sacred functions of priestly ministry discharged. Men speak of the versatility of genius, or a capacity to turn quickly from one thing to another. But the most versatile genius that was ever possessed could not enable a man to pass from an unhallowed arena of literary, commercial, or political competition, into the holy retirement of the sanctuary of the divine presence; nor could it ever adjust the eye that had become dimmed by the influence of such scenes, so as to enable it to discern, with priestly accuracy, the difference "between holy and unholy, and between unclean and clean." No, my reader, God's priests must keep themselves apart from "wine and strong drink." Theirs is a path of holy separation and abstraction. They are to be raised far above the influence of earthly joy as well as earthly sorrow. If they have anything to do with "strong wine," it is only that it may "be poured unto the Lord for a drink offering, in the holy place" (Num. 28:7). In other words, the joy of God's priests is not the joy of earth, but the joy of heaven, the joy of the sanctuary. "The joy of the Lord is their strength."

Would that all this holy instruction were more deeply pondered by us! We, surely, stand much in need of it. If our priestly responsibilities are not duly attended to, all must be deranged. When we contemplate the camp of Israel, we may observe three circles, and the innermost of these circles had its centre in the sanctuary. There was first the circle of men of war (Numb. 1, 2). Then the circle of Levites round about the tabernacle (Numb. 3, 4). And, lastly, the innermost circle of priests, ministering in the holy place. Now, let it be remembered that the believer is called to move in all those circles. He enters into conflict, as a man of war (Eph. 6:11-17; 1 Tim. 1:18; 6:12; 2 Tim. 4:7). He serves, as a Levite, in the midst of his brethren, according to his measure and sphere (Matt. 25:14, 15; Luke 19:12, 13). Finally, he sacrifices and worships, as a priest, in the holy place (Heb. 13:15, 16; 1 Peter 2:5, 9).

The last of these shall endure for ever. And, moreover, it is as we are enabled, now, to move aright in that holy circle, that all other relations and responsibilities are rightly discharged. Hence, every thing that incapacitates us for our priestly functions – every thing that draws us off from the centre of that innermost circle, in which it is our privilege to move – every thing, in short, that tends to derange our priestly relation, or dim our priestly vision, must, of necessity, unfit us for the service which we are called to render, and for the warfare which we are called to wage.

These are weighty considerations. Let us dwell upon them. The heart must be kept right – the conscience pure – the eye single – the spiritual vision undimmed. The soul's business in the holy place must be faithfully and diligently attended to, else we shall go all wrong. Private communion with God must be kept up, else we shall be fruitless, as servants, and defeated, as men of war. It is vain for us to bustle about, and run hither and thither, in what we call service, or indulge in vapid words about Christian armour and Christian warfare. If we are not keeping our priestly garments unspotted, and if we are not keeping ourselves free from all that would excite nature, we shall, assuredly, break down. The *priest* must keep his heart with all diligence, else the *Levite* will fail, and the *warrior* will be defeated.

It is, let me repeat it, the business of each one to be fully aware of what it is that to him proves to be "wine and strong drink" – what it is that produces excitement – that blunts his spiritual perception, or dims his priestly vision. It may be an auction mart, a cattle-show, a newspaper. It may be the merest trifle. But no matter what it is, if it tends to excite, it will disqualify us for priestly ministry; and if we are disqualified as priests, we are unfit for everything, inasmuch as our success in every department and in every sphere must ever depend upon our cultivating a spirit of worship.

Let us, then, exercise a spirit of self-judgment – a spirit of watchfulness over our habits, our ways, and our associations; and when we, by grace, discover anything that tends, in the smallest degree, to unfit us for the elevated exercises of the sanctuary, let us put it away from us, cost what it may. Let us not suffer ourselves to be the slaves of a habit. Communion with God should be dearer to our hearts than all beside; and just in proportion as we prize that communion, shall we watch and pray against anything that would rob us of it – everything that would excite, ruffle, or unhinge.[20]

The inalienable portion of the priests

"And Moses spake unto Aaron, and unto Eleazar, and unto Ithamar, his sons that were left, Take the meat offering that remaineth of the offerings of the Lord made by fire, and eat it without leaven beside the altar; for it is most holy: and ye shall eat it in the holy place, because it is thy due, and thy sons' due, of the sacrifices of the Lord made by fire; for so I am commanded" (ver. 12, 13).

There are few things in which we are more prone to fail than in the maintenance of the divine standard, when human failure has set in. Like David, when the Lord made a breach upon Uzza, because of his failure in putting his hand to the ark, "He was afraid of God that day, saying, How shall I bring the ark of God home to me?" (1 Chron. 13:12). It is exceedingly difficult to bow to the divine judgment, and, at the same time, to hold fast the divine ground. The temptation is to lower the standard, to come down from the lofty elevation, to take human ground. We must ever carefully guard against this evil, which is all the more dangerous as wearing the garb of modesty, self-distrust, and humility. Aaron and his sons, notwithstanding all that had occurred, were to eat the meat offering in the holy place. They were to do so, not because all had gone on in perfect order, but "because it is thy due," and "so I am commanded." Though there had been failure, yet their place was in the tabernacle; and those who were there had certain "dues" founded upon the divine commandment. Though man had failed ten thousand times over, the word of the Lord could not fail; and that word had secured certain privileges for all true priests, which it was their place to enjoy. Were God's priests to have nothing to eat, no priestly food, because failure had set in? Were those that were left to be allowed to starve, because Nadab and Abihu had offered "strange fire?" This would never do. God is faithful, and He can never allow any one to be empty in His blessed presence. The prodigal may wander, and squander, and come to poverty; but it must ever hold good that "in my Father's house is bread enough and to spare."

"And the wave breast and the heave shoulder shall ye eat in a clean place; thou, and thy sons, and thy daughters with thee: for they be thy due, and thy sons' due, which are *given* out of the sacrifices of peace offerings of the children of Israel . . . by *a statute for ever; as the Lord hath commanded*" (Ver. 14, 15). What strength and stability we have here! All the members of the priestly family, "daughters" as well as "sons" – all, whatever be the measure of energy or capacity, are to feed upon "the breast" and "the shoulder," the affections and the strength of the true Peace Offering, as raised from the dead, and presented, in resurrection, before God. This precious privilege is theirs as, "given, by a statute for ever, as the Lord hath commanded." This makes all "sure and steadfast," come what may. Men may fail, and come short; strange fire may be offered, but God's priestly family must never be deprived of the rich and gracious portion which divine love has provided, and divine faithfulness secured, "by a statute for ever."

However, we must distinguish between those privileges which belonged to all the members of Aaron's family, "daughters" as well as "sons," and those which could only be enjoyed by the male portion of the family. This point has already been referred to, in the notes on the offerings. There are certain blessings which are the common portion of all believers, simply as such; and there are those which demand a higher measure of spiritual attainment and priestly energy to apprehend and enjoy. Now, it is worse than vain, yea, it is impious, to set up for the enjoyment of this higher measure, when we really have it not. It is one thing to hold fast the privileges which are "given" of God, and can never be taken away, and quite another to assume a measure of spiritual capacity to which we have never attained. No doubt, we ought to desire earnestly the very highest measure of priestly communion – the most elevated order of priestly privilege. But, then, desiring a thing, and assuming to have it, are very different.

Omission in service

This thought will throw light upon the closing paragraph of our chapter. "And Moses diligently sought the goat of the sin offering, and, behold, it was burnt: and he was angry with Eleazar and Ithamar, the sons of Aaron which were left, saying, Wherefore have ye not eaten the sin offering in the holy place, seeing it is most holy, and God hath given it to you to bear the iniquity of the congregation, to make atonement for them before the Lord? Behold, the blood of it was not brought in within the holy place: ye should indeed have eaten it in the holy place, as I commanded And Aaron said unto Moses, Behold, this day have they offered their sin offering and their burnt offering before the Lord; and such things have befallen me; and if I had eaten the sin offering today, should it have been accepted in the sight of the Lord? And when Moses heard that, he was content."

The "daughters" of Aaron were not permitted to eat of "the sin offering." This high privilege belonged only to the "sons," and it was a type of the most elevated form of priestly service. To eat of the sin offering was the expression of full identification with the offerer, and this demanded an amount of priestly capacity and energy which found its type in "the sons of Aaron." On the occasion before us, however, it is very evident that Aaron and his sons were not in a condition to rise to this high and holy ground. They ought to have been, but they were not. "Such things have befallen me," said Aaron. This, no doubt, was to be deplored; but, yet, "when Moses heard it, he was content." It is far better to be real in the confession of our failure and shortcoming, than to put forth pretensions to spiritual power which are wholly without foundation.

Thus, then, the tenth chapter of the Book of Leviticus opens with positive sin, and closes with negative failure. Nadab and Abihu offered "strange fire;" and Eleazar and Ithamar were unable to eat the sin offering. The former was met by divine judgment; the latter, by divine forbearance. There could be no allowance for "strange fire." It was positively flying in the face of God's plain commandment. There is, obviously, a wide difference between a deliberate rejection of a plain command, and mere inability to rise to the height of a divine privilege. The former is open dishonour done to God; the latter is a forfeiture of one's own blessing. There should be neither the one nor the other, but the difference between the two is easily traced.

May the Lord, in His infinite grace, ever keep us abiding in the secret retirement of His holy presence, abiding in His love, and feeding upon His truth. Thus shall we be preserved from "strange fire," and "strong drink" – from false worship of every kind, and fleshly excitement, in all its forms. Thus, too, shall we be enabled to carry ourselves aright in every department of priestly ministration, and to enjoy all the privileges of our priestly position. The communion of a Christian is like a sensitive plant. It is easily hurt by the rude influences of an evil world. It will expand beneath the genial action of the air of heaven; but must firmly shut itself up from the chilling breath of time and sense. Let us remember these things, and ever seek to keep close within the sacred precincts of the divine presence. There, all is pure, safe, and happy.

> Far from a world of grief and sin,
> With God eternally shut in.

---

[18] Lest any reader should be troubled with a difficulty in reference to the souls of Nadab, and Abihu, I would say that no such question ought ever to be raised. In such cases as Nadab and Abihu, in Leviticus 10; Korah and his company, in Numbers 16; the whole congregation, Joshua and Caleb

excepted, whose carcasses fell in the wilderness, Numbers 14 and Hebrews 3; Achan and his family, Joshua 7; Ananias and Sapphira, Acts 5; those who were judged for abuses at the Lord's table, 1 Cor. 11. In all such cases, the question of the soul's salvation is never raised. We are simply called to see, in them, the solemn actings of God, in government in the midst of His people. This relieves the mind from all difficulty. Jehovah dwelt, of old, between the Cherubim, to judge His people in everything; and God the Holy Ghost dwells, now, in the church, to order and govern, according to the perfection of His presence. He was so really and personally present that Ananias and Sapphira could lie to Him, and He could execute judgment upon them. It was as positive and as immediate an exhibition of His actings in government as we have in the matter of Nadab and Abihu, or Achan, or any other.

This is a great truth to get hold of. God is not only *for* His people, but *with* them, and *in* them. He is to be counted upon, for everything, whether it be great or small. He is present to comfort and help. He is there to chasten and judge. He is there "for exigence of every hour." He is sufficient. Let faith count upon Him. "Where two or three are gathered together in my name, there am I" (Matt. 18:20). And, assuredly, where He is, we want no more.

[19] Some have thought that, owing to the special place which this direction about wine occupies, Nadab and Abihu must have been under the influence of strong drink, when they offered the "strange fire." But, be this as it may, we have to be thankful for a most valuable principle, in reference to our conduct, as spiritual priests. We are to refrain from everything which would produce the same effect upon our spiritual man, as strong drink produces upon the physical man.

It needs hardly to be remarked that the Christian should be *most jealous* over himself as to the use of wine or strong drink. Timothy, as we know, needed an apostolic recommendation to induce him even to touch it, for his health's sake. (1 Tim. 5) A beauteous proof of Timothy's habitual self-denial, and of the thoughtful love of the Spirit, in the apostle. I must confess that one's moral sense is offended by seeing Christians making use of strong drink in cases where it is, very manifestly, not medicinal. I rarely, if ever, see a spiritual person indulge in such a thing. One trembles to see a Christian the mere slave of a habit, whatever that habit may be. It proves that he is not keeping his body in subjection, and he is in great danger of being "disapproved" (1 Cor. 9:27).

[20] Some, perhaps, may think that the wording of Lev. 10:9 affords a warrant for *occasional* indulgence in those things which tend to excite the natural mind, inasmuch as it is said, "Do not drink wine nor strong drink . . . when ye go into the tabernacle of the congregation." To this we may reply, that the sanctuary is not a place which the Christian is, *occasionally*, to visit, but a place in which he is, *habitually*, to serve and worship. It is the sphere in which he should "live, and move, and have his being." The more we live in the presence of God, the less can we bear to be out of it; and no one who knows the deep joy of being there could lightly indulge in anything that would take or keep him hence. There is not that object within the compass of earth which would, in the judgment of a spiritual mind, be an equivalent for one hour's fellowship with God.

Chapter 11

THE LAW CONCERNING CLEAN AND UNCLEAN ANIMALS

God gives adequate directions

The Book of Leviticus may be termed "the priest's guide book." This is very much its character. It is full of principles for the guidance of such as desire to live in the enjoyment of priestly nearness to God. Had Israel gone on with Jehovah, according to the grace in which He had brought them up, out of the land of Egypt, they should have been to Him "a kingdom of priests and a holy nation" (Ex. 19:6). This, however, they failed to do. They put themselves at a distance. They got under law and failed to keep it. Hence, Jehovah had to take up a certain tribe, and from that tribe a certain family, and from that family a certain man, and to him and to his house, was granted the high privilege of drawing nigh, as priests unto God.

Now, the privileges of such a position were immense; but it had its heavy responsibilities, likewise. There would be the ever-recurring demand for the exercise of a discerning mind. "The priest's lips should keep knowledge, and they should seek the law at his mouth: for he is the messenger of the Lord of hosts" (Mal. 2:7). The priest was not only to bear the judgment of the congregation, before the Lord, but also to expound the ordinances of the Lord to the congregation. He was to be the ever-ready medium of communication between Jehovah and the assembly. He was not merely to know the mind of God, for himself, but be able also to interpret that mind to the people. All this would demand, of necessity, constant watching, constant waiting, constant hanging over the page of inspiration, that he might drink in, to his very soul, all the precepts, the judgments, the statutes, the laws, the commandments, and the ordinances of the God of Israel, so as to be able to instruct the congregation, in reference to "those things which ought to be done."

There was no room left for the play of fancy, the working of imagination, the introduction of man's plausible inferences, or the cunning devices of human expediency. Everything was laid down, with the divine precision and commanding authority of a "thus saith the Lord." Minute and elaborate as was the detail of sacrifices, rites, and ceremonies, nothing was left for man's brain to originate. He was not even permitted to decide upon the kind of sacrifice to be offered, upon any given occasion; nor yet as to the mode in which such sacrifice was to be presented. Jehovah took care of everything. Neither the congregation nor the priest had any authority whatsoever, to decree, enact, or suggest so much as a single item throughout all the vast array of ordinances in the Mosaic economy. *The word of the Lord settled all.* Man had *only to obey.*

This, to an obedient heart, was nothing short of an unspeakable mercy. It is quite impossible to overestimate the privilege of being permitted to betake oneself to the oracles of God, and there find the most ample guidance as to all the details of one's faith and service, day by day. All that we need is a broken will, a mortified mind, a single eye. The divine guide book is as full as we can possibly desire. We want no more. To imagine, for a moment, that anything is left for man's wisdom to supply, must be regarded as a flagrant insult offered to the sacred canon. No one can read the Book of Leviticus, and not be struck with the extraordinary painstaking, on the part of Israel's God, to furnish His people with the most minute instruction upon every point connected with His service and worship. The most cursory reader of the book might, at least, bear away with him this touching and interesting lesson.

And, truly, if ever there was a time when this self-same lesson needed to be read out in the ears of the professing church, this is the time. On all hands, the divine sufficiency of Holy Scripture is called in question. In some cases this is openly and deliberately done; in others it is, with less frankness, hinted, insinuated, implied, and inferred. The Christian mariner is told, directly, or indirectly, that the divine chart is insufficient for all the intricate details of his voyage – that such changes have taken place in the ocean of life, since that chart was made, that, in many cases, it is entirely deficient for the purposes of modern navigation. He is told that the currents, tides, coasts, strands, and shores of that ocean are quite different, now, from what they were some centuries ago, and that, as a necessary consequence, he must have recourse to the aids which modern navigation supplies, in order to make up for the deficiencies in the old chart, which is, as a matter of course, admitted to have been perfect at the time it was made.

Now, I earnestly desire that the Christian reader should be able, with clearness and decision, to meet this grievous dishonour done to the precious volume of inspiration, every line of which comes to him fresh from his Father's bosom, through the pen of God the Holy Ghost. I desire that he should meet it, whether it comes before him in the shape of a bold and blasphemous statement, or a learned and plausible inference. Whatever garb it wears, it owes its origin to the enemy of Christ, the enemy of the Bible, the enemy of the soul. If, indeed, the Word of God be not sufficient, then where are we? or whither shall we turn? To whom shall we betake ourselves for aid, if our Father's book be, in any respect, defective? God says that His book can "furnish us *thoroughly* to *all* good works" (2 Tim. 3:17). Man says, no; there are many things about which the Bible is silent, which, nevertheless, we need to know. Whom am I to believe? God or man? Our reply to any one who questions the divine sufficiency of Scripture, is just this, "either you are not a 'man of God,' or else that for which you want a warrant is not 'a good work,' " This is plain. No one can possibly think otherwise, with his eye resting on 2 Timothy 3:17.

Oh! for a deeper sense of the fullness, majesty, and authority of the Word of God! We very much need to be braced up on this point. We want such a deep, bold, vigorous, influential, and abiding sense of the supreme authority of the divine canon, and of its absolute completeness for every age, every clime, every position, every department – personal, social, and ecclesiastical, as shall enable us to withstand every attempt of the enemy to depreciate the value of that inestimable treasure. May our hearts enter more into the spirit of those words of the Psalmist, "Thy word is true *from the beginning:* and every one of thy righteous judgments *endureth for ever"* (Psalm 119:160).

The foregoing train of thought is awakened by the perusal of the eleventh chapter of the Book of Leviticus. Therein we find Jehovah entering, in most marvellous detail, into a description of beasts, birds, fishes, and reptiles, and furnishing His people with various marks by which they were to know what was clean and what was unclean. We have the summing up of the entire contents of this remarkable chapter in the two closing verses. "This is the law of the beasts, and of the fowl, and of every living creature that moveth in the waters, and of every creature that creepeth upon the earth; *to make a difference* between the unclean and the clean, and between the beast that may be eaten and the beast that may not be eaten."

Animals which chew the cud and which divide the hoof

With regard to beasts, two things were essential to render them clean, they should chew the cud and divide the hoof. "Whatsoever parteth the hoof, and is cloven footed, and cheweth the cud among the beasts, that shall ye eat." Either of these marks would, of itself, have been wholly insufficient to constitute ceremonial cleanness. The two should go together. Now, while these two marks were quite sufficient for the guidance of an Israelite, as to the cleanness or uncleanness of an animal, without any reference as to why or wherefore such marks were given, or what they meant, yet is the Christian permitted to enquire into the spiritual truth wrapped up in these ceremonial enactments.

What, then, are we to learn from those two features in a clean animal? The chewing of the cud expresses the natural process of "inwardly digesting" that which one eats; while the divided hoof sets forth the character of one's outward walk. There is, as we know, an intimate connexion between the two, in the Christian life. The one who feeds upon the green pastures of the Word of God, and inwardly digests what he takes in – the one who is enabled to combine calm meditation with prayerful study, will, without doubt, manifest that character of outward walk which is to the praise of Him who has graciously given us His word to form our habits and govern our ways.

It is to be feared that many who *read the Bible* do not *digest the word*. The two things are widely different. One may read chapter after chapter, book after book, and not digest so much as a single line. We may read the Bible as part of a dull and profitless routine; but, through lack of the ruminating powers – the digestive organs, we derive no profit whatsoever. This should be carefully looked into. The cattle that browse on the green may teach us a wholesome lesson. They, first, diligently gather up the refreshing pasture, and then calmly lie down to chew the cud. Striking and beautiful picture of a Christian feeding upon and inwardly digesting the precious contents of the volume of inspiration. Would that there were more of this amongst us! Were we more accustomed to betake ourselves to the Word as the necessary pasture of our souls, we should, assuredly, be in a more vigorous and healthy condition. Let us beware of reading the Bible as a dead form – a cold duty – a piece of religious routine.

The same caution is needful in reference to the public exposition of the Word. Let those who expound Scripture to their fellows, first feed and digest for themselves. Let them read and ruminate, in private, not merely for others, but for themselves. It is a poor thing for a man to be continually occupied in procuring food for other people, and he himself dying of starvation. Then, again, let those who attend upon the public ministry of the Word, see that they are not doing so mechanically, as by the force of mere religious habit, but with an earnest desire to "read, mark, learn, and inwardly digest" what they hear. Then will both teachers and taught be well-conditioned, the spiritual life nourished and sustained, and the true character of outward walk exhibited.

The internal life and the external walk

But, be it remembered, that the chewing of the cud must never be separated from the divided hoof. If one but partially acquainted with the priest's guide book – unpractised in the divine ceremonial, happened to see an animal chewing the cud, he might hastily pronounce him clean. This would have been a serious error. A more careful reference to the divine directory would, at once, show that he must mark the animal's *walk* – that he must note the impression made by each movement – that he must look for the result of the divided hoof. "Nevertheless, these shall ye not eat, of them that chew the cud, or of them that divide the hoof: as the camel because he cheweth the cud, but divideth not the hoof; he is unclean unto you," &c., &c. (ver. 4-6).

In like manner, the divided hoof was insufficient, if not accompanied by the chewing of the cud. "The swine, though he divide the hoof, and be cloven footed, yet he cheweth not the cud; he is unclean to you" (ver. 7). In a word, then, the two things were inseparable in the case of every clean animal; and, as to the spiritual application, it is of the very last importance, in a practical point of view. The inward life and the outward walk must go together. A man may profess to love and feed upon – to study and ruminate over the Word of God – the pasture of the soul; but, if his footprints along the pathway of life are not such as the Word requires, he is not clean. And, on the other hand, a man may seem to walk with pharisaic blamelessness; but if his walk be not the result of the hidden life, it is worse than worthless. There must be the divine principle within which feeds upon and digests the rich pasture of God's Word, else the impression of the footstep will be of no avail. The value of each depends upon its inseparable connexion with the other.

We are, here, forcibly reminded of a solemn passage in the First Epistle of John, in which the apostle furnishes us with the two marks whereby we may know those that are of God. "In this the children of God are manifest, and the children of the devil: whosoever *doeth not righteousness,* is not of God, neither he that *loveth not his brother"* (1 John 3:10). Here we have the two grand characteristics of the eternal life, of which all true believers are possessed, namely, "righteousness" and "love". The outward and the inward. Both must be combined. Some professing Christians are all for love, so called; and some for righteousness. Neither can exist, in a divine way, without the other. If that which is called love exist without practical righteousness, it will, in reality, be but a lax, soft, easy-going habit of mind, which will tolerate all manner of error and evil. And, if that which is called righteousness exist without love, it will be a stern, proud, pharisaic, self-sufficient temper of soul resting upon the miserable basis of personal reputation. But where the divine life is in energy, there will ever be the inward charity combined with genuine practical righteousness. The two elements are essential in the formation of true Christian character. There must be the love that will express itself in reference to the very feeblest development of that which is of God; and, at the same time, the holiness that shrinks, with intense abhorrence, from all that is of Satan.

Creatures living in water

We shall now pass on to the consideration of that which the Levitical ceremonial taught with respect to "all that are in the waters." Here again, we find the double mark. "These shall ye eat of all that are in the waters: whatsoever hath fins and scales in the waters, in the seas, and in the rivers, them shall ye eat. And all that have not fins and scales in the seas, and in the rivers, of all that move in the waters, and of any living thing which is in the waters, they shall be an abomination unto you" (ver. 9, 10). Two things were necessary to render a fish ceremonially clean, namely, "fins and scales," which, obviously, set forth a certain fitness for the sphere and element in which the creature had to move.

But, doubtless, there was more than this. I believe it is our privilege to discern, in the natural properties with which God has endowed those creatures which move in the waters, certain spiritual qualities which belong to the Christian life. If a fish needs a "fin" to enable him to move through the waters and "scales" to resist the action thereof, so does the believer need that spiritual capacity which enables him to move onward through the scene with which he is surrounded, and, at the same time, to resist its influence – to prevent its penetrating – to keep it out. These are precious qualities. The fin and the scale are pregnant with meaning – full of practical instruction to the Christian. They exhibit to us, in ceremonial garb, two things which we specially need, namely, spiritual energy to move onward through the element which surrounds us, and the power to preserve us from its action. The one will not avail without the other. It is of no use to possess a capacity to get on, through the world, if we are not proof against the world's influence; and though we may seem to be able to keep the world out, yet if we have not the motive power, we are defective. The "fins" would not do without the "scales," nor the "scales" without the "fins" Both were required, to render a fish ceremonially clean; and we, in order to be properly equipped, require to be encased against the penetrating influence of an evil world; and, at the same time, to be furnished with a capacity to pass rapidly on.

The whole deportment of a Christian should declare him a pilgrim and a stranger here. "*Onward*" must be his motto – ever and only, onward. Let his locality and his circumstances be what they may, he is to have his eye fixed on a home beyond this perishing, passing world. He is furnished, by grace, with spiritual ability to go forward – to penetrate, energetically, through all, and carry out the earnest aspirations of his heaven-born spirit. And, while thus vigorously pushing his way onward – while "forcing his passage to the skies," he is to keep his inward man fenced round about, and fast closed up against all external influences.

Oh! for more of the onward bent, the upward tendency! For more holy fixedness of soul, and profound retirement from this vain world! We shall have reason to bless the Lord for our meditations amid the ceremonial shadows of the Book of Leviticus, if we are led, thereby, to long more intensely after those graces which, though so dimly portrayed there, are, nevertheless, so manifestly needful for us.

Birds

From verse 13 to verse 24 of our chapter, we have the law with respect to birds. All of the carnivorous kind, that is, all that fed on flesh, were unclean. The omnivorous, or those who could eat anything, were unclean. All those which, though furnished with power to soar into the heavens, would, nevertheless, grovel upon the earth, were unclean. As to the latter class, there were some exceptional cases (ver. 21, 22); but the general rule, the fixed principle, the standing ordinance was as distinct as possible; "all fowls that creep, going upon all fours, shall be an abomination unto you." (Ver. 20) All this is very simple in its instruction to us. Those fowls that could feed upon flesh; those that could swallow anything or everything; and all grovelling fowls, were to be unclean to the Israel of God, because so pronounced by the God of Israel; nor can the spiritual mind have any difficulty in discerning the fitness of such an ordinance. We can not only trace in the habits of the above three classes of fowl the just ground of their being pronounced unclean; but we can also see in them the striking exhibition of that, in nature, which is to be strenuously guarded against by every true Christian. Such an one is called to refuse everything of a carnal nature. Moreover, he cannot feed, promiscuously, upon everything that comes before him. He must "try the things that differ:" He must "take heed what he hears." He must exercise a discerning mind, a spiritual judgment, a heavenly taste. Finally, he must use his wings. He must rise on the pinions of faith, and find his place in the celestial sphere to which he belongs. In short, there must be nothing grovelling, nothing promiscuous, nothing unclean, for the Christian.

As to "creeping things," the following was the general rule: "And every creeping thing that creepeth upon the earth shall be an abomination; it shall not be eaten" (ver. 41). How wonderful to think of the condescending grace of Jehovah! He could stoop to give directions about a crawling reptile. He would not leave His people at a loss as to the most trivial affair. The priest's guide book contained the most ample instructions as to everything. He desired to keep His people free from the defilement consequent upon touching, tasting, or handling anything that was unclean. They were not their own, and hence they were not to do as they pleased. They belonged to Jehovah; His name was called upon them; they were identified with Him. His word was to be their grand regulating standard, in every case. From it they were to learn the ceremonial *status* of beasts, birds, fishes, and creeping things. They were not to think their own thoughts, to exercise their own reasoning powers, or be guided by their own imaginations, in such matters. *God's Word was to be their sole directory.* Other nations might eat what they pleased; but Israel enjoyed the high privilege of eating that only which was pleasing to Jehovah.

The holiness of God and the holiness of the believer

Nor was it as to the mere matter of *eating* anything that was unclean that the people of God were so jealously guarded. Bare *contact* was forbidden (see ver. 8, 24, 26-28, 31-41). It was impossible for a member of the Israel of God to touch that which was unclean without contracting defilement. This is a principle largely unfolded, both in the law and the prophets. "Thus saith the Lord of hosts, ask ye now the priests concerning the law, saying, if one bear holy flesh in the skirt of his garment, and with his skirt do touch bread, or pottage, or wine, or oil, or any meat, shall it be holy? And the priests answered and said, No. Then said Haggai, If one that is unclean by a dead body touch any of these, shall it be unclean? And the priests answered and said, It shall be unclean" (Hag. 2:11-13). Jehovah would have His people holy in all things. They were neither to eat nor touch anything that was unclean. "Ye shall not make yourselves abominable with any creeping thing that creepeth, neither shall ye make yourselves unclean with them, that ye should be defiled thereby." Then follows the powerful reason for all this careful separation. *"For I am the Lord your God:* ye shall therefore sanctify yourselves, and ye shall be holy; *for I am holy:* neither shall ye defile yourselves with any manner of creeping thing that creepeth upon the earth. For I am the Lord that bringeth you up out of the land of Egypt, to be *your God*: ye shall therefore be holy, *for I am holy"* (Ver. 43-45).

It is well to see that the personal holiness of God's people – their entire separation from all manner of uncleanness, flows out of their relationship to Him. It is not upon the principle of "stand by thyself, I am holier than thou;' but simply this, "God is holy," and therefore all who are brought into association with Him must be holy, likewise. It is, in every way, worthy of God that *His* people should be holy. "Thy testimonies are very sure; holiness becometh thy house, O Lord, for ever." What else save holiness could become the house of such an One as Jehovah? If any one had asked an Israelite, of old, "Why do you shrink so from that reptile which crawls along the path?" He would have replied, "Jehovah is holy; and I belong to Him. He has said 'Touch not.' " So, also, now, if a Christian be asked why he walks apart from the ten thousand things in which the men of this world participate, his answer is simply to be, *"My Father is holy."* This is the true foundation of personal holiness. The more we contemplate the divine character, and enter into the power of our relationship to God, in Christ, by the energy of the Holy Ghost, the holier we must, of necessity, be. There can be no progress in the condition of holiness into which the believer is introduced; but there is, and ought to be, progress in the apprehension, experience, and practical exhibition of that holiness. These things should never be confounded. All believers are in the same condition of holiness or sanctification; but their practical measure may vary to any conceivable degree. This is easily understood. The condition arises out of our *being brought* nigh to God, by the blood of the cross; the practical measure will depend upon our *keeping* nigh, by the power of the Spirit. It is not a man setting up for something superior in himself – for a greater degree of personal sanctity than is ordinarily possessed – for being, in any wise, better than his neighbours. All such pretensions are utterly contemptible, in the judgment of every right-thinking person. But then, if God, in His exceeding grace, stoop down to our low estate, and lift us into the holy elevation of His blessed presence, in association with Christ, has He not a right to prescribe what our character is to be, as thus brought nigh? Who could think of calling in question a truth so obvious? And, further, are we not bound to aim at the maintenance of that character which He prescribes? Are we to be accused of presumption for so doing? Was it presumption in an Israelite to refuse to touch "a creeping thing?" Nay, it would have been presumption of the most daring and dangerous character to have done so. True, he might not have been able to make an uncircumcised stranger understand or appreciate the reason of his conduct; but this was not his province. Jehovah had said, "Touch not," not because an Israelite was holier in himself than a stranger; but because Jehovah was holy, and Israel belonged to Him. It needed the eye and the heart of a circumcised disciple of the law of God, in order to discern what was clean and what was not. An alien knew no difference. Thus it must ever be. It is only Wisdom's children that can justify her and approve her heavenly ways.

Obsolete ordinances

Ere turning from Leviticus 11, my reader might, with much spiritual profit, compare it with the tenth chapter of Acts, ver. 11-16. How strange is must have appeared to one who had, from his earliest days, been taught in the principles of the Mosaic ritual, to see a vessel descending from heaven, "wherein were *all manner* of four-footed beasts of the earth, and wild beasts, and *creeping things,* and fowls of the air;" and not only to see such a vessel, so filled, but also to hear a voice, saying, "Rise, Peter; kill, and eat." How wonderful! No examination of hoofs or habits! There was no need of this. The vessel and its contents had come from heaven. This was enough. The Jew might ensconce himself behind the narrow enclosures of the Jewish ritual, and exclaim, "Not so, Lord; for I have never eaten anything that is common or unclean;" but, then, the tide of divine grace was rising, majestically, above all such enclosures, in order to embrace, in its mighty compass, "all manner" of objects, and bear them upward to heaven, in the power and on the authority of those precious words, "What God hath cleansed, that call not thou common." It mattered not what was in the vessel, if God had cleansed it. The Author of the Book of Leviticus was about to raise the thoughts of His servant above the barriers which that book had erected, into all the magnificence of heaven's grace. He would teach him that true cleanness – the cleanness which heaven demanded, was no longer to consist in chewing the cud, dividing the hoof, or any such ceremonial marks, but in being washed in the blood of the Lamb, which cleanseth from all sin, and renders the believer clean enough to tread the sapphire pavement of the heavenly courts.

This was a noble lesson for a Jew to learn. It was a divine lesson, before the light of which the shadows of the old economy must pass away. The hand of sovereign grace has thrown open the door of the kingdom; but not to admit anything that is unclean. This could not be. Nothing unclean can enter heaven. But, then, a cloven hoof was no longer to be the criterion; but *"what God hath cleansed."* When God cleanses a man, he must needs be clean. Peter was about to be sent to open the kingdom to the Gentiles, as he had already opened it to the Jews; and his Jewish heart needed to be enlarged. He needed to get above the dark shadows of a by-gone age, into the meridian light that was shining from an open heaven, in virtue of a completed sacrifice. He needed to get out of the narrow current of Jewish prejudices, and be borne upon the bosom of that mighty tide of grace which was about to roll through the length and breadth of a lost world. He had to learn, too, that the standard by which true cleanness must be regulated, was no longer carnal, ceremonial, and earthly, but spiritual, moral, and heavenly. Assuredly, we may say, these were noble lessons for the apostle of the circumcision to learn upon the housetop of Simon the tanner. They were eminently calculated to soften, to expand, and elevate a mind which had been trained amid the contracting influences of the Jewish system. We bless the Lord for these precious lessons. We bless Him for the large and wealthy place in which He has set us, by the blood of the cross. We bless Him that we are no longer hemmed round about by "touch not this; taste not that; handle not the other thing; but that His word assures us that "every creature of God is good, and nothing to be refused, if it be received with thanksgiving: for it is sanctified by the word of God and prayer" (1 Tim. 4:4, 5).

Chapter 12

PURIFICATION OF THE WOMAN WHO HAS HAD A CHILD

Man conceived and born in sin

This brief section reads out to us, after its own peculiar fashion, the double lesson of "man's ruin and God's remedy." But though the fashion is peculiar, the lesson is most distinct and impressive. It is, at once, deeply humbling and divinely comforting. The effect of all scripture, when interpreted to one's own soul, directly, by the power of the Holy Ghost, is to lead us out of self to Christ. Wherever we see our fallen nature – at whatever stage of its history we contemplate it, whether in its conception, at its birth, or at any point along its whole career, from the womb to the coffin, it wears the double stamp of iniquity and defilement. This is, sometimes, forgotten amid the glitter and glare, the pomp and fashion, the wealth and splendour of human life. The mind of man is fruitful in devices to cover his humiliation. In various ways he seeks to ornament and gild, and put on an appearance of strength and glory; but it is all vain. He has only to be seen as he enters this world, a poor helpless creature; or, as he passes away from it, to take his place with the clod of the valley, in order to have a most convincing proof of the hollowness of all his pride, the vanity of all his glory. Those whose path through this world has been brightened by what man calls glory, have entered in nakedness and helplessness, and retreated amid disease and death.

Nor is this all. It is not merely helplessness that belongs to man – that characterises him as he enters this life. There is defilement also. "Behold," says the psalmist," I was shapen in iniquity, and in sin did my mother conceive me" (Ps. 51:5). "How can he be clean that is born of a woman?" (Job 25:4). In the chapter before us, we are taught that the conception and birth of "a man child," involved "seven days" of ceremonial defilement to the mother, together with thirty-three days of separation from the sanctuary; and these periods were doubled in the case of "a maid child." Has this no voice? Can we not read, herein, an humbling lesson? Does it not declare to us, in language not to be misunderstood, that man is "an unclean thing," and that he needs the blood of atonement to cleanse him? Truly so. Man may imagine that he can work out a righteousness of his own. He may vainly boast of the dignity of human nature. He may put on a lofty air, and assume a haughty bearing, as he moves across the stage of life; but if he would just retire for a few moments, and ponder over the short section of our book which now lies open before us, his pride, pomp, dignity, and righteousness would speedily vanish; and, instead thereof, he might find the solid basis of all true dignity, as well as the ground of divine righteousness, in the cross of our Lord Jesus Christ.

The shadow of this cross passes before us in a double way in our chapter; first, in the circumcision of the "man child," whereby he became enrolled as a member of the Israel of God; and, secondly, in the burnt offering and sin offering, whereby the mother was restored from every defiling influence, rendered fit, once more, to approach the sanctuary, and to come in contact with holy things. "And when the days of her purifying are fulfilled, for a son, or for a daughter, she shall bring a lamb of the first year for a burnt offering, and a young pigeon or a turtle dove, for a sin offering, unto the door of the tabernacle of the congregation, unto the priest; who shall offer it before the Lord, and make an atonement for her; and she shall be cleansed from the issue of her blood. This is the law for her that hath born a male or a female" (ver. 6, 7). The death of Christ, in its two grand aspects, is here introduced to our thoughts, as the only thing which could possibly meet, and perfectly remove, the defilement connected with man's natural birth. The burnt offering presents the death of Christ, according to the divine estimate thereof; the sin offering, on the other hand, presents the death of Christ, as bearing upon the sinner's need.

The blood of atonement within the reach of all

"And if she be not able to bring a lamb, then she shall bring two turtles, or two young pigeons; the one for a burnt offering, and the other for a sin offering; and the priest shall make an atonement for her, and she shall be clean." Nothing but blood-shedding could impart cleanness. The cross is the only remedy for man's infirmity, and man's defilement. Wherever that glorious work is apprehended, by faith, there is perfect cleanness enjoyed. Now, the apprehension may be feeble – the faith may be but wavering – the experience may be shallow; but, let the reader remember, for his soul's joy and comfort, that it is not the depth of his experience, the stability of his faith, or the strength of his apprehension, but the divine value, the changeless efficacy of the blood of Jesus. This gives great rest to the heart. The sacrifice of the cross is the same to every member of the Israel of God, whatever be his *status* in the assembly. The tender considerateness of our ever gracious God is seen in the fact that the blood of a turtle dove was as efficacious for the poor, as the blood of a bullock for the rich. The full value of the atoning work was alike maintained and exhibited in each. Had it not been so, the humble Israelite, if involved in ceremonial defilement, might, as she gazed upon the well-stocked pastures of some wealthy neighbour, exclaim, "Alas! what shall I do? How shall I be cleansed? How shall I get back to my place and privilege in the assembly? I have neither flock nor herd. I am poor and needy." But, blessed be God, the case of such an one was fully met. A pigeon or turtle dove was quite sufficient. The same perfect and beautiful grace shines forth, in the case of the leper, in chapter 14 of our book: "And *if he be poor and cannot get so much*, then he shall take, &c . . . And he shall offer the one of the turtle doves, or of the young pigeons, *such as he can get; even such as he is able to get* . . . This is the law of him in whom is the plague of leprosy, *whose hand is not able to get* that which pertaineth to his cleansing" (Ver. 21, 30-32).

Grace meets the needy one just where he is, and as he is. The atoning blood is brought within the reach of the very lowest, the very poorest, the very feeblest. All who need it can have it. "If he be poor" – what then? Let him be cast aside? Ah no; Israel's God could never so deal with the poor and needy. There is ample provision for all such in the gracious expression, "such as he can get; even such as he is able to get." Most exquisite grace! "To the poor the Gospel is preached." None can say, "the blood of Jesus was beyond me." Each can be challenged with the inquiry, "how near would you have it brought to you?" "I bring *near* my righteousness." How "near?" So near, that it is "to him that worketh not, but believeth on him that justifieth the ungodly" (Rom. 4:5). Again, "the word is *nigh* thee." How "nigh?" So nigh "that if thou shalt confess with thy mouth, the Lord Jesus, and shalt believe in thine heart that God hath raised him from the dead, thou shalt be saved" (Rom. 10:9). So also that most touching and beautiful invitation, "Ho, every one that thirsteth, come ye to the waters, and *he that hath no money"* (Isa. 55:1).

What matchless grace shines in the expressions, "to him that *worketh not,"* and, "he that hath *no money!"* They are as like God as they are unlike man. Salvation is as free as the air we breathe. Did we create the air? Did we mingle its component parts? No; but we enjoy it, and, by enjoying it, get power to live and act by Him who made it. So is it in the matter of salvation. We get it without a fraction, without an effort. We feed upon the wealth of another; we rest in the work finished by another; and, moreover, it is by so feeding and resting, that we are enabled to work for Him on whose wealth we feed, and in whose work we rest. This is a grand Gospel paradox, perfectly inexplicable to legality, but beautifully plain to faith. Divine grace delights in making provision for those who are "not able" to make provision for themselves.

The downstooping of the Lord Jesus

But, there is another invaluable lesson furnished by this twelfth chapter of Leviticus. We not only read, herein, the grace of God to the poor, but, by comparing its closing verse with Luke 2:24, we learn the amazing depth to which God stooped in order to manifest that grace. The Lord Jesus Christ, God manifest in the flesh, the pure and spotless Lamb, the Holy One, who knew no sin, was "made of a woman," and that woman – wondrous mystery! – having borne in her womb, and brought forth, that pure and perfect, that holy and spotless human body, had to undergo the usual ceremonial, and accomplish the days of her purification, according to the law of Moses. And not only do we read divine grace in the fact of her having thus to purify herself, but also the mode in which this was accomplished. "And to offer a sacrifice according to that which is said in the law of the Lord, *a pair of turtle doves or two young pigeons.*" From this simple circumstance we learn that the reputed parents of our blessed Lord Jesus were so poor, as to be obliged to take advantage of the gracious provision made for those whose means did not afford "a lamb for a burnt offering." What a thought! The Lord of Glory, the most High God, Possessor of heaven and earth, the One to whom pertained "the cattle upon a thousand hills" – yea, the wealth of the universe – appeared in the world which His hands had made, in the narrow circumstances of humble life. The Levitical economy had made provision for the poor, and the mother of Jesus availed herself thereof. Truly, there is a profound lesson in this for the human heart. The Lord Jesus did not make his appearance, in this world, in connexion with the great or the noble. He was pre-eminently a poor man. He took His place with the poor. "For ye know the grace of our Lord Jesus Christ, that, though he was rich, yet for our sakes he became poor, that ye through his poverty might be rich" (2 Cor. 8:9).

May it ever be our joy to feed upon this precious grace of our Lord Jesus Christ, by which we have been made rich for time and for eternity. He emptied Himself of all that love could give, that we might be filled. He stripped Himself, that we might be clothed. He died, that we might live. He, in the greatness of His grace, travelled down from the height of divine wealth into the depth of human poverty, in order that we might be raised from the dunghill of nature's ruin, to take our place amid the princes of His people, for ever. Oh! that the sense of this grace, wrought in our hearts by the power of the Holy Ghost, may constrain us to a more unreserved surrender of ourselves to Him, to whom we owe our present and everlasting felicity, our riches, our life, our all!

Chapters 13 & 14

THE LEPER

The responsibility of the priest

Of all the functions which, according to the Mosaic ritual, the priest had to discharge, none demanded more patient attention, or more strict adherence to the divine guide-book, than the discernment and proper treatment of leprosy. This fact must be obvious to every one who studies, with any measure of care, the very extensive and important section of our book at which we have now arrived.

There were two things which claimed the priest's vigilant care, namely, the purity of the assembly, and the grace which could not admit of the exclusion of any member, save on the most clearly-established grounds. Holiness could not permit any one to remain in who ought to be out; and, on the other hand, grace would not have any one out who ought to be in. Hence, therefore, there was the most urgent need, on the part of the priest, of watchfulness, calmness, wisdom, patience, tenderness, and enlarged experience. Things might seem trifling which, in reality, were serious; and things might look like leprosy which were not it at all. The greatest care and coolness were needed. A judgment rashly formed, a conclusion hastily arrived at, might involve the most serious consequences, either as regards the assembly or some individual member thereof.

This will account for the frequent occurrence of such expressions as the following, namely, "The priest shall look;" – "The priest shall shut up him that hath the plague *seven days*;" – "And the priest shall look on him the seventh day;" – "Then the priest shall shut him up *seven days more*;" – "And the priest *shall look on him again* the seventh day;" – "And the priest shall *see him*;" – "Then the priest shall *consider*." No case was to be hastily judged, or rashly decided. No opinion was to be formed from mere hearsay. Personal observation, priestly discernment, calm reflection, strict adherence to the written word – the holy, infallible guide book – all these things were imperatively demanded of the priest, if he would form a sound judgment of each case. He was not to be guided by his own thoughts, his own feelings, his own wisdom, in any thing. He had ample guidance in the word, if only he was subject thereto. Every point, every feature, every movement, every variation, every shade and character, every peculiar symptom and affection – all was provided for, with divine fullness and forethought; so that the priest only needed to be acquainted with, and subject to, the word in all things, in order to be preserved from ten thousand mistakes.

Thus much as to the priest and his holy responsibilities.

We shall now consider the disease of leprosy, as developed in a person, in a garment, or in a house.

Looking at this disease in a physical point of view, nothing can possibly be more loathsome; and being, so far as man is concerned, totally incurable, it furnishes a most vivid and appalling picture of sin – sin in one's nature – sin in his circumstances – sin in an assembly. What a lesson for the soul in the fact that such a vile and humiliating disease should be used as a type of moral evil, whether in a member of God's assembly, in the circumstances of any member, or in the assembly itself!

Leprosy in a man

I. And first, then, as to leprosy in a person; or, in other words, the working of moral evil, or of that which might seem to be evil, in any member of the assembly. This is a matter of grave and solemn import – a matter demanding the utmost vigilance and care on the part of all who are concerned in the good of souls and in the glory of God, as involved in the well-being and purity of His assembly as a whole, or of each individual member thereof.

It is important to see that, while the broad principles of leprosy and its cleansing apply, in a secondary sense, to any sinner, yet, in the scripture now before us, the matter is presented in connexion with those who were God's recognised people. The person who is here seen as the subject of priestly examination, is a member of the assembly of God. It is well to apprehend this. God's assembly must be kept pure, because it is His dwelling-place. No leper can be allowed to remain within the hallowed precincts of Jehovah's habitation.

But, then, mark the care, the vigilance, the perfect patience, inculcated upon the priest, lest anything that was not leprosy might be treated as such, or lest anything that really was leprosy might be suffered to escape. Many things might appear "in the skin" – the place of manifestation – "like the plague of leprosy," which, upon patient, priestly investigation, would be found to be merely superficial. This was to be carefully attended to. Some blemish might make its appearance, upon the surface, which, though demanding the jealous care of the one who had to act for God, was not, in reality, defiling. And, yet, that which seemed but a superficial blemish might prove to be something deeper than the skin, something below the surface, something affecting the hidden springs of the constitution. All this claimed the most intense care on the part of the priest (see ver. 2-11). Some slight neglect, some trifling oversight, might lead to disastrous consequences. It might lead to the defilement of the assembly, by the presence of a confirmed leper, or to the expulsion, for some superficial blemish, of a genuine member of the Israel of God.

Now, there is a rich fund of instruction in all this for the people of God. There is a difference between personal infirmity and the positive energy of evil – between mere defects and blemishes in the outward character, and the activity of sin in the members. No doubt, it is important to watch against our infirmities; for, if not watched, judged, and guarded against, they may become the source of positive evil (see ver. 14-28).

Everything of nature must be judged and kept down. We must not make any allowance for personal infirmity, *in ourselves*, though we should make ample allowance for it *in others*. Take, for example, the matter of an irritable temper. I should judge it in myself; I should make allowance for it in another. It may, like "the burning boil," in the case of an Israelite (ver. 19, 20), prove the source of real defilement – the ground of exclusion from the assembly. Every form of weakness must be watched, lest it become an occasion of sin. "A bald forehead" was not leprosy, but it was that in which leprosy might appear, and, hence, it had to be watched. There may be a hundred things which are not, in themselves, sinful, but which may become the occasion of sin, if not diligently looked after. Nor is it merely a question of what, in our estimation, may be termed blots, blemishes, and personal infirmities, but even of what our hearts might feel disposed to boast of. Wit, humour, vivacity of spirit and temper; all these may become the source and centre of defilement. Each one has something to guard against – something to keep him ever upon the watch-tower. How happy it is that we have a Father's heart to come to and count on, with respect to all such things! We have the precious privilege of coming, at all times, into the presence of unrebuking, unupbraiding love, there to tell out all, and obtain grace to help in all, and full victory over all. We need not be discouraged, so long as we see such a motto inscribed on the door of our Father's treasury, "He giveth more grace." Precious motto! It has no limit. It is bottomless and boundless.

We shall now proceed to inquire what was done in every case in which the plague of leprosy was unquestionably and unmistakably defined. The God of Israel could bear with infirmity, blemish, and failure; but the moment it became a case of defilement, whether in the head, the beard, the forehead, or any other part, it could not be tolerated in the holy assembly. "The leper, in whom the plague is, his clothes shall be rent, and his head bare, and he shall put a covering upon his upper lip, and shall cry, Unclean, unclean.

All the days wherein the plague shall be in him he shall be defiled; he is unclean: he shall dwell alone; without the camp shall his habitation be" (ver. 45, 46). Here was the leper's condition – the leper's occupation – the leper's place. With rent garments, bare head, and covered lip; crying, Unclean, unclean; and dwelling outside, in the dreary solitude, the dismal desert waste. What could be more humiliating, what more depressing than this? "He shall dwell alone." He was unfit for communion or companionship. He was excluded from the only spot, in all the world, in which Jehovah's presence was known or enjoyed.

Reader, behold, in the poor, solitary leper, a vivid type of one in whom sin is working. This is really what it means. It is not, as we shall see presently, a helpless, ruined, guilty, convicted sinner, whose guilt and misery have come thoroughly out, and who is, therefore, a fit subject for the love of God, and the blood of Christ. No; we see in the excluded leper, one in whom sin is actually working – one in whom there is the positive energy of evil. This is what defiles and shuts out from the enjoyment of the divine presence and the communion of saints. So long as sin is working, there can be no fellowship with God, or with His people. "He shall dwell alone; without the camp shall his habitation be." How long? "All the days wherein *the plague* shall be *in* him." This is a great practical truth. The energy of evil is the death-blow to communion. There may be the outward appearance, the mere form, the hollow profession; but communion there can be none, so long as the energy of evil is there. It matters not what the character or amount of the evil may be, if it were but the weight of a feather, if it were but some foolish thought, so long as it continues to work, it must hinder communion, it must cause a suspension of fellowship. It is when it rises to a head, when it comes to the surface, when it is brought thoroughly out, that it can be perfectly met and put away by the grace of God and by the blood of the Lamb.

A man totally covered in leprosy

This leads us to a deeply-interesting point in connexion with the leper – a point which must prove a complete paradox to all save those who understand God's mode of dealing with sinners. "And if a leprosy break out abroad in the skin, and the leprosy cover all the skin of him that hath the plague, from his head even to his foot, wheresoever the priest looketh; then the priest shall consider; and, behold, if the leprosy have covered all his flesh, he shall pronounce him clean that hath the plague: it is all turned white: he is clean" (chap. 13:12, 13) The moment a sinner is in his true place before God, the whole question is settled. Directly his real character is fully brought out, there is no further difficulty. He may have to pass through much painful exercise, ere he reaches this point – exercise consequent upon his refusal to take his true place – to bring out "all the truth," with respect to what he is; but the moment he is brought to say, from his heart, *"just as I am,"* the free grace of God flows down to him. "When I kept silence, my bones waxed old, through my roaring all the day long. For day and night thy hand was heavy upon me: my moisture is turned into the drought of summer" (Ps. 32:3, 4). How long did this painful exercise continue? Until the whole truth was brought out – until all that which was working inwardly came fully to the surface. "I acknowledged my sin unto thee, and mine iniquity have I not hid. I said, I will confess my transgressions unto the Lord; and thou forgavest the iniquity of my sin" (ver. 5).

It is deeply interesting to mark the progress of the Lord's dealing with the leprous man, from the moment that the suspicion is raised, by certain features in the place of manifestation, until the disease covers the whole man, "from the crown of the head unto the sole of the foot." There was no haste, and no indifference. God ever enters the place of judgment with a slow and measured pace; but when He does enter, He must act according to the claims of His nature. He can patiently investigate. He can wait for "seven days;" and should there be the slightest variation in the symptoms, He can wait for "seven days more;" but, the moment it is found to be the positive working of leprosy, there can be no toleration. "Without the camp shall his habitation be." How long? Until the disease comes fully to the surface. "If the leprosy have covered *all* his flesh, he shall pronounce him clean." This is a most precious and interesting point. The very smallest speck of leprosy was intolerable to God; and yet, when the whole man was covered, from head to foot, he was pronounced clean – that is, he was a proper subject for the grace of God and the blood of atonement.

Thus is it, in every case, with the sinner. God is "of purer eyes than to behold evil, and cannot look upon iniquity" (Hab. 1:13;); and yet, the moment a sinner takes his true place, as one thoroughly lost, guilty, and undone – as one in whom there is not so much as a single point on which the eye of Infinite Holiness can rest with complacency – as one who is so bad, that he cannot, possibly, be worse, there is an immediate, a perfect, a divine settlement of the entire matter. The grace of God deals with sinners; and when I know myself to be a sinner, I know myself to be one whom Christ came to save. The more clearly any one can prove me to be a sinner, the more clearly he establishes my title to the love of God, and the work of Christ. "For Christ also hath once suffered for sins, the just for the unjust, that he might bring us to God" (1 Peter 3:18). Now, if I am "unjust;" I am one of those very people for whom Christ died, and I am entitled to all the benefits of His death. "There is not a just man upon earth;" and, inasmuch as I am "upon earth," it is plain that I am "unjust;" and it is equally plain that Christ died for me – that he suffered for my sins. Since, therefore, Christ died for me, it is my happy privilege to enter into the immediate enjoyment of the fruits of His sacrifice. This is as plain as plainness itself. It demands no effort whatsoever. I am not called to be anything but just what I am. I am not called to feel, to experience, to realize anything. The word of God assures me that Christ died for me just as I am; and if He died for me I am as safe as He is

Himself. There is nothing against me. Christ met all. He not only suffered for my "*sins*," but He "made an end of *sin*." He abolished the entire system in which, as a child of the first Adam, I stood, and He has introduced me into a new position, in association with Himself, and there I stand, before God, free from all charge of sin, and all fear of judgment.

> Just as I am – without one plea,
> But that thy blood was shed for me,
> And that thou bidst me come to thee,
> O Lamb of God, I come!

How do I know that His blood was shed for me? By the Scriptures. Blessed, solid, eternal ground of knowledge! Christ suffered for sins. I have gotten sins. Christ died "the just for the unjust." I am unjust. Wherefore, the death of Christ appropriates itself to me, as fully, as immediately, and as divinely, as though I were the only sinner upon earth. It is not a question of my appropriation, realization, or experience. Many souls harass themselves about this. How often has one heard such language as the following, "Oh! I believe that Christ died for sinners, but I cannot *realize* that my sins are forgiven. I cannot apply, I cannot appropriate, I do not experience the benefit of Christ's death." All this is self and not Christ. It is feeling and not Scripture. If we search from cover to cover of the blessed volume, we shall not find a syllable about being saved by realization, experience, or appropriation. The Gospel applies itself to all who are on the ground of being lost. Christ died for sinners. That is just what I am. Wherefore, He died for me. How do I know this? Is it because I feel it? By no means. How then? By the word of God. "Christ died for our sins, according to the Scriptures; he was buried and rose again the third day, according to the Scriptures" (1 Cor. 15:3, 4). Thus it is all "according to the Scriptures." If it were according to our feelings, we should be in a deplorable way, for our feelings are hardly the same for the length of a day; but the scriptures are ever the same.

"For ever, O Lord, thy word is settled in heaven." "Thou hast magnified thy word above all thy name."

No doubt, it is a very happy thing to realize, to feel, and to experience; but, if we put these things in the place of Christ, we shall neither have them nor the Christ that yields them. If I am occupied with Christ, I shall realize; but if I put my realization in place of Christ, I shall have neither the one nor the other. This is the sad condition of thousands. Instead of resting on the stable authority of "the Scriptures," they are ever looking into their own hearts, and, hence, they are always uncertain and, as a consequence, always unhappy. A condition of doubt is a condition of torture. But how can I get rid of my doubt? Simply by relying on the divine authority of "the Scriptures." Of what do the Scriptures testify? Of Christ (John 5). They declare that Christ died for our sins, and that He was raised again for our justification (Rom. 4). This settles everything. The self-same authority that tells me I am unjust, tells me also that Christ died for me. Nothing can be plainer than this. If I were anything else than unjust, the death of Christ could not be for me at all, but being unjust, it is divinely fitted, divinely intended, and divinely applied to me. If I am occupied with anything in, of, or about myself, it is plain I have not entered into the full spiritual application of Lev. 13:12, 13. I have not come to the Lamb of God, *just as I am.*" It is when the leper is covered from head to foot that he is on the true ground. It is there and there alone that grace can meet him. "Then the priest shall consider; and, behold, if the leprosy have covered all his flesh, he shall pronounce him clean that hath the plague: it is all turned white: he is clean." Precious truth! "Where sin abounded grace did much more abound." So long as I think there is a single spot which is not covered with the direful disease, I have not come to the end of myself. It is when my true condition is fully disclosed to my view, that I really understand the meaning of salvation by grace.

The force of all this will be more fully apprehended when we come to consider the ordinances connected with the cleansing of the leper, in chapter 14 of our book. We shall, now, briefly enter upon the question of leprosy in a garment, as presented in chapter 13:47-59.

Leprosy in a garment

II. The garment or skin suggests to the mind the idea of a man's circumstances or habits. This is a deeply practical point. We are to watch against the working of evil in our ways just as carefully as against evil in ourselves. The same patient investigation is observable with respect to a garment as in the case of a person. There is no haste; neither is there any indifference. "The priest shall look upon the plague, and shut up it that hath the plague seven days." There must be no indifference, no indolence, no carelessness. Evil may creep into our habits and circumstances, in numberless ways; and, hence, the moment we perceive anything of a suspicious nature, it must be submitted to a calm, patient process of priestly investigation. It must be "shut up seven days," in order that it may have full time to develop itself perfectly.

"And he shall look on the plague on the seventh day: if the plague be spread in the garment, either in the warp, or in the woof, or in a skin, or in any work that is made of skin, the plague is a fretting leprosy; it is unclean. He shall therefore burn that garment." The wrong habit must be given up, the moment I discover it. If I find myself in a thoroughly wrong position, I must abandon it. The burning of the garment expresses the act of judgment upon evil, whether in a man's habits or circumstances. There must be no trifling with evil. In certain cases the garment was to be "washed," which expresses the action of the Word of God upon a man's habits. "Then the priest shall command that they wash the thing wherein the plague is, and he shall shut it up *seven days more*." There is to be patient waiting in order to ascertain the effect of the Word. "And the priest shall look on the plague, after that it is washed; and, behold, if the plague have not changed . . . thou shalt burn it in the fire." When there is any thing radically and irremediably bad in one's position or habits, the whole thing is to be given up. "And if the priest look, and, behold, the plague be somewhat dark: after the washing of it; then he shall rend it out of the garment." The Word may produce such an effect as that the wrong features in a man's character, or the wrong points in his position, shall be given up, and the evil be got rid of; but if the evil continue, after all, the whole thing must be condemned and set aside.

There is a rich mine of practical instruction in all this. We must look well to the position which we occupy, the circumstances in which we stand, the habits we adopt, the character we wear. There is special need of watchfulness. Every suspicious symptom and trait must be sedulously guarded, lest it should prove, in the sequel, to be "a fretting" or "spreading leprosy," whereby we ourselves and many others may be defiled. We may be placed in a position attached to which there are certain wrong things which can be given up, without entirely abandoning the position; and, on the other hand, we may find ourselves in a situation in which it is impossible to "abide with God." Where the eye is single, the path will be plain. Where the one desire of the heart is to enjoy the divine presence, we shall easily discover those things which tend to deprive us of that unspeakable blessing.

May our hearts be tender and sensitive. May we cultivate a deeper, closer walk with God; and may we carefully guard against every form of defilement, whether in person, in habit, or in association!

The cleansing of the leper

We shall, now, proceed to consider the beauteous and significant ordinances connected with the cleansing of the leper, in which we shall find some of the most precious truths of the gospel presented to us.

"And the Lord spake unto Moses, saying, This shall be the law of the leper in the day of his cleansing: he shall be brought unto the priest: and the priest shall go forth out of the camp" (chap. 14:1-3). We have already seen the place which the leper occupied. He was outside the camp, in the place of moral distance from God – from His sanctuary and His assembly. Moreover, he dwelt in dreary solitude, in a condition of uncleanness. He was beyond the reach of human aid; and, as for himself, he could only communicate defilement to every one and every thing he touched. It was, therefore, obviously impossible that he could do anything to cleanse himself. If, indeed, he could *only* defile by his very touch, how could he possibly cleanse himself? How could he contribute towards, or co-operate in, his cleansing? Impossible. As an unclean leper, he could not do so much as a single thing for himself; *all* had to be done *for* him. He could not make his way to God, but God could make His way to him. He was shut up to God. There was no help for him, either in himself or in his fellow-man. It is clear that one leper could not cleanse another; and it is equally clear that if a leper touched a clean person he rendered him unclean. His *only* resource was in God. He was to be a debtor to grace for everything.

Hence we read, "The priest shall go forth out of the camp. It is not said, "the leper shall go." This was wholly out of the question. It was of no use talking to the leper about going or doing. He was consigned to dreary solitude; whither could he go? He was involved in helpless defilement; what could he do? He might long for fellowship and long to be clean; but his longings were those of a lonely helpless leper. He might make efforts after cleansing; but his efforts could but prove him unclean, and tend to spread defilement. Before ever he could be pronounced "clean," a work had to be wrought for him – a work which he could neither do nor help to do – a work which had to be wholly accomplished by another. The leper was called to "stand still," and behold the priest doing a work in virtue of which the leprosy could be perfectly cleansed. The priest accomplished *all*. The leper did *nothing*.

The two birds

"Then shall the priest command to take for him that is to be cleansed, two birds, alive and clean, and cedarwood, and scarlet, and hyssop. And the priest shall command that one of the birds be killed in an earthen vessel over running water." In the priest going forth from the camp – forth from God's dwelling place – we behold the blessed Lord Jesus coming down from the bosom of the Father, His eternal dwelling-place, into this polluted world of ours, where He beheld us sunk in the polluting leprosy of sin. He, like the good Samaritan, "came where we were." He did not come half-way, merely. He did not come nine-tenths of the way. He came all the way. This was indispensable. He could not, consistently with the holy claims of the throne of God, have bidden our leprosy to depart had He remained in the bosom. He could call worlds into existence by the word of His mouth; but when leprous sinners had to be cleansed, something more was needed. "God so loved the world that he gave his only begotten Son." When worlds were to be framed, God had but to speak. When sinners had to be saved, He had to give His Son. "In this was manifested the love of God toward us, because that God sent his only begotten Son into the world, that we might live through Him. Herein is love, not that we loved God, but that he loved us, and sent his Son to be the propitiation for our sins" (1 John 4:9, 10).

But there was far more to be accomplished than the mission and incarnation of the Son. It would have availed the leper but little indeed, had the priest merely gone forth from the camp and looked upon his low and forlorn condition. Blood shedding was essentially necessary ere leprosy could be removed. The death of a spotless victim was needed. "Without shedding of blood is no remission" (Heb. 9:22). And, be it observed, that the shedding of blood was the real basis of the leper's cleansing. It was not a mere circumstance which, in conjunction with others, contributed to the leper's cleansing. By no means. The giving up of the life was the grand and all-important fact. When this was accomplished the way was open; every barrier was removed; God could deal in perfect grace with the leper. This point should be distinctly laid hold of, if my reader would fully enter into the glorious doctrine of the blood.

"And the priest shall command that one of the birds be killed in an earthen vessel over running water." Here we have the acknowledged type of the death of Christ, "who, through the eternal Spirit, offered himself without spot to God." "He was crucified in weakness" (Heb. 9; 2 Cor. 13). The greatest, the mightiest, the most glorious, the most momentous work that ever was accomplished, throughout the wide universe of God, was wrought "in weakness." Oh! my reader, how terrible a thing must sin be, in the judgment of God, when His own beloved Son had to come down from heaven, and hang upon yonder cursed tree, a spectacle to men, to angels, and to devils, in order that you and I might be forgiven! And what a type of sin have we in leprosy! Who would have thought that that little "bright spot" appearing on the person of some member of the congregation was a matter of such grave consequence? But, ah! that little "bright spot" was nothing less than the energy of evil, in the place of manifestation. It was the index of the dreadful working of sin in the nature; and ere that person could be fitted for a place in the assembly, or for the enjoyment of communion with a holy God, the Son of God had to leave those bright heavens, and descend into the lowest parts of the earth, in order to make a full atonement for that which exhibited itself merely in the form of a little "bright spot." Let us remember this. Sin is a dreadful thing in the estimation of God. He cannot tolerate so much as a single sinful thought. Before one such thought could be forgiven, Christ had to die upon the cross. The most trifling sin, if any sin can be called trifling, demanded nothing less than the death of God's Eternal and Co-equal Son. But, eternal praise be to God, what sin demanded, redeeming love freely gave; and now God is infinitely more glorified in the forgiveness of sins than He could have been had Adam maintained his original innocency. God is more glorified in the salvation, the pardon, the justification, the preservation, and final glorification of guilty man, than He could have been in maintaining an innocent man in the enjoyment of creation blessings. Such is the precious mystery of redemption. May our hearts enter, by the power of the Holy Ghost, into the living and profound depths of this wondrous mystery!

"As for the living bird, he shall take it, and the cedar wood, and the scarlet, and the hyssop, and shall dip them and the living bird in the blood of the bird that was killed over the running water. And he shall sprinkle upon him that is to be cleansed from the leprosy seven times, and shall pronounce him clean, and shall let the living bird loose into the open field." The blood being shed, the priest can enter directly and fully upon his work. Up to this, we read, "the priest shall command;" but now he acts immediately himself. The death of Christ is the basis of His priestly ministration. Having entered with His own blood into the holy place, He acts as our Great High Priest, applying to our souls all the precious results of His atoning work, and maintaining us in the full and divine integrity of the position into which His sacrifice has introduced us. "For every high priest is ordained to offer gifts and sacrifices: wherefore it is of necessity that this man have somewhat also to offer. For if he were on earth he should not be a priest" (Heb. 8:3, 4).

We could hardly have a more perfect type of the resurrection of Christ than that presented in "the living bird let loose into the open field." It was not let go until after the death of its companion; for the two birds typify one Christ, in two stages of His blessed work, namely, death and resurrection. Ten thousand birds let loose would not have availed for the leper. It was that living bird, mounting upward into the open heavens, bearing upon his wing that significant token of accomplished atonement – it was that which told out the great fact that the work was done – the ground cleared, the foundation laid. Thus is it in reference to our blessed Lord Jesus Christ. His resurrection declares the glorious triumph of redemption.

"He rose again the third day according to the Scriptures." "He was raised again for our justification." It is this that sets the burdened heart free, and liberates the struggling conscience. The Scriptures assure me that Jesus was nailed to the cross under the weight of my sins; but the same Scriptures assure me that He rose from the grave without one of those sins upon Him. Nor is this all. The same Scriptures assure me that all who put their trust in Jesus are as free from all charge of guilt as He is; that there is no more wrath or condemnation for them than for Him; that they are in Him, one with Him, accepted in Him; co-quickened, co-raised, co-seated with Him. Such is the peace-giving testimony of the Scriptures of truth – such, the record of God who cannot lie (see Rom. 6:6-11; Rom. 8:1-4; 2 Cor. 5:21; Eph. 2:5, 6; Col. 2:10-15, 1 John 4:17).

The cedar wood, scarlet and hyssop

But we have another most important truth set before us in verse 6 of our chapter. We not only see our full deliverance from guilt and condemnation, as beautifully exhibited in the living bird let loose, but we see also our entire deliverance from all the attractions of earth and all the influences of nature. "The scarlet" would be the apt expression of the former, while "the cedar wood and hyssop" would set forth the latter. The cross is the end of all this world's glory. God presents it as such, and the believer recognises it as such. "God forbid that I should glory, save in the cross of our Lord Jesus Christ, whereby the world is crucified unto me, and I unto the world" (Gal. 6:14).

Then, as to the "cedar wood and hyssop," they present to us, as it were, the two extremes of nature's wide range. Solomon "spake of trees, from the cedar tree that is in Lebanon even unto the hyssop that springeth out of the wall" (1 Kings 4:33). From the lofty cedar which crowns the sides of Lebanon, down to the lowly hyssop – the wide extremes and all that lies between – nature, in all its departments, is brought under the power of the cross; so that the believer sees, in the death of Christ, the end of all his guilt, the end of all earth's glory, and the end of the whole system of nature – the entire old creation. And with what is he to be occupied? With Him who is the Antitype of that living bird, with blood-stained feathers, ascending into the open heavens. Precious, glorious, soul-satisfying object! A risen, ascended, triumphant, glorified Christ, who has passed into the heavens, bearing in His sacred Person the marks of an accomplished atonement. It is with Him we have to do. We are shut up to Him. He is God's exclusive object. He is the centre of heaven's joy, the theme of angels' song. We want none of earth's glory, none of nature's attractions. We can behold them all, together with our sin and guilt, for ever set aside by the death of Christ. We can well afford to dispense with earth and nature, inasmuch as we have gotten, instead thereof "the unsearchable riches of Christ."

Sprinkling the blood on the leper

"And he shall sprinkle upon him that is to be cleansed from the leprosy, seven times, and shall pronounce him clean, and shall let the bird loose into the open field." The more deeply we ponder over the contents of chap. 13 the more clearly we shall see how utterly impossible it was for the leper to do anything towards his own cleansing. All he could do was to "put a covering upon his upper lip;" and all he could say was, "Unclean, unclean." It belonged to God, and to Him alone, to devise and accomplish a work whereby the leprosy could be perfectly cleansed; and, further, it belonged to God, and to Him alone, to pronounce the leper "clean." Hence it is written, "the priest shall sprinkle;" and "he shall pronounce him clean." It is not said, "the leper shall sprinkle, and pronounce, or imagine himself, clean." This would never do. God was the Judge – God was the Healer – God was the Cleanser. He alone knew what leprosy was, how it could be put away, and when to pronounce the leper clean. The leper might have gone on all his days covered with leprosy, and yet be wholly ignorant of what was wrong with him. It was the word of God – the Scriptures of truth – the divine Record, that declared the full truth as to leprosy; and nothing short of the selfsame authority could pronounce the leper clean, and that, moreover, only, on the solid and indisputable ground of death and resurrection. There is the most precious connexion between the three things in verse 7: the blood is sprinkled, the leper pronounced clean, and the living bird let loose. There is not so much as a single syllable about what the leper was to do, to say, to think, or to feel. It was enough that he was a leper; a fully revealed, a thoroughly judged leper, covered from head to foot. This sufficed for him; all the rest pertained to God.

It is of all importance, for the anxious inquirer after peace, to enter into the truth unfolded in this branch of our subject. So many are tried by the question of *feeling, realizing,* and *appropriating,* instead of seeing, as in the leper's case, that the sprinkling of the blood was as independent and as divine as the shedding of it. It is not said, "The leper shall apply, appropriate, or realize, and then he shall be clean." By no means. The plan of deliverance was divine; the provision of the sacrifice was divine; the shedding of the blood was divine; the sprinkling of the blood was divine; the record as to the result was divine: in short, it was all divine.

It is not that we should undervalue realization, or, to speak more correctly, communion, through the Holy Ghost, with all the precious results of Christ's work for us. Far from it: we shall see, presently, the place assigned thereto, in the divine economy. But then, we are no more saved by realization, than the leper was cleansed by it. The gospel, by which we are saved, is that "Christ died for our sins, according to the Scriptures; and that he was buried, and that he rose again the third day, according to the Scriptures." There is nothing about realization here. No doubt, it is happy to realise. It is a very happy thing for one, who was just on the point of being drowned, to realise himself in a life-boat; but, clearly, he is saved by the boat and not by his realization. So it is with the sinner that believes on the Lord Jesus Christ. He is saved by death and resurrection. Is it because he realizes it? No; but because God says it. It is *"according to the Scriptures."* Christ died and rose again; and, on that ground, God pronounces him clean.

> "No condemnation, O, my soul!
> *'Tis God that speaks the word."*

This gives immense peace to the soul. I have to do with God's plain record, which nothing can ever shake. That record has reference to God's own work. It is He Himself, who has wrought all that was needful, in order to my being pronounced clean in His sight. My pardon no more depends upon my realization than upon any "works of righteousness that I have done;" and it no more depends upon my works of righteousness than it does upon my crimes. In a word, it depends, exclusively, upon the death and resurrection of Christ. How do I know it? God tells me. It is "according to the Scriptures."

There are, perhaps, few things which disclose the deep-seated legality of our hearts, more strikingly, than this oft-raised question of realization. We *will* have in something of self, and thus so sadly mar our peace and liberty in Christ. It is mainly because of this that I dwell, at such length, upon the beautiful ordinance of the cleansing of the leper, and especially on the truth unfolded in chapter 14:7. It was the priest that sprinkled the blood; and it was the priest that pronounced the leper clean. Thus it is in the case of the sinner. The moment he is on his true ground, the blood of Christ and the word of God apply themselves without any further question or difficulty whatever. But the moment this harassing question of realization is raised, the peace is disturbed, the heart depressed, and the mind bewildered. The more thoroughly I get done with self, and become occupied with Christ, as presented in "the Scriptures," the more settled my peace will be. If the leper had looked at himself, when the priest pronounced him clean, would he have found any basis for the declaration? Surely not. The sprinkled blood was the basis of the divine record, and not anything in, or connected with, the leper. The leper was not asked how he felt, or what he thought. He was not questioned as to whether he had a deep sense of the vileness of his disease. He was an acknowledged leper; that was enough. It was for such an one the blood was shed; and that blood made him clean. How did he know this? Was it because he felt it? No; but because the priest, on God's behalf, and by His authority told him so. The leper was pronounced clean on the very same ground that the living bird was let loose. The same blood which stained the feathers of that living bird was sprinkled upon the leper. This was a perfect settlement of the whole affair, and that, too, in a manner entirely independent of the leper, the leper's thoughts, his feelings, and his realization. Such is the type. And when we look from the type to the Antitype, we see that our blessed Lord Jesus Christ entered heaven, and laid on the throne of God the eternal record of an accomplished work, in virtue of which the believer enters also. This is a most glorious truth, divinely calculated to dispel from the heart of the anxious inquirer every doubt, every fear, every bewildering thought, and every harassing question. A risen Christ is God's exclusive object, and He sees every believer in Him. May every awakened soul find abiding repose in this emancipating truth.

He shall tarry abroad out of his tent seven days

"And he that is to be cleansed shall wash his clothes, and shave off all his hair, and wash himself in water, that he may be clean: and after that he shall come into the camp, and shall tarry abroad out of his tent seven days" (ver. 8). The leper, being pronounced clean, can begin to do what he could not even have attempted to do before, namely, to cleanse himself, cleanse his habits, shave off all his hair; and, having done so, he is privileged to take his place in the camp – the place of ostensible, recognized, public relationship with the God of Israel, whose presence in that camp it was which rendered the expulsion of the leper needful. The blood having been applied in its expiating virtue, there is the washing of water, which expresses the action of the word on the character, the habits, the ways, so as to render the person, not only in God's view, but also in the view of the congregation, morally and practically fit for a place in the public assembly.

But, be it observed, the man, though sprinkled with blood and washed with water, and thus entitled to a position in the public assembly, was not permitted to enter his own tent. He was not permitted to enter upon the full enjoyment of those private, personal privileges, which belonged to his own peculiar place in the camp. In other words, though knowing redemption through the shed and sprinkled blood, and owning the word as the rule, according to which his person and all his habits should be cleansed and regulated, he had yet to be brought, in the power of the Spirit, into full, intelligent communion with his own special place, portion, and privileges in Christ.

I speak according to the doctrine of the type; and I feel it to be of importance to apprehend the truth unfolded therein. It is too often overlooked. There are many, who own the blood of Christ as the alone ground of pardon, and the word of God as that whereby alone their habits, ways, and associations are to be cleansed and ordered, who, nevertheless, are far from entering, by the power of the Holy Ghost, into communion with the preciousness and excellency of that One, Whose blood has put away their sins, and whose word is to cleanse their practical habits. They are in the place of ostensible and actual relationship; but not in the power of personal communion. It is perfectly true, that all believers are in Christ, and, as such, entitled to communion with the very highest truths. Moreover, they have the Holy Ghost, as the power of communion. All this is divinely true; but, then, there is not that entire setting aside of all that pertains to nature, which is really essential to the power of communion with Christ, in all the aspects of His character and work. In point of fact, this latter will not be fully known to any until "the eighth day" – the day of resurrection-glory, when we shall know even as we are known. Then, indeed, each one for himself, and all together, shall enter into the full, unhindered power of communion with Christ, in all the precious phases of His Person, and features of His character, unfolded from verse 10 to 20 of our chapter. Such is the hope set before us; but, even now, in proportion as we enter, by faith, through the mighty energy of the indwelling Spirit, into the death of nature and all pertaining thereto, we can feed upon and rejoice in Christ as the portion of our souls, in the place of individual communion.

"But it shall be on the seventh day, that he shall shave all his hair off his head, and his beard, and his eyebrows, even all his hair he shall shave off: and he shall wash his clothes, also he shall wash his flesh in water, and he shall be clean" (ver. 9). Now, it is clear, that the leper was just as clean, in God's judgment, on the first day, when the blood was sprinkled upon him, in its sevenfold or perfect efficacy, as he was on the seventh day. Wherein, then, was the difference? Not in his actual standing and condition, but in his personal intelligence and communion. On the seventh day, he was called to enter into the full and complete abolition of all that pertained to nature. He was called to apprehend that, not merely was nature's leprosy to be put away, but nature's ornaments – yea, all that was natural – all that belonged to the old condition.

It is one thing to know, as a doctrine, that God sees my nature to be dead, and it is quite another thing for me to "reckon" myself as dead – to put off, practically, the old man and his deeds – to mortify my members which are on the earth. This, probably, is what many godly persons mean when they speak of progressive sanctification. They mean a right thing, though they do not put it exactly as the Scriptures do. The leper was pronounced clean, the moment the blood was sprinkled upon Him; and yet he had to cleanse himself. How was this? In the former case, he was clean, in the judgment of God; in the latter, he was to be clean practically, in his own personal intelligence, and in his manifested character. Thus it is with the believer. He is, as one with Christ, "washed, sanctified, and justified" – "accepted" – "complete" (1 Cor. 6:11; Eph. 1:6; Col 2:10). Such is his unalterable standing and condition before God. He is as perfectly sanctified as he is justified, for Christ is the measure of both the one and the other, according to God's judgment and view of the case. But, then, the believer's apprehension of all this, in his own soul, and his exhibition thereof in his habits and ways, open up quite another line of things. Hence it is we read, "Having therefore these promises, dearly beloved, let us *cleanse ourselves* from all filthiness of the flesh and spirit, perfecting holiness in the fear of God" (2 Cor. 7:1). It is because Christ has cleansed us by His precious blood that therefore we are called to "cleanse ourselves" by the application of the word, through the Spirit. "This is he that came by water and blood, Jesus Christ; not by water only, but by water and blood. And it is the Spirit that beareth witness because the Spirit is truth. For there are three that bear record, the Spirit, and the water, and the blood: and these three agree in one" (1 John 5:6-8). Here we have atonement by the blood, cleansing by the word, and power by the Spirit, all founded upon the death of Christ, and all vividly foreshadowed in the ordinances connected with the cleansing of the leper.

The eighth day and its offerings

"And on the eighth day he shall take two he lambs without blemish, and one ewe lamb of the first year without blemish, and three tenth deals of fine flour for a meat offering, mingled with oil, and one log of oil. And the priest that maketh him clean shall present the man that is to be made clean, and those things, before the Lord, at the door of the tabernacle of the congregation. And the priest shall take one he lamb, and offer him for a trespass offering, and the log of oil, and wave them for a wave offering before the Lord" (ver. 10-12). The entire range of offerings is here introduced; but it is the trespass offering which is first killed, inasmuch as the leper is viewed as an actual trespasser. This is true in every case. As those, who have trespassed against God, we need Christ as the one who atoned, on the cross, for those trespasses. "Himself bare our *sins* in his own body on the tree." The first view which the sinner gets of Christ is as the Antitype of the trespass offering.

"And the priest shall take some of the blood of the trespass offering, and the priest shall put it upon the tip of the right ear of him that is to be cleansed, and upon the thumb of his right hand, and upon the great toe of his right foot." "*The ear*" – that guilty member which had so frequently proved a channel of communication for vanity, folly, and even uncleanness – that ear must be cleansed by the blood of the trespass offering. Thus all the guilt, which I have ever contracted by that member, is forgiven according to God's estimate of the blood of Christ. "*The right hand,*" which had, so frequently, been stretched forth for the execution of deeds of vanity, folly, and even uncleanness, must be cleansed by the blood of the trespass offering. Thus all the guilt, which I have ever contracted by that member, is forgiven, according to God's estimate of the blood of Christ. "*The foot,*" which had so often run in the way of vanity, folly, and even uncleanness, must now be cleansed by the blood of the trespass offering, so that all the guilt, which I have ever contracted by that member, is forgiven, according to God's estimate of the blood of Christ. Yes; *all, all, all* is forgiven – all is cancelled – all forgotten – all sunk as lead in the mighty waters of eternal oblivion. Who shall bring it up again? Shall angel, man, or devil, be able to plunge into those unfathomed and unfathomable waters, to bring up from thence those trespasses of "foot," "hand," or "ear," which redeeming love has cast thereinto? Oh! no; blessed be God, they are gone, and gone for ever. I am better off, by far, than if Adam had never sinned. Precious truth! To be washed in the blood is better far than to be clothed in innocency.

But God could not rest satisfied with the mere blotting out of trespasses, by the atoning blood of Jesus. This, in itself, is a great thing; but there is something greater still.

"And the priest shall take some of the log of oil, and pour it into the palm of his own left hand: and the priest shall dip his right finger in the oil that is in his left hand, and shall sprinkle of the oil with his finger seven times before the Lord. And of the rest of the oil that is in his hand shall the priest put upon the tip of the right ear of him that is to be cleansed, and upon the thumb of his right hand, and upon the great toe of his right foot, upon the blood of the trespass offering; and the remnant of the oil that is in the priest's hand, he shall pour upon the head of him that is to be cleansed; and the priest shall make an atonement for him before the Lord" (ver. 15-18). Thus, not only are our members cleansed by the blood of Christ, but also consecrated to God, in the power of the Spirit. God's work is not only negative, but positive. The ear is no longer to be the vehicle for communicating defilement, but to be "swift to hear" the voice of the Good Shepherd. The hand is no longer to be used as the instrument of unrighteousness, but to be stretched forth in acts of righteousness, grace, and true holiness. The foot is no longer to tread in folly's paths, but to run in the way of God's holy commandments. And, finally, the whole man is to be dedicated to God in the energy of the Holy Ghost.

It is deeply interesting to see that "the oil" was put "upon the blood of the trespass offering." The blood of Christ is the divine basis of the operations of the Holy Ghost. The blood and the oil go together. As sinners we could know nothing of the latter save on the ground of the former. The oil could not have been put upon the leper until the blood of the trespass offering had first been applied. "In whom also, after that ye believed, ye were sealed with that Holy Spirit of promise." The divine accuracy of the type evokes the acclamation of the renewed mind. The more closely we scrutinise it – the more of the light of Scripture we concentrate upon it – the more its beauty, force, and precision, are perceived and enjoyed. All, as might justly be expected, is in the most lovely harmony with the entire analogy of the word of God. There is no need for any effort of the mind. Take Christ as the key to unlock the rich treasury of the types; explore the precious contents by the light of Inspiration's heavenly lamp; let the Holy Ghost be your interpreter; and you cannot fail to be edified, enlightened, and blessed.

"And the priest shall offer the sin offering, and make an atonement for him that is to be cleansed from his uncleanness." Here we have a type of Christ, not only as the bearer of our trespasses, but also as the One, who made an end of *sin*, root and branch; the One, who destroyed the entire system of sin – "The Lamb of God, who taketh away the sin of the world." "The propitiation for the whole world." As the trespass offering, Christ put away all my trespasses. As the sin offering, He met the great root from whence those trespasses emanated. He met all; but it is as the trespass offering I first know Him, because it is as such I first need Him. It is the "conscience of sins" that first troubles me. This is divinely met by my precious Trespass Offering. Then, as I get on, I find that all these sins had a root, a parent stem, and that root or stem I find within me. This, likewise, is divinely met by my precious Sin Offering. The order, as presented in the leper's case, is perfect. It is precisely the order which we can trace in the actual experience of every soul. The trespass offering comes first, and then the sin offering.

"And afterward he shall kill the burnt offering." This offering presents the highest possible aspect of the death of Christ. It is Christ offering Himself without spot to God, without special reference to either trespasses or sin. It is Christ in voluntary devotedness, walking to the cross, and there offering Himself as a sweet savour to God.

"And the priest shall offer the burnt offering and the meat offering upon the altar: and the priest shall make an atonement for him, and he shall be clean" (ver. 20). The meat offering typifies "the man Christ Jesus" in His perfect human life. It is intimately associated, in the case of the cleansed leper, with the burnt offering; and so it is in the experience of every saved sinner. It is when we know our *trespasses* are forgiven, and the root or principle of *sin* judged, that we can, according to our measure, by the power of the Spirit, enjoy communion with God about that blessed One, who lived a perfect human life, down here, and then offered Himself without spot to God on the cross. Thus, the four classes of offerings are brought before us in their divine order, in the cleansing of the leper – namely, the trespass offering, the sin offering, the burnt offering, and the meat offering, each exhibiting its own specific aspect of our blessed Lord Jesus Christ.

Here closes the record of the Lord's dealings with the leprous man; and, oh! what a marvellous record it is! What an unfolding of the exceeding hatefulness of sin, the grace and holiness of God, the preciousness of Christ's Person, and the efficacy of His work! Nothing can be more interesting than to mark the footprints of divine grace forth from the hallowed precincts of the sanctuary, to the defiled place where the leper stood, with bare head, covered lip, and rent garments. God visited the leper where he was; but He did not leave him there. He went forth prepared to accomplish a work, in virtue of which he could bring the leper into a higher place, and higher communion than ever he had known before. On the ground of this work, the leper was conducted from his place of defilement and loneliness to the very door of the tabernacle of the congregation, the priestly place, to enjoy priestly privileges (comp. Exod. 29:20, 21, 32). How could he ever have climbed to such an elevation! Impossible For anything he could do, he might have languished and died in his leprosy, had not the sovereign grace of the God of Israel stooped to lift him from the dunghill, to set him among the princes of His people. If ever there was a case in which the question of human effort, human merit, and human righteousness, could be fully tried and perfectly settled, the leper is, unquestionably, that case. Indeed it were a sad loss of time to discuss such a question in the presence of such a case.

It must be obvious, to the most cursory reader, that nought but free grace, reigning through righteousness, could meet the leper's condition and the leper's need. And how gloriously and triumphantly did that grace act! It travelled down into the deepest depths, that it might raise the leper to the loftiest heights. See what the leper lost, and see what he gained! He lost all that pertained to nature, and he gained the blood of atonement and the grace of the Spirit. I mean typically. Truly, he was a gainer, to an incalculable amount. He was infinitely better off than if he had never been thrust forth from the camp. Such is the grace of God! Such the power and value, the virtue and efficacy, of the blood of Jesus!

How forcibly does all this remind us of the prodigal, in Luke 15! In him, too, leprosy had wrought and risen to a head. He had been afar off in the defiled place, where his own sins and the intense selfishness of the far country had created a solitude around him. But, blessed for ever be a Father's deep and tender love, we know how it ended. The prodigal found a higher place, and tasted higher communion than ever he had known before. "The fatted calf" had never been slain for him before. "The best robe" had never been on him before. And how was this? Was it a question of the prodigal's merit? Oh! no; it was simply a question of the Father's love.

Dear reader, let me ask, can you ponder over the record of God's dealings with the leper, in Leviticus 14, or the Father's dealings with the prodigal, in Luke 15, and not have an enlarged sense of the love that dwells in the bosom of God, that flows through the Person and work of Christ, that is recorded in the Scriptures of truth, and brought home to the heart by the Holy Ghost? Lord grant us a deeper and more abiding fellowship with Himself!

From verse 21 to 32 we have "the law of him in whom is the plague of leprosy, whose hand is not able to get that which pertaineth to his cleansing." This refers to the sacrifices of "the eighth day," and not to the "two birds alive and clean." These latter could not be dispensed with in any case, because they set forth the death and resurrection of Christ as the alone ground on which God can receive a sinner back to Himself. On the other hand, the sacrifices of "the eighth day," being connected with the soul's communion, must, in some degree, be affected by the measure of the soul's apprehension. But, whatever that measure may be, the grace of God can meet it with those peculiarly-touching words, *"such as he is able to get."* And, not only so, but "the two turtle doves" conferred the same privileges on the "poor," as the two lambs conferred upon the rich, inasmuch as both the one and the other pointed to "the precious blood of Christ," which is of infinite, changeless, and eternal efficacy in the judgment of God. All stand before God on the ground of death and resurrection. All are brought into the same place of nearness; but all do not enjoy the same measure of communion – all have not the same measure of apprehension of the preciousness of Christ in all the aspects of His work. They might, if they would; but they allow themselves to be hindered, in various ways. Earth and nature, with their respective influences, act prejudicially; The Spirit is grieved, and Christ is not enjoyed as He might be. It is utterly vain to expect that, if we are living in the region of nature, we can be feeding upon Christ. No; there must be self-emptiness, self-denial, self-judgment, if we would habitually feed upon Christ. It is not a question of salvation. It is not a question of the leper introduced into the camp – the place of recognised relationship. By no means. It is only a question of the soul's communion, of its enjoyment of Christ. As to this, the largest measure lies open to us. We may have communion with the very highest truths; but, if our measure be small, the unupbraiding grace of our Father's heart breathes in the sweet words, *"such as he is able to get."* The title of all is the same, however our capacity may vary; and, blessed be God, when we get into His presence, all the desires of the new nature, in their utmost intensity, are satisfied; all the powers of the new nature, in their fullest range, are occupied. May we prove these things in our souls' happy experience, day by day!

Leprosy in a house

We shall close this section with a brief reference to the subject of leprosy in a house.

III. The reader will observe, that a case of leprosy, in a person, or in a garment, might occur in the wilderness; but, in the matter of a house, it was, of necessity, confined to the land of Canaan. "When ye be come into the land of Canaan, which I give to you for a possession, and I put the plague of leprosy in a house of the land of your possession, . . . then the priest shall command that they empty the house, before the priest go into it to see the plague, that all that is in the house be not made unclean; and afterward the priest shall go in to see the house. And he shall look on the plague; and, behold, if the plague be in the walls of the house with hollow strakes, greenish or reddish, which in sight are lower than the wall; then the priest shall go out of the house to the door of the house, and shut up the house seven days."

Looking at the house as the type of an assembly, we have some weighty principles presented to us as to the divine method of dealing with moral evil, or suspicion of evil, in a congregation. We observe the same holy calmness and perfect patience with respect to the house, as we have already seen, in reference to the person or the garment. There was no haste, and no indifference, either as regards the house, the garment, or the individual. The man who had an interest in the house was not to treat with indifference any suspicious symptoms appearing in the wall thereof; neither was he to pronounce judgment himself upon such symptoms. It belonged to the priest to investigate and to judge. The moment that anything of a questionable nature made its appearance, the priest assumed a judicial attitude with respect to the house. The house was under judgment, though not condemned. The perfect period was to be allowed to run its course, ere any decision could be arrived at. The symptoms might prove to be merely superficial, in which case there would be no demand for any action whatever.

"And the priest shall *come again the seventh day,* and shall *look*: and, behold, if the plague be spread in the walls of the house, then the priest shall command that they take away the stones in which the plague is, and they shall cast them into an unclean place without the city." The whole house was not to be condemned. The removal of the leprous stones was first to be tried.

"And if the plague come again, and break out in the house, after that he hath taken away the stones, and after that he hath scraped the house, and after that it is plastered; then the priest shall come and look; and, behold, if the plague be spread in the house, it is a fretting leprosy in the house: it is unclean. And he shall break down the house, the stones of it, and the timber thereof, and all the mortar of the house; and he shall carry them forth out of the city into an unclean place." The case was hopeless, the evil irremediable, the whole building was annihilated.

"Moreover, he that goeth into the house all the while that it is shut up shall be unclean until the even. And he that lieth in the house shall wash his clothes; and he that eateth in the house shall wash his clothes." This is a solemn truth. *Contact defiles!* Let us remember this. It was a principle largely inculcated under the Levitical economy; and, surely, it is not less applicable now.

"And if the priest shall come in, and look upon it, and, behold, the plague hath not spread in the house, after the house was plastered; then the priest shall pronounce the house clean, because the plague is healed." The removal of the defiled stones, &c., had arrested the progress of the evil, and rendered all further judgment needless. The house was no longer to be viewed as in a judicial place; but, being cleansed by the application of the blood, it was again fit for occupation.

Judgment of evil in an assembly

And, now, as to the moral of all this. It is, at once, interesting, solemn, and practical. Look, for example, at the church at Corinth. It was a spiritual house, composed of spiritual stones; but, alas! the eagle eye of the apostle discerned upon its walls certain symptoms of a most suspicious nature. Was he indifferent? Surely not. He had imbibed far too much of the spirit of the Master of the house to admit, for one moment, of any such thing. But he was no more hasty than indifferent. He commanded the leprous stone to be removed, and gave the house a thorough scraping. Having acted thus faithfully, he patiently awaited the result. And what was that result? All that the heart could desire. "Nevertheless, God, that comforteth those that are cast down, comforted us by the coming of Titus; and not by his coming only, but by the consolation wherewith he was comforted in you, when he told us your earnest desire, your mourning, your fervent mind toward me; so that I rejoiced the more . . . *In all things ye have approved yourselves to be clear in this matter*" (comp. 1 Cor. 5 with 2 Cor. 7:11). This is a lovely instance. The zealous care of the apostle was amply rewarded; the plague was stayed, and the assembly delivered from the defiling influence of unjudged moral evil.

Take another solemn example. "And to the angel of the church in Pergamos write: These things saith he that hath the sharp sword with two edges; I know thy works, and where thou dwellest, even where Satan's seat is; and thou holdest fast my name, and hast not denied my faith, even in those days wherein Antipas was my faithful martyr, who was slain among you, where Satan dwelleth. But I have a few things against thee, because thou hast there them that hold the doctrine of Balaam, who taught Balak to cast a stumbling block before the children of Israel, to eat things sacrificed unto idols, and to commit fornication. So hast thou also them that hold the doctrine of the Nicolaitanes, which thing I hate. Repent; or else I will come unto thee quickly, and will fight against them with the sword of my mouth" (Rev. 2:12-16). Here the divine Priest stands in a judicial attitude with respect to His house at Pergamos. He could not be indifferent to symptoms so alarming; but He patiently and graciously gives time to repent. If reproof or warning, and discipline, prove unavailing, judgment must take its course.

These things are full of practical teaching as to the doctrine of the assembly. The seven churches of Asia afford various striking illustrations of the house under priestly judgment. We should ponder them deeply and prayerfully. They are of immense value. We should never sit down, at ease, so long as anything of a suspicious nature is making its appearance in the assembly. We may be tempted to say, "It is none of my business;" but it is the business of every one who loves the Master of the house to have a jealous, godly care, for the purity of that house; and if we shrink from the due exercise of this care, it will not be for our honour or profit, in the day of the Lord.

I shall not pursue this subject any further in these pages and shall merely remark, in closing this section, that I do not doubt, in the least, that this whole subject of leprosy has a great dispensational bearing, not only upon the house of Israel, but also upon the professing church.

Chapter 15

CEREMONIAL UNCLEANNESS

What is inherent in human nature

This chapter treats of a variety of ceremonial uncleannesses of a much less serious nature than leprosy. This latter would seem to be presented as the expression of the deep-seated energy of nature's evil; whereas, chap. 15 details a number of things which are merely unavoidable infirmities, but which, as being, in any measure the outflow of nature, were defiling, and needed the provisions of divine grace. The divine presence in the assembly demanded a high order of holiness and moral purity. Every movement of nature had to be counteracted. Even things which, so far as man was concerned, might seem to be unavoidable weaknesses, had a defiling influence, and required cleansing, because Jehovah was in the camp. Nothing offensive, nothing unsightly, nothing in any way uncomely, should be suffered within the pure, unsullied and sacred precincts of the presence of the God of Israel. The uncircumcised nations around would have understood nothing of such holy ordinances; but Jehovah would have Israel holy, because He was Israel's God. If they were to be privileged and distinguished by having the presence of a holy God, they would need to be a holy people.

Nothing can be more calculated to elicit the soul's admiration than the jealous care of Jehovah over all the habits and practices of His people. At home and abroad, asleep and awake, by day and by night, He guarded them. He attended to their food, He attended to their clothing, He attended to their most minute and private concerns. If some trifling spot appeared upon the person, it had to be instantly and carefully looked into. In a word, nothing was overlooked which could, in any wise, affect the well-being or purity of those with whom Jehovah had associated Himself, and in whose midst He dwelt. He took an interest in their most trivial affairs. He carefully attended to everything connected with them, whether publicly, socially, or privately.

This, to an uncircumcised person, would have proved an intolerable burden. For such an one to have a God of infinite holiness about his path, by day, and about his bed, by night, would have involved an amount of restraint beyond all power of endurance; but to a true lover of holiness, a lover of God, nothing could be more delightful. Such an one rejoices in the sweet assurance that God is always near; and he delights in the holiness which is, at once, demanded and secured by the presence of God.

Reader, say, is it thus with you? Do you love the divine presence and the holiness which that presence demands? Are you indulging in anything incompatible with the holiness of God's presence? Are your habits of thought, feeling, and action, such as comport with the purity and elevation of the sanctuary? Remember, when you read this fifteenth chapter of Leviticus, that it was written for your learning. You are to read it in the Spirit, for to you it has a spiritual application. To read it in any other way is to wrest it to your own destruction, or, to use a ceremonial phrase, "to seethe a kid in its mother's milk."

Do you ask, "what am I to learn from such a section of Scripture? What is its application to me?' In the first place, let me ask, do you not admit that it was written for your learning? This, I imagine, you will not question, seeing the inspired apostle so expressly declares that, "*whatsoever* things were written aforetime were written for our learning" (Rom.15:4). Many seem to forget this important statement, at least, in so far as the book of Leviticus is concerned. They cannot conceive it possible, that they are to learn anything from the rites and ceremonies of a by-gone age, and particularly from such rites and ceremonies as the fifteenth of Leviticus records. But, when we remember, that God the Holy Ghost has written this very chapter – that every paragraph, every verse, every line of it "is given by inspiration of God, and is profitable," it should lead us to inquire what it means. Surely, what God has written His child should read. No doubt, there is need of spiritual power to know *how*, and spiritual wisdom to know *when*, to read such a chapter; but the same holds good with respect to any chapter. One thing is certain, if we were sufficiently spiritual, sufficiently heavenly, sufficiently abstracted from nature, and elevated above earth, we should deduce nought but purely spiritual principles and ideas from this and kindred chapters. If an angel from heaven were to read such sections, how should he regard them? Only in a spiritual and heavenly light; only as the depositories of the purest and highest morality. And why should not we do the same? I believe we are not aware of what positive contempt we pour upon the sacred Volume by suffering any portion of it to be so grossly neglected as the book of Leviticus has been. If this book ought not to be read, surely it ought not to have been written. If it be not "profitable," surely it ought not to have had a place assigned it in the canon of divine inspiration; but, inasmuch as it hath pleased "the only wise God" to write this book, it surely ought to please His children to read it.

No doubt, spiritual wisdom, holy discernment, and that refined moral sense, which only communion with God can impart – all these things would be needed in order to form a judgment as to when such scripture ought to be read. We should feel strongly disposed to question the sound judgment and refined taste of a man, who could stand up and read the fifteenth of Leviticus, in the midst of an ordinary congregation. But why? Is it because it is not "divinely inspired," and, as such, "profitable?" By no means; but because the generality of persons are not sufficiently spiritual to enter into its pure and holy lessons.

What, then, are we to learn from the chapter before us? In the first place, we learn to watch, with holy jealousy, everything that emanates from nature. Every movement of, and every emanation from, nature is defiling. Fallen human nature is an impure fountain, and all its streams are polluting. It cannot send forth anything that is pure, holy, or good. This is a lesson frequently inculcated in the Book of Leviticus, and it is impressively taught in this chapter.

The water and the blood

But, blessed be the grace that has made such ample provision for nature's defilement! This provision is presented under two distinct forms, throughout the entire of the book of God, and throughout this section of it in particular – namely, "water and blood." Both these are founded upon the death of Christ. The blood that expiates and the water that cleanses flowed from the pierced side of a crucified Christ (comp. John 19:34, with 1 John 5:6). "The blood of Jesus Christ his Son cleanseth us from all sin." (1 John 1:7) And the word of God cleanseth our practical habits and ways (Ps.119:9; Eph.5:26). Thus, we are maintained in fitness for communion and worship, though passing through a scene where all is defiling, and carrying with us a nature, every movement of which leaves a soil behind.

It has been already remarked that our chapter treats of a class of ceremonial defilements less serious than leprosy. This will account for the fact that atonement is here foreshadowed, not by a bullock or a lamb, but by the lowest order of sacrifice – namely, "two turtle doves." But, on the other hand, the cleansing virtue of the Word is continually introduced, in the ceremonial actions of "washing," "bathing," and "rinsing." "Wherewithal shall a young man *cleanse* his way? By taking heed thereto according to thy *word*." "Husbands, love your wives, even as Christ also loved the Church, and gave himself for it; that he might *sanctify and cleanse it with the washing of water by the word.*" Water held a most important place in the Levitical system of purification, and, as a type of the Word, nothing can be more interesting or instructive.

Thus we can gather up the most valuable points from this fifteenth chapter of Leviticus. We learn, in a very striking manner, the intense holiness of the divine presence. Not a soil, not a stain, not a speck can be tolerated, for a moment, in that thrice-hallowed region. "Thus shall ye separate the children of Israel from their uncleanness, that they die not in their uncleanness, when they defile my tabernacle that is among them" (ver. 31).

Again, we learn that human nature is the overflowing fountain of uncleanness. It is hopelessly defiled; and not only defiled, but defiling. Awake or asleep, sitting, standing, or lying, nature is defiled and defiling. Its very touch conveys pollution. This is a deeply-humbling lesson for proud humanity; but thus it is. The Book of Leviticus holds up a faithful mirror to nature. It leaves "flesh" nothing to glory in. Men may boast of their refinement, their moral sense, their dignity. Let them study the third book of Moses, and there they will see what it is all really worth, in God's estimation.

Finally, we learn, afresh, the expiatory value of the blood of Christ, and the cleansing, purifying, sanctifying virtues of the precious word of God. When we think of the unsullied purity of the sanctuary, and then reflect upon nature's irremediable defilement, and ask the question, "However can *we* enter and dwell *there*?" the answer is found in "the blood and water" which flowed from the side of a crucified Christ – a Christ who gave up His life unto death for us, that we might live by Him. "There are three that bear record in earth, the Spirit, and the water, and the blood: and," blessed be God, "these three agree in one." The Spirit does not convey to our ears a message diverse from that which we find in the Word; and both the Word and the Spirit declare to us the preciousness and efficacy of the blood.

Can we not, therefore, say that the fifteenth chapter of Leviticus was "written for our learning?" Has it not its own distinct place in the divine canon? Assuredly. There would be a blank were it omitted. We learn in it what we could not learn in the same way, anywhere else. True, all Scripture teaches us the holiness of God, the vileness of nature, the efficacy of the blood, the value of the Word; but the chapter upon which we have been pondering presents these great truths to our notice, and presses them upon our hearts in a manner quite peculiar to itself.

May *every section* of our Father's Volume be precious to our hearts. May *every one* of His testimonies be sweeter to us than honey and the honeycomb, and may *"every one* of his righteous judgments" have its due place in our souls.

Chapter 16

THE GREAT DAY OF ATONEMENT

A way still closed

This chapter unfolds some of the weightiest principles of truth which can possibly engage the renewed mind. It presents the doctrine of atonement with uncommon fullness and power. In short, we must rank the sixteenth chapter of Leviticus amongst the most precious and important sections of Inspiration; if indeed it be allowable to make comparisons where all is divine.

Looking at this chapter, historically, it furnished a record of the transactions of the great day of atonement in Israel, whereby Jehovah's relationship with the assembly was established and maintained, and all the sins, failures, and infirmities of the people fully atoned for, so that the Lord God might dwell among them. The blood which was shed upon this solemn day formed the basis of Jehovah's throne in the midst of the congregation. In virtue of it, a holy God could take up His abode in the midst of the people, notwithstanding all their uncleanness. "The tenth day of the seventh month" was a unique day in Israel. There was no other day in the year like it. The sacrifices of this one day formed the ground of God's dealing in grace, mercy, patience, and forbearance.

Furthermore, we learn from this portion of inspired history, "that the way into the holiest of all was not yet made manifest." God was hidden behind a veil and man was at a distance. "And the Lord spake unto Moses after the death of the two sons of Aaron, when they offered before the Lord, and died; and the Lord said unto Moses, Speak unto Aaron thy brother, that he come not at all times unto the holy place within the veil before the mercy seat, which is upon the ark, that he die not: for I will appear in the cloud upon the mercy seat."

The way was not open for man to approach, at all times, into the divine presence, nor was there any provision, in the entire range of the Mosaic ritual, for his abiding there continually. God was shut in from man; and man was shut out from God, nor could "the blood of bulls and goats" open a permanent meeting place; "A sacrifice of nobler name and richer blood" was needed to accomplish this. "For the law having a shadow of good things to come, and not the very image of the things, can never with those sacrifices which they offered year by year continually make the comers thereunto perfect. For then would they not have ceased to be offered? Because that the worshippers once purged should have had no more conscience of sins. But in those sacrifices there is a remembrance again made of sins every year. For it is not possible that the blood of bulls and of goats should take away sins" (Heb. 10:1-4). Neither the Levitical priesthood nor the Levitical sacrifices, could yield perfection. Insufficiency was stamped on the latter, infirmity on the former, imperfection on both. An imperfect man could not be a perfect priest; nor could an imperfect sacrifice give a perfect conscience. Aaron was not competent or entitled to take his seat within the vail, nor could the sacrifices which he offered rend that vail.

Thus much as to our chapter, historically. Let us now look at it typically.

Aaron, a type of Christ

"Thus shall Aaron come into the holy place: with a young bullock for a *sin* offering, and a ram for a *burnt* offering" (ver. 3). Here, we have the two grand aspects of Christ's atoning work, as that which perfectly maintains the divine glory, and perfectly meets man's deepest need. There is no mention, throughout all the services of this unique and solemn day, of a *meat* offering, or a *peace* offering. The perfect human life of our blessed Lord is not foreshadowed, here, nor is the communion of the soul with God, consequent upon His accomplished work, unfolded. In a word, the one grand subject is "atonement," and that in a double way namely, first, as meeting all the claims of God – the claims of His nature – the claims of His character – the claims of His throne; and, secondly, as perfectly meeting all man's guilt and all his necessities. We must bear these two points in mind, if we would have a clear understanding of the truth presented in this chapter, or of the doctrine of the great day of atonement. "Thus shall Aaron come into the holy place," with atonement, as securing the glory of God, in every possible way, whether as respects His counsels of redeeming love toward the church, toward Israel, and toward the whole creation, or in reference to all the claims of His moral administration; and with atonement as fully meeting man's guilty and needy condition. These two aspects of the atonement will continually present themselves to our view as we ponder the precious contents of our chapter. Their importance cannot possibly be overestimated.

"He shall put on the holy linen coat, and he shall have the linen breeches upon his flesh, and he shall be girded with a linen girdle, and with the linen mitre shall he be attired: these are holy garments; therefore shall he wash his flesh in water, and so put them on (ver. 4). Aaron's person, washed in pure water, and robed in the white linen garments, furnishes a lovely and impressive type of Christ entering upon the work of atonement. He is seen to be *personally and characteristically* pure and spotless. "For their sakes I sanctify myself, that they also might be sanctified through the truth" (John 17:19). It is peculiarly precious to be called, as it were, to gaze upon the Person of our divine Priest, in all His essential holiness. The Holy Ghost delights in every thing that unfolds Christ to the view of His people; and wherever we behold Him, we see Him to be the same spotless, perfect, glorious, precious, peerless Jesus, "the fairest among ten thousand, yea, altogether lovely." He did not need to *do* or to *wear* anything, in order to be pure and spotless. He needed no pure water, no fine linen. He was, intrinsically and practically, "the holy One of God." What Aaron *did*, and what he *wore* – the washing and the robing, are but the faint shadows of what Christ *is*. The law had only a "shadow," and "not the very image of good things to come." Blessed be God, we have not merely the shadow, but the eternal and divine reality – Christ Himself.

Aaron and his house

"And he shall take of the congregation of the children of Israel two kids of the goats for a sin offering, and one ram for a burnt offering. And Aaron shall offer his bullock of the sin offering, which is for himself, and make atonement for himself and for his house" (ver. 5, 6). Aaron and his house represent the Church, not indeed as the "one body," but as a priestly house. It is not the Church as we find it developed in Ephesians and Colossians, but rather as we find it in the First Epistle of Peter, in the following well-known passage: "Ye also, as lively stones, are built up a *spiritual house,* an holy priesthood, to offer up spiritual sacrifices, acceptable to God by Jesus Christ" (chap. 2:5). So also in Hebrews: "But Christ as a Son over His own house; *whose house are we,* if we hold fast the confidence and the rejoicing of the hope firm unto the end" (chap. 3:6). We must ever remember that there is no revelation of the mystery of the Church in the Old Testament. Types and shadows there are, but no revelation. That wondrous mystery of Jew and Gentile forming "one body," "one new man," and united to a glorified Christ in heaven, could not, as is obvious, be revealed until Christ had taken His place above. Of this mystery Paul was, pre-eminently, made a steward and a minister, as he tells us in Ephesians 3:1-12, a passage which I would commend to the prayerful attention of the Christian reader.

Two goats – one lot for the Lord

"And he shall take the two goats, and present them before the Lord at the door of the tabernacle of the congregation. And Aaron shall cast lots upon the two goats; one lot for the Lord, and the other lot for the scapegoat. And Aaron shall bring the goat upon which the Lord's lot fell, and offer him for a sin offering. But the goat, on which the lot fell to be the scapegoat, shall be presented alive before the Lord, to make an atonement with him, and to let him go for a scapegoat into the wilderness" (ver. 7-10). In these two goats, we have the two aspects of atonement already referred to. "The Lord's lot" fell upon one; and the people's lot fell upon the other. In the case of the former, it was not a question of the persons or the sins which were to be forgiven, nor of God's counsels of grace toward His elect. These things, I need hardly say, are of infinite moment; but they are not involved in the case of "the goat on which the Lord's lot fell." This latter typifies the death of Christ as that wherein God has been perfectly glorified, with respect to sin in general. This great truth is fully set forth in the remarkable expression, "the Lord's lot." God has a peculiar portion in the death of Christ – a portion quite distinct – a portion which would hold eternally good even though no sinner were ever to be saved. In order to see the force of this, it is needful to bear in mind how God has been dishonoured in this world. His truth has been despised. His authority has been contemned. His majesty has been slighted. His law has been broken. His claims have been disregarded. His name has been blasphemed. His character has been traduced.

Now, the death of Christ has made provision for all this. It has perfectly glorified God in the very place where all these things have been done. It has perfectly vindicated the majesty, the truth, the holiness, the character of God. It has divinely met all the claims of His throne. It has atoned for *sin*. It has furnished a divine remedy for all the mischief which sin introduced into the universe. It affords a ground on which the blessed God can act in grace, mercy, and forbearance toward all. It furnishes a warrant for the eternal expulsion and perdition of the prince of this world. It forms the imperishable foundation of God's moral government. In virtue of the cross, God can act according to His own sovereignty. He can display the matchless glories of His character, and the adorable attributes of His nature. He might, in the exercise of inflexible justice, have consigned the human family to the lake of fire, together with the devil and his angels. But, in that case, where would be His love, His grace, His mercy, His kindness, His long-suffering, His compassion, His patience, His perfect goodness?

Then, on the other hand, had these precious attributes been exercised, in the absence of atonement, where were the justice, the truth, the majesty, the holiness, the righteousness, the governmental claims, yea, the entire moral glory of God? How could "mercy and truth meet together?" or "righteousness and peace kiss each other" How could "truth spring out of the earth" or "righteousness look down from heaven?" Impossible. Nought save the atonement of our Lord Jesus Christ could have fully glorified God; but that has glorified Him. It has reflected the full glory of the divine character, as it never could have been reflected amid the brightest splendours of an unfallen creation. By means of that atonement, in prospect and retrospect, God has been exercising forbearance toward this world, for well nigh six thousand years. In virtue of that atonement, the most wicked, daring, and blasphemous of the sons of men "live, move, and have their being;" eat, drink, and sleep. The very morsel which yonder open blaspheming infidel puts into his mouth, he owes to the atonement which he knows not, but impiously ridicules. The sunbeams and showers which fertilise the fields of the atheist, reach him in virtue of the atonement of Christ. Yea, the very breath which the infidel and the atheist spend in blaspheming God's revelation, or denying His existence, they owe to the atonement of Christ. Were it not for that precious atonement, instead of blaspheming upon earth, they would be weltering in hell.

Let not my reader misunderstand me, I speak not here of the forgiveness or salvation of persons. This is quite another thing, and stands connected, as every true Christian knows, with the confession of the name of Jesus, and the hearty belief that God raised Him from the dead (Rom. 10). This is plain enough, and fully understood; but it is in no wise involved in that aspect of the atonement which we are, at present, contemplating, and which is so strikingly foreshadowed by "the goat on which the Lord's lot fell." God's pardoning and accepting a sinner is one thing; His bearing with that man, and showering temporal blessings upon him, is quite another. Both are in virtue of the cross, but in a totally different aspect and application thereof.

The consequence of the atonement for the whole of humanity

Nor is this distinction, by any means, unimportant. Quite the opposite. Indeed, so important is it that where it is overlooked, there must be confusion as to the full doctrine of atonement. Nor is this all. A clear understanding of God's ways in government, whether in the past, the present, or the future, will be found involved in this profoundly interesting point. And, finally, in it will be found the key wherewith to expound a number of texts in which many Christians find considerable difficulty. I shall just adduce two or three of these passages as examples.

"Behold the Lamb of God, which taketh away the *sin* of the world" (John 1:29). With this we may connect a kindred passage in John's first epistle, in which the Lord Jesus Christ is spoken of as "the propitiation for the whole world" (1 John 2:2).[21] In both these passages the Lord Jesus is referred to as the One who has perfectly glorified God with respect to "*sin*" and "*the world*," in their broadest acceptation. He is here seen as the great Antitype of "the goat on which the Lord's lot fell." This gives us a most precious view of the atonement of Christ, and one which is too much overlooked, or not clearly apprehended. Whenever the question of *persons* and the forgiveness of *sins* is raised, in connexion with these and kindred passages of scripture, the mind is sure to get involved in insuperable difficulties.

So, also, with respect to all those passages in which God's grace to the world at large is presented. They are founded upon that special aspect of the atonement with which we are more immediately occupied. "Go ye into *all the world,* and preach the gospel *to every creature"* (Mark 16). "God so loved *the world,* that he gave his only begotten Son, that whosoever believeth in him might not perish, but have everlasting life. For God sent not his Son into the world to condemn *the world;* but that the world through him might be saved" (John 3:16, 17). "I exhort, therefore, that first of all, supplications, prayers, intercessions, and giving of thanks, be made for *all men;* for kings, and for all that are in authority; that we may lead a quiet and peaceable life in all godliness and honesty. For this is good and acceptable in the sight of God our Saviour; who will have *all men* to be saved, and to come unto the knowledge of the truth. For there is one God, and one mediator between God and men, the man Christ Jesus; who gave himself a *ransom for all,* to be testified in due time" (1 Tim. 2:1-6). "For the *grace of God* that bringeth salvation hath appeared *to all men"* (Titus 2:11). "But we see Jesus, who was made a little lower than the angels, for the suffering of death, crowned with glory and honour; that he by *the grace of God* should taste death *for every man* (Heb. 2:9). "The Lord is not slack concerning his promise, as some men count slackness; but is long-suffering to usward, not willing that *any* should perish, but that *all* should come to repentance" (2 Peter 3:9).

God is glorified and is able to show grace

There is no need whatsoever for seeking to avoid the plain sense of the above and similar passages. They bear a clear and unequivocal testimony to divine grace toward all, without the slightest reference to man's responsibility, on the one hand, or to God's eternal counsels, on the other. These things are just as clearly, just as fully, just as unequivocally, taught in the word. Man is responsible, and God is sovereign. All who bow to Scripture admit these things. But, at the same time, it is of the very last importance to recognise the wide aspect of the grace of God, and of the cross of Christ. It glorifies God and leaves man *wholly* without excuse. Men argue about God's decrees and man's incompetency to believe without divine influence. Their arguments prove that they do not want God; for did they only want Him, He is near enough to be found of them. The grace of God, and the atonement of Christ, are as wide as they could desire. *"Any"* – *"every"* – *"whosoever"* – and *"all,"* are God's own words; and I should like to know who is shut out. If God sends a message of salvation to a man, He surely intends it for him; and what can be more wicked and impious than to reject God's grace, and make Him a liar, and then give His secret decrees as a reason for so doing. It would be, in a certain sense, honest for a man to say at once, "The fact is, I do not believe God's word, and I do not want His grace or His salvation." One could understand this; but for men to cover their hatred of God and His truth with the drapery of a false because one-sided theology, is the very highest character of wickedness. It is such as to make us feel, of a truth, that the devil is never more diabolical than when he appears with the Bible in his hand.

If it be true that men are prevented, by God's secret decrees and counsels, from receiving the gospel which He has commanded to be preached to them, then on what principle of righteousness will they be "punished with everlasting destruction" for not obeying that gospel? (2 Thess. 1:6-10). Is there a single soul throughout all the gloomy regions of the lost who blames God's counsels for his being there? Not one. Oh! no; God has made such ample provision in the atonement of Christ, not only for the salvation of those that believe, but also for the aspect of His grace toward those that reject the gospel, that there is no excuse. It is not because a man *cannot*, but because he *will not* believe that he "shall be punished with everlasting destruction." Never was there a more fatal mistake than for a man to ensconce himself behind God's decrees while deliberately and intelligently refusing God's grace; and this is all the more dangerous, because supported by the dogmas of a one-sided theology. God's grace is free to all; and if we ask, How is this? the answer is, "Jehovah's lot" fell upon the true victim, in order that He might be perfectly glorified as to sin, in its widest aspect, and be free to act in grace toward all, and "preach the gospel to every creature." This grace and this preaching must have a solid basis, and that basis is found in the atonement; and though man should reject, God is glorified in the exercise of grace, and in the offer of salvation, because of the basis on which both the one and the other repose. He *is* glorified, and He *shall* be glorified, throughout eternity's countless ages. "Now is my soul troubled; and what shall I say? Father, save me from this hour: but for this cause came I unto this hour. Father, glorify thy name. Then came there a voice from heaven, saying, I have both glorified it, and will glorify it again . . . Now is the judgment of this world: now shall the prince of this world be cast out. And I, if I be lifted up from the earth, will draw all unto me" (John 12:27-32).

Thus far we have been occupied only with one special point, namely, "the goat on which the Lord's lot fell;" and a cursory reader might suppose that the next thing in order would be the scape-goat, which gives us the other great aspect of the death of Christ, or its application to the sins of the people. But no: ere we come to that, we have the fullest confirmation of that precious line of truth which has been before us, in the fact that the blood of the slain goat, together with the blood of the bullock, was sprinkled upon, and before, Jehovah's throne, in order to show that all the claims of that throne were answered in the blood of atonement, and full provision made for all the demands of God's moral administration.

The blood of atonement carried within the veil

"And Aaron shall bring the bullock of the sin offering which is for himself, and shall make an atonement for himself, and for his house, and shall kill the bullock of the sin offering which is for himself. And he shall take a censer full of burning coals of fire from off the altar before the Lord, and his hands full of sweet incense beaten small, and bring it within the vail. And he shall put the incense upon the fire before the Lord, that the cloud of the incense may cover the mercy-seat that is upon the testimony, that he die not." Here we have a most vivid and striking presentation indeed. The blood of atonement is carried in within the veil, into the holiest of all, and there sprinkled upon the throne of the God of Israel. The cloud of the divine presence was there; and in order that Aaron might appear in the immediate presence of the glory, and not die, "the cloud of incense" ascends and "covers the mercy-seat," on which the blood of atonement was to be sprinkled "seven times." The "*sweet* incense beaten *small*" expresses the fragrance of Christ's Person – the sweet odour of His most precious sacrifice.

"And he shall take of the blood of the bullock, and sprinkle it with his finger upon the mercy-seat eastward; and before the mercy-seat shall he sprinkle of the blood with his finger seven times. Then shall he kill the goat of the sin offering that is for the people, and bring his blood within the vail, and do with that blood as he did with the blood of the bullock, and sprinkle it upon the mercy-seat, and before the mercy-seat" (ver. 14, 15). "Seven" is the perfect number; and in the sprinkling of the blood seven times before the mercy-seat we learn that whatever be the application of the atonement of Christ, whether as to things, to places, or to persons, it is perfectly estimated in the divine presence. The blood which secures the salvation of the Church – the "house" of the true Aaron; the blood which secures the salvation of the "congregation" of Israel; the blood which secures the final restoration and blessedness of the whole creation – that blood has been presented before God, sprinkled and accepted according to all the perfectness, fragrance, and preciousness of Christ. In the power of that blood God can accomplish all His eternal counsels of grace. He can save the Church, and raise it into the very loftiest heights of glory and dignity, despite of all the power of sin and Satan. He can restore Israel's scattered tribes – He can unite Judah and Ephraim – He can accomplish all the promises made to Abraham, Isaac, and Jacob. He can save and bless untold millions of the Gentiles. He can restore and bless the wide creation. He can allow the beams of His glory to lighten up the universe for ever. He can display, in the view of angels, men, and devils, His own eternal glory – the glory of His character – the glory of His nature – the glory of His works – the glory of His government. All this He can do, and will do; but the one solitary pedestal upon which the stupendous fabric of glory shall rest, for ever, is the blood of the cross – that precious blood, dear Christian reader, which has spoken peace, divine and everlasting peace, to your heart and conscience, in the presence of Infinite Holiness. The blood which is sprinkled upon the believer's conscience has been sprinkled "seven times" before the throne of God. The nearer we get to God, the more importance and value we find attached to the blood of Jesus. If we look at the brazen altar, we find the blood there; if we look at the brazen laver, we find the blood there; if we look at the golden altar, we find the blood there; if we look at the vail of the tabernacle, we find the blood there: but in no place do we find so much about the blood, as within the veil, before Jehovah's throne, in the immediate presence of the divine glory.

> "In heaven His blood for ever speaks,
> In God the Father's ears."

"And he shall make an atonement for the holy place, because of the uncleanness of the children of Israel, and because of their transgressions in all their sins: and so shall he do for the tabernacle of the congregation, that remaineth among them in the midst of their uncleanness." The same truth meets us all along. The claims of the sanctuary must be provided for. Jehovah's courts, as well as His throne, must bear witness to the value of the blood. The tabernacle, in the midst of Israel's uncleanness, must be fenced round about by the divine provisions of atonement. Jehovah provided, in all things, for His own glory. The priests and their priestly service, the place of worship, and all therein, must stand in the power of the blood. The Holy One could not have remained, for a moment, in the midst of the congregation, were it not for the power of the blood! It was that which left Him free to dwell, and act, and rule, in the midst of an erring people.

The way into the holiest of all is open

"And there shall be no man in the tabernacle of the congregation when he goeth in to make an atonement in the holy place, until he come out, and have made an atonement for himself, and for his household, and for all the congregation of Israel" (ver. 17). Aaron needed to offer up sacrifice for his own sins, as well as for the sins of the people. He could only enter into the sanctuary in the power of the blood. We have, in verse 17, a type of the atonement of Christ in its application both to the church and to the congregation of Israel. The church now enters into the holiest by the blood of Jesus (Heb. 10). As to Israel, the vail is still on their hearts (2 Cor. 3). They are still at a distance, although full provision has been made in the cross for their forgiveness and restoration when they shall turn to the Lord. This entire period is, properly speaking, the day of atonement. The true Aaron is gone in with His own blood, into heaven itself, now to appear in the presence of God for us. By and by, He will come forth to lead the congregation of Israel into the full results of His accomplished work. Meanwhile, His house, that is to say, all true believers, are associated with Him, having boldness to enter into the holiest, being brought nigh by the blood of Jesus.

"And he shall go out unto the altar that is before the Lord, and make an atonement for it; and shall take of the blood of the bullock, and of the blood of the goat, and put it upon the horns of the altar round about. And he shall sprinkle of the blood upon it with his finger seven times, and cleanse it, and hallow it from the uncleanness of the children of Israel" (ver. 18, 19). Thus the atoning blood was sprinkled everywhere, from the throne of God within the vail, to the altar which stood in the court of the tabernacle of the congregation. "It was therefore necessary that the patterns of things in the heavens should be purified with these; but the heavenly things themselves with better sacrifices than these. For Christ is not entered into the holy places made with hands, which are the figures of the true; but into heaven itself, now to appear in the presence of God for us: nor yet that He should offer Himself often, as the high priest entereth into the holy place every year with blood of others; for then must He often have suffered since the foundation of the world; but now *once* in the end of the world (at the end of everything earthly, everything human) hath he appeared to put away sin by the sacrifice of Himself. And as it is appointed unto men once to die, but after this the judgment: so Christ was once offered to bear the sins of many; and unto them that look for Him shall He appear the second time, without sin, unto salvation" (Heb. 9:23-28).

There is but one way into the holiest of all, and that is a blood-sprinkled way. It is vain to strive to enter by any other. Men may attempt to work themselves in, to pray themselves in, to buy themselves in, to get in by a pathway of ordinances, or it may be of half-ordinances, half-Christ; but it is of no use. God speaks of *one* way, and but one, and that way has been thrown open through the rent vail of the Saviour's flesh. Along that way have the millions of the saved passed, from age to age. Patriarchs, prophets, apostles, martyrs, saints in every age, from Abel downwards, have trod that blessed way, and found thereby sure and undisputed access. The *one* sacrifice of the Cross is divinely sufficient for all. God asks no more, and He can take no less. To add anything thereto is to cast dishonour upon that with which God has declared himself well pleased, yea, in which He is infinitely glorified. To diminish anything therefrom is to deny man's guilt and ruin, and offer an indignity to the justice and majesty of the eternal Trinity.

The goat Azazel or the goat let go

"And when he hath made an end of reconciling the holy place, and the tabernacle of the congregation, and the altar, he shall bring the live goat. And Aaron shall lay both his hands upon the head of the live goat, and confess over him *all* the iniquities of the children of Israel, and *all* their transgressions in *all* their sins, putting them upon the head of the goat, and shall send him away by the hand of a fit man into the wilderness. And the goat shall bear upon him *all* their iniquities unto a land not inhabited: and he shall let go the goat in the wilderness."

Here, then, we have the other grand idea attached to the death of Christ – namely, the full and final forgiveness of the people. If the death of Christ forms the foundation of the glory of God, it also forms the foundation of the perfect forgiveness of sins to all who put their trust in it. This latter, blessed be God, is but a secondary, an inferior application of the atonement, though our foolish hearts would fain regard it as the very highest possible view of the cross to see in it that which puts away all our sins. This is a mistake. God's glory is the first thing; our salvation is the second. To maintain God's glory was the chief, the darling object of the heart of Christ. This object He pursued from first to last, with an undeviating purpose and unflinching fidelity. "Therefore doth my Father love me, because I lay down my life, that I might take it again" (John 10:17). "Now is the Son of Man glorified, and God is glorified in Him. If God be glorified in him, God shall also glorify him in himself, and shall straightway glorify him" (John 13:31, 32). "Listen, O isles, unto me; and hearken, ye people from far: the Lord hath called me from the womb; from the bowels of my mother hath he made mention of my name. And he hath made my mouth like a sharp sword; in the shadow of his hand hath he hid me, and made me a polished shaft: in his quiver hath he hid me; and said unto me, Thou art my servant, O Israel, in whom *I will be glorified"* (Isaiah 49:1-3).

Thus, the glory of God was the paramount object of the Lord Jesus Christ, in life and in death. He lived and died to glorify His Father's name. Does the Church lose anything by this? Nay. Does Israel? Nay. Do the Gentiles? Nay. In no way could their salvation and blessedness be so perfectly provided for as by being made subsidiary to the glory of God. Hearken to the divine response to Christ, the true Israel, in the sublime passage just quoted. "It is a light thing that thou shouldest be my servant to raise up the tribes of Jacob, and to restore the preserved of Israel: I will also give thee for a light to the Gentiles, that thou mayest be my salvation to the ends of the earth."

And is it not a blessed thing to know that God is glorified in the putting away of our sins. We may ask, Where are our sins? Put away. By what? By that act of Christ upon the cross in which God has been eternally glorified. Thus it is. The two goats, on the day of atonement, give the double aspect of the one act. In the one, we see God's glory maintained; in the other, sins put away. The one is as perfect as the other. We are as perfectly forgiven as God is perfectly glorified, by the death of Christ. Was there one single point in which God was not glorified in the cross? Not one. Neither is there one single point in which we are not perfectly forgiven. I say "we;" for albeit the congregation of Israel is the primary object contemplated in the beautiful and impressive ordinance of the scape-goat; yet does it hold good, in the fullest way, with respect to every soul that believes on the Lord Jesus Christ, that he is as perfectly forgiven as God is perfectly glorified, by the atonement of the cross. How many of the sins of Israel did the scape-goat bear away? *"All."* Precious word! Not one left behind. And whither did he bear them? "Into a land not inhabited" – a land where they could never be found, because there was no one there to look for them. Could any type be more perfect? Could we possibly have a more graphic picture of Christ's accomplished sacrifice, in its primary and secondary aspects? Impossible. We can hang with intense admiration over such a picture, and, as we gaze, exclaim, "Of a truth, the pencil of the Master is here!"

Reader, pause here, and say, do you know that *all* your sins are forgiven, according to the perfection of Christ's sacrifice? If you simply *believe* on His name they are so. They are all gone, and gone for ever. Say not, as so many anxious souls do, "I fear I do not *realize*." There is no such word as "realize" in the entire gospel. We are not saved by realization, but by Christ; and the way to get Christ in all His fullness and preciousness is to believe – *"only believe!"* And what will be the result? "The worshippers once purged should have no more conscience of sins." Observe this. "No more conscience of sins." This must be the result, inasmuch as Christ's sacrifice is perfect – so perfect, that God is glorified therein. Now, it must be obvious to you that Christ's work does not need your realization to be added to it to make it perfect. This could not be. We might as well say that the work of creation was not complete until Adam realized it in the garden of Eden. True, he did realize; but what did he realize? A perfect work. Thus let it be with your precious soul this moment, if it has never been so before. May you, now and evermore, repose, in artless simplicity, upon the One who has, by one offering, perfected for ever them that are sanctified! And how are they sanctified? Is it by realization? By no means. How then? By the perfect work of Christ.

The prophetic aspect for Israel

Having sought – alas! most feebly – to unfold the doctrine of this marvellous chapter, so far as God has given me light upon it, there is just one point further to which I shall merely call my reader's attention, ere I close this section. It is contained in the following quotation: "And this shall be a statute for ever unto you, that in the seventh month, on the tenth day of the month, ye shall afflict your souls, and do no work at all, whether it be one of your own country, or a stranger that sojourneth among you. For on that day shall the priest make an atonement for you, to cleanse you, that ye may be clean from *all* your sins *before the Lord.* It shall be a *Sabbath of rest* and ye shall *afflict your souls,* by a statute for ever" (ver. 29-31).

This shall have its full accomplishment in the saved remnant of Israel by and by, as foretold by the prophet Zechariah: "And I will pour upon the house of David, and upon the inhabitants of Jerusalem, the spirit of grace and of supplications; and they shall look upon me whom they have pierced, and they shall mourn for him, as one mourneth for his only son, and shall be in bitterness for him, as one that is in bitterness for his firstborn. *In that day* shall there be *a great mourning* in Jerusalem, as the mourning of Hadadrimmon in the valley of Megiddon . . . *In that day* there shall be *a fountain opened* to the house of David, and to the inhabitants of Jerusalem, for sin and for uncleanness . . . And it shall come to pass *in that day* that the light shall not be clear (in one place) and dark: (in another:) but it shall be one day, (the true and long-expected sabbath,) which shall be known to the Lord, not day nor night: but it shall come to pass, that at evening time it shall be light. And it shall be *in that day* that living waters shall go out from Jerusalem; half of them toward the former sea, and half of them toward the hinder sea: in summer and in winter shall it be. And THE LORD SHALL BE KING OVER ALL THE EARTH: *in that day* shall there be one Lord, and his name one . . . *In that day* shall there be upon the bells of the horses, HOLINESS UNTO THE LORD . . . And *in that day* there shall be no more the Canaanite in the house of the Lord of hosts" (Zech. 12 – 14).

What a day that will be! No marvel that it should be so frequently and so emphatically introduced in the above glowing passage. It will be a bright and blessed "Sabbath of rest" when the mourning remnant shall gather, in the spirit of true penitence, round the open fountain, and enter into the full and final results of the great day of atonement. They shall "afflict their souls," no doubt; for how could they do otherwise, while fixing their repentant gaze "upon him whom they have pierced?" But, oh! what a Sabbath they will have! Jerusalem will have a brimming cup of salvation, after her long and dreary night of sorrow. Her former desolations shall be forgotten, and her children, restored to their long-lost dwellings, shall take down their harps from the willows, and sing once more the sweet songs of Zion beneath the peaceful shade of the vine and fig tree.

Blessed be God, the time is at hand. Every setting sun brings us nearer to that blissful Sabbath. The word is, "Surely, I come quickly;" and all around seems to tell us that "the days are at hand, and the effect of every vision." May we be "sober, and watch unto prayer!" May we keep ourselves unspotted from the world; and thus, in the spirit of our minds, the affections of our hearts, and the experience of our souls, be ready to meet the heavenly Bridegroom! Our place for the present is outside the camp. Thank God that it is so! It would be an unspeakable loss to be inside. The same cross which has brought us inside the vail has cast us outside the camp. Christ was cast out thither, and we are with Him there; but He has been received up into heaven, and we are with Him there. Is it not a mercy to be outside of all that which has rejected our blessed Lord and Master? Truly so; and the more we know of Jesus, and the more we know of this present evil world, the more thankful we shall be to find our place outside of it all *with Him*.

---

[21] The reader will observe, in the above passage, that the words "the sins of" are introduced by the translators, and are not inspired. The divine accuracy of the passage is completely lost by retaining those uninspired words. The doctrine laid down is surely this – In the first clause of the verse, Christ is set forth as the propitiation for His people's actual *sins*; but in the last clause, it is not a question of *sins* or of *persons* at all, but of *sin* and the *world* in general. In fact, the whole verse presents Christ as the Antitype of the two goats, as the One who has borne His people's sins; and, also, as the One who has perfectly glorified God with respect to sin in general, and made provision for dealing in grace with the world at large, and for the final deliverance and blessing of the whole creation.

Chapter 17

THE BLOOD

Life belongs to God

In this chapter the reader will find two special points, namely – first, that life belongs to Jehovah; and, secondly, that the power of atonement is in the blood. The Lord attached peculiar importance to both these things. He would have them impressed upon every member of the congregation.

"And the Lord spake unto Moses, saying, Speak unto Aaron, and unto his sons, and unto all the children of Israel, and say unto them, This is the thing which the Lord hath commanded, saying, What man soever there be of the house of Israel, that killeth an ox, or lamb, or goat, in the camp, or that killeth it out of the camp, and bringeth it not unto the door of the tabernacle of the congregation, to offer an offering unto the Lord, before the tabernacle of the Lord; blood shall be imputed unto that man; he hath shed blood; and that man shall be cut off from among his people." This was a most solemn matter; and we may ask what was involved in offering a sacrifice otherwise than in the manner here prescribed? It was nothing less than robbing Jehovah of His rights, and presenting to Satan that which was due to God. A man might say, "Can I not offer a sacrifice in one place as well as another?" The answer is, "Life belongs to God, and His claim thereto must be recognised in the place which He has appointed – before the tabernacle of the Lord." That was the only meeting place between God and man. To offer elsewhere proved that the heart did not want God.

The moral of this is plain. There is one place where God has appointed to meet the sinner, and that is the cross – the antitype of the brazen altar. There and there alone has God's claim upon the life been duly recognised. To reject this meeting-place is to bring down judgment upon oneself – it is to trample under foot the just claims of God, and to arrogate to oneself a right to life which all have forfeited. It is important to see this.

"And the priest shall sprinkle the blood upon the altar of the Lord, at the door of the tabernacle of the congregation, and burn the fat for a sweet savour unto the Lord." The blood and the fat belonged to God. The blessed Jesus fully recognised this. He surrendered His life to God, and all his hidden energies were devoted to Him likewise. He voluntarily walked to the altar and there gave up His precious life; and the fragrant odour of His intrinsic excellency ascended to the throne of God. Blessed Jesus! it is sweet, at every step of our way, to be reminded of Thee.

It is the blood which makes atonement for the soul

The second point above referred to is clearly stated in verse 11. "For the life of the flesh is in the blood and I have given it to you upon the altar, to make an atonement for your souls: for IT IS THE BLOOD THAT MAKETH AN ATONEMENT FOR THE SOUL." The connexion between the two points is deeply interesting. When man duly takes his place as one possessing no title whatsoever to life – when he fully recognises God's claims upon him, then the divine record is, "I have given you the life to make an atonement for your soul." Yes; atonement is God's gift to man; and, be it carefully noted, that this atonement is in the blood, and *only* in the blood. "It is the *blood* that maketh an atonement for the soul." It is not the blood *and* something else. The word is most explicit. It attributes atonement exclusively to *the blood*. "Without shedding of *blood* there is no remission" (Heb. 9:22). It was the *death* of Christ that rent the vail. It is "by *the blood* of Jesus" we have "boldness to enter into the holiest." "We have redemption through his *blood*, the forgiveness of sins" (Eph. 1:7; Col. 1:14). "Having made peace by *the blood* of his cross." "Ye who were afar off are made nigh by *the blood* of his cross." "*The blood* of Jesus Christ his Son cleanseth us from all sin" (1 John 1:7). "They washed their robes and made them white in *the blood* of the Lamb" (Rev. 7). "They overcame him by *the blood* of the Lamb" (Rev. 12).

I would desire to call my reader's earnest attention to the precious and vital doctrine of the blood. I am anxious that he should see its true place. The blood of Christ is the foundation of everything. It is the ground of God's righteousness in justifying an ungodly sinner that believes on the name of the Son of God; and it is the ground of the sinner's confidence in drawing nigh to a holy God who is of purer eyes than to behold evil. God would be just in the condemnation of the sinner; but, through the death of Christ, He can be just and the justifier of him that believeth – a just God and a Saviour. The righteousness of God is His consistency with Himself – His acting in harmony with His revealed character. Hence, were it not for the cross, His consistency with Himself would, of necessity, demand the death and judgment of the sinner; but in the cross that death and judgment were borne by the sinner's Surety, so that the same divine consistency is perfectly maintained while a holy God justifies an ungodly sinner through faith. *It is all through the blood of Jesus* – nothing less – nothing more – nothing different. "It is the blood that maketh an atonement for the soul." This is conclusive. This is God's simple plan of justification. Man's plan is much more cumbrous, much more roundabout. And not only is it cumbrous and roundabout, but it attributes righteousness to something quite different from what I find in the word. If I look from Genesis 3 down to the close of Revelation, I find the blood of Christ put forward as the alone ground of righteousness. We get pardon, peace, life, righteousness, all by the blood, and nothing but the blood. The entire book of Leviticus, and particularly the chapter upon which we have just been meditating, is a commentary upon the doctrine of the blood. It seems strange to have to insist upon a fact so obvious to every dispassionate teachable student of holy Scripture. Yet so it is. Our minds are prone to slip away from the plain testimony of the word. We are ready to adopt opinions without ever calmly investigating them in the light of the divine testimonies. In this way we get into confusion, darkness, and error.

May we all learn to give the blood of Christ its due place! It is so precious in God's sight that He will not suffer anything else to be added to or mingled with it. "The life of the flesh is in the blood, and I have given it to you upon the altar, to make an atonement for your souls: for *it is the blood that maketh an atonement for the soul.*"

Chapters 18-20

DETAILED INSTRUCTIONS

The holiness required of those who belong to the people of God

This section sets before us, in a very remarkable manner, the personal sanctity and moral propriety which Jehovah looked for, on the part of those whom He had graciously introduced into relationship with Himself and, at the same time, it presents a most humiliating picture of the enormities of which human nature is capable.

"And the Lord spake unto Moses, saying, Speak unto the children of Israel, and say unto them, *I am the Lord your God.*" Here we have the foundation of the entire superstructure of moral conduct which these chapters present. Israel's actings were to take their character from the fact that Jehovah was *their* God. They were called to comport themselves in a manner worthy of so high and holy a position. It was God's prerogative to set forth the special character and line of conduct becoming a people with whom He was pleased to associate His name. Hence the frequency of the expressions – "I am the Lord." "I am the Lord your God." "I the Lord your God am holy." Jehovah was their God, and He was holy; hence, therefore, they were called to be holy likewise. His name was invoked in their character and acting.

This is the true principle of holiness for the people of God in all ages. They are to be governed and characterised by the revelation which He has made of Himself. Their conduct is to be founded upon what He is, not upon what they are in themselves. This entirely sets aside the principle expressed in the words, "Stand by thyself, I am holier than thou;" a principle so justly repudiated by every sensitive mind. It is not a comparison of one man with another; but a simple statement of the line of conduct which God looks for in those who belong to Him. "After the doings of the land of Egypt, wherein ye dwelt, shall ye not do; and after the doings of the land of Canaan, whither I bring you, shall ye not do; neither shall ye walk in their ordinances." The Egyptians and the Canaanites were all wrong. How was Israel to know this? Who told them? How came they to be right, and all besides wrong? These are interesting inquiries; and the answer is as simple as the questions are interesting. Jehovah's word was the standard by which all questions of right and wrong were to be definitely settled in the judgment of every member of the Israel of God. It was not, by any means, the judgment of an Israelite in opposition to the judgment of an Egyptian or of a Canaanite; but it was the judgment of God above *all*. Egypt might have her practices and her opinions, and so might Canaan; but Israel were to have the opinions and practices laid down in the word of God. "Ye shall do my judgments, and keep mine ordinances, to walk therein: I am the Lord your God. Ye shall therefore keep my statutes and my judgments; which, if a man do, he shall live in them: I am the Lord."

It will be well for my reader to get a clear, deep, full, practical sense of this truth. The word of God must settle every question and govern every conscience. There must be no appeal from its solemn and weighty decision. When God speaks, every heart must bow. Men may form and hold their opinions; they may adopt and defend their practices; but one of the finest traits in the character of "the Israel of God" is profound reverence for, and implicit subjection to, "every word that proceedeth out of the mouth of the Lord." The exhibition of this valuable feature may, perhaps, lay them open to the charge of dogmatism, superciliousness, and self-sufficiency, on the part of those who have never duly weighed the matter; but, in truth, nothing can be more unlike dogmatism than simple subjection to the plain truth of God; nothing more unlike superciliousness than reverence for the statements of inspiration; nothing more unlike self-sufficiency than subjection to the divine authority of holy scripture.

True, there will ever be the need of carefulness as to the tone and manner in which we set forth the authority for our convictions and our conduct. It must be made manifest, so far as it may be, that we are wholly governed, not by our own opinions, but by the word of God. There is great danger of attaching an importance to an opinion merely because *we* have adopted it. This must be carefully guarded against. *Self* may creep in and display its deformity in the defence of our opinions as much as in anything else; but we must disallow it, in every shape and form, and be governed, in all things, by "Thus saith the Lord."

But, then, we are not to expect that everyone will be ready to admit the full force of the divine statutes and judgments. It is as persons walk in the integrity and energy of the divine nature that the word of God will be owned, appreciated, and reverenced. An Egyptian or a Canaanite would have been wholly unable to enter into the meaning or estimate the value of these statutes and judgments, which were to govern the conduct of the circumcised people of God; but that did not, in any wise, affect the question of Israel's obedience. They were brought into a certain relationship with Jehovah, and that relationship had its distinctive privileges and responsibilities. "I am the Lord *your* God." This was to be the ground of their conduct. They were to act in a way worthy of the One who had become *their* God, and made them *His* people. It was not that they were a whit better than other people. By no means. The Egyptians or Canaanites might have considered that the Israelites were setting themselves up as something superior in refusing to adopt the habits of either nation. But, no; the foundation of their peculiar line of conduct and tone of morality was laid in these words, "*I* am the Lord *your God.*"

In this great and practically-important fact, Jehovah set before His people a ground of conduct which was immovable, and a standard of morality which was as elevated, and as enduring, as the eternal throne itself. The moment He entered into a relationship with a people, their ethics were to assume a character and tone worthy of Him. It was no longer a question as to what they were, either in themselves or in comparison with others; but of what God was in comparison with all. This makes a material difference. To make *self* the ground of action or the standard of ethics is not only presumptuous folly, but it is sure to set one upon a descending scale of action. If self be my object, I must, of necessity, sink lower and lower every day; but if, on the other hand, I set the Lord before me, I shall rise higher and higher as, by the power of the Holy Ghost, I grow in conformity to that perfect model which is unfolded to the gaze of faith in the sacred pages of inspiration. I shall, undoubtedly, have to prostrate myself in the dust, under a sense of how infinitely short I come of the mark set before me; but, then, I can never consent to the setting up of a lower standard, nor can I ever be satisfied until I am conformed in all things to Him who was my Substitute on the cross, and is my Model in the glory.

What man is capable of doing

Having said thus much on the main principle of the section before us – a principle of unspeakable importance to Christians, in a practical point of view – I feel it needless to enter into anything like a detailed exposition of statutes which speak for themselves in most obvious terms. I would merely remark that those statutes range themselves under two distinct heads, namely, first, those which set forth the shameful enormities which the human heart is capable of devising; and, secondly, those which exhibit the exquisite tenderness and considerate care of the God of Israel.

As to the first, it is manifest that the Spirit of God could never enact laws for the purpose of preventing evils that have no existence. He does not construct a dam where there is no flood to be resisted. He does not deal with abstract ideas, but with positive realities. Man is, in very deed, capable of perpetrating each and every one of the shameful crimes referred to in this most faithful section of the Book of Leviticus. If he were not, why should he be told not to do so. Such a code would be wholly unsuitable for angels, inasmuch as they are incapable of committing the sins referred to; but it suits man, because he has gotten the seeds of those sins in his nature. This is deeply humbling. It is a fresh declaration of the truth that man is a total wreck. From the crown of his head to the sole of his foot, there is not so much as a single speck of moral soundness, as looked at in the light of the divine presence. The being for whom Jehovah thought it needful to write Leviticus 18 – 20 must be a vile sinner; but that being is *man* – the writer and reader of these lines. How plain it is, therefore, that "they that are in the flesh *cannot* please God" (Rom. 8). Thank God, the believer is "not in the flesh, but in the Spirit." He has been taken completely out of his old creation-standing, and introduced into the new creation, in which the moral evils aimed at in this our section can have no existence. True, he has gotten the old nature; but it is his happy privilege to "reckon" it as a dead thing, and to walk in the abiding power of the new creation, wherein "all things are of God." This is Christian liberty – even liberty to walk up and down in that fair creation where no trace of evil can ever be found; hallowed liberty to walk in holiness and purity before God and man; liberty to tread those lofty walks of personal sanctity whereon the beams of the divine countenance ever pour themselves in living lustre. Reader, this is Christian liberty. It is liberty, not to commit sin, but to taste the celestial sweets of a life of true holiness and moral elevation. May we prize more highly than we have ever done this precious boon of heaven – Christian liberty!

Consideration for the poor and the stranger

And, now, one word as to the second class of statutes contained in our section – namely, those which so touchingly bring out divine tenderness and care. Take the following:

"and when ye reap the harvest of your land, thou shalt not wholly reap the corners of thy field, neither shalt thou gather the gleanings of thy harvest. And thou shalt not glean thy vineyard, neither shalt thou gather every grape of thy vineyard; *thou shalt leave them for the poor and stranger:* I am the Lord your God" (chap. 19:9, 10). This ordinance will meet us again in chapter 23, but there we shall see it in its dispensational bearing. Here, we contemplate it morally, as unfolding the precious grace of Israel's God. He would think of "the poor and stranger;" and He would have His people think of them likewise. When the golden sheaves were being reaped, and the mellow clusters gathered, "the poor and stranger" were to be remembered by the Israel of God, because Jehovah was the God of Israel. The reaper and the grape-gatherer were not to be governed by a spirit of grasping covetousness, which would bare the corners of the field and strip the branches of the vine, but rather by a spirit of large-hearted, genuine benevolence, which would leave a sheaf and a cluster "for the poor and stranger," that they, too, might rejoice in the unbounded goodness of Him whose paths drop fatness, and on whose open hand all the sons of want may confidently wait.

The Book of Ruth furnishes a fine example of one who fully acted out this most benevolent statute. "And Boaz said unto her, (Ruth,) At meal-time come thou hither, and eat of the bread, and dip thy morsel in the vinegar. And she sat beside the reapers: and he reached her parched corn, and she did eat, and was sufficed and left. And when she was risen up to glean, Boaz commanded his young men, saying, Let her glean even among the sheaves, and reproach her not: *and let fall also some of the handfuls of purpose for her,* and leave them, that she may glean them, and rebuke her not" (Ruth 2:14-16). Most touching and beautiful grace! Truly, it is good for our poor selfish hearts to be brought in contact with such principles and such practices. Nothing can surpass the exquisite refinement of the words, "let fall also some of the handfuls of purpose for her." It was, evidently, the desire of this noble Israelite that "the stranger" might have abundance, and have it, too, rather as the fruit of her own gleaning than of his benevolence. This was the very essence of refinement. It was putting her in immediate connexion with, and dependence upon, the God of Israel, who had fully recognised and provided for "the gleaner." Boaz was merely acting out that gracious ordinance of which Ruth was reaping the benefit. The same grace that had given him the field gave her the gleanings. They were both debtors to grace. She was the happy recipient of Jehovah's goodness. He was the honoured exponent of Jehovah's most gracious institution. All was in most lovely moral order. The creature was blessed and God was glorified. Who would not own that it is good for us to be allowed to breathe such an atmosphere?

The worker's just wages

Let us now turn to another statute of our section. "Thou shalt not defraud thy neighbour, neither rob him: the wages of him that is hired shall not abide with thee all night until the morning" (chap. 19:13). What tender care is here! The High and Mighty One that inhabiteth eternity can take knowledge of the thoughts and feelings that spring up in the heart of a poor labourer. He knows and takes into account the expectations of such an one in reference to the fruit of his day's toil. The wages will, naturally, be looked for. The labourer's heart counts upon them; the family meal depends upon them. Oh! let them not be held back. Send not the labourer home with a heavy heart, to make the heart of his wife and family heavy likewise. By all means, give him that for which he has wrought, to which he has a right, and on which his heart is set. He is a husband, he is a father; and he has borne the burden and heat of the day that his wife and children may not go hungry to bed. Disappoint him not. Give him his due. Thus does our God take notice of the very throbbings of the labourer's heart, and make provision for his rising expectations. Precious grace! Most tender, thoughtful, touching, condescending love! The bare contemplation of such statutes is sufficient to throw one into a flood of tenderness. Could any one read such passages and not be melted? Could any one read them and thoughtlessly dismiss a poor labourer, not knowing whether he and his family have wherewithal to meet the cravings of hunger?

Nothing can be more painful to a tender heart than the lack of kindly consideration for the poor, so often manifested by the rich. These latter can sit down to their sumptuous repast after dismissing from their door some poor industrious creature who had come seeking the just reward of his honest labour. They think not of the aching heart with which that man returns to his family, to tell them of the disappointment to himself and to them. Oh! it is terrible. It is most offensive to God, and to all who have drunk, in any measure, into His grace. If we would know what God thinks of such acting, we have only to hearken to the following accents of holy indignation: "Behold, the hire of the labourers who have reaped down your fields, which is of you kept back by fraud, crieth: and the cries of them that have reaped have entered into the ears of the Lord of Sabaoth" (James 5:4). "The Lord of Sabaoth" hears the cry of the aggrieved and disappointed labourer. His tender love tells itself forth in the institutions of His moral government; and even though the heart should not be melted by the grace of those institutions, the conduct should, at least, be governed by the righteousness thereof. God will not suffer the claims of the poor to be heartlessly tossed aside by those who are so hardened by the influence of wealth as to be insensible to the appeals of tenderness, and who are so far removed beyond the region of personal need as to be incapable of feeling for those whose lot it is to spend their days amid exhausting toil or pinching poverty. The poor are the special objects of God's care. Again and again He makes provision for them in the statutes of His moral administration; and it is particularly declared of Him who shall, ere long, assume, in manifested glory, the reins of government, that "He shall deliver the needy when he crieth;

the poor also, and him that hath no helper. He shall spare the poor and needy, and shall save the souls of the needy. He shall redeem their souls from deceit and violence; and precious shall their blood be in his sight" (Psalm 72:12-14).

May we profit by the review of those precious and deeply practical truths! May our hearts be affected, and our conduct influenced by them. We live in a heartless world; and there is a vast amount of selfishness in our own hearts. We are not sufficiently affected by the thought of the need of others. We are apt to forget the poor in the midst of our abundance. We often forget that the very persons whose labour ministers to our personal comfort are living, it may be, in the deepest poverty. Let us think of these things. Let us beware of "grinding the faces of the poor." If the Jews of old were taught by the statutes and ordinances of the Mosaic economy, to entertain kindly feelings toward the poor, and to deal tenderly and graciously with the sons of toil, how much more ought the higher and more spiritual ethics of the Gospel dispensation produce in the hearts and lives of Christians a large-hearted benevolence toward every form of human need.

True, there is urgent need of prudence and caution, lest we take a man out of the honourable position in which he was designed and fitted to move – namely, a position of dependence upon the fruits, the precious and fragrant fruits, of honest industry. This would be a grievous injury instead of a benefit. The example of Boaz should instruct in this matter. He allowed Ruth to glean; but he took care to make her gleaning profitable. This is a very safe and a very simple principle. God intends that man should work at something or another, and we run counter to Him when we draw our fellow out of the place of dependence upon the results of patient industry, into that of dependence upon the results of false benevolence. The former is as honourable and elevating as the latter is contemptible and demoralising. There is no bread so sweet to the taste as that which is nobly earned; but then those who earn their bread should get enough. A man will feed and care for his horses; how much more his fellow, who yields him the labour of his hands from Monday morning till Saturday night.

But, some will say, "There are two sides to this question." Unquestionably there are; and, no doubt, one meets with a great deal amongst the poor which is calculated to dry up the springs of benevolence and genuine sympathy. There is much which tends to steel the heart, and close the hand; but, one thing is certain – it is better to be deceived in ninety-nine cases out of a hundred than to shut up the bowels of compassion against a single worthy object. Our heavenly Father causes His sun to shine upon the evil and on the good; and sendeth rain upon the just and upon the unjust. The same sunbeams that gladden the heart of some devoted servant of Christ are poured upon the path of some ungodly sinner; and the self-same shower that falls upon the tillage of a true believer, enriches also the furrows of some blaspheming infidel. This is to be our model. "Be ye, therefore, perfect, even as your Father which is in heaven is perfect." (Matt. 5:48) It is only as we set the Lord before us, and walk in the power of His grace, that we shall be able to go on, from day to day, meeting with a tender heart and an open hand every possible form of human misery. It is only as we ourselves are drinking at the exhaustless fountain of divine love and tenderness, that we shall be able to go on ministering to human need unchecked by the oft-repeated manifestation of human depravity. Our tiny springs would soon be dried up were they not maintained in unbroken connexion with that ever-gushing source.

The attitude towards the deaf and the blind

The statute which next presents itself for our consideration, exemplifies, most touchingly, the tender care of the God of Israel. "Thou shalt not curse the deaf, nor put a stumbling-block before the blind, but shalt fear thy God: I am the Lord" (ver. 14). Here, a barrier is erected to stem the rising tide of irritability with which uncontrolled nature would be almost sure to meet the personal infirmity of deafness. How well we can understand this! Nature does not like to be called upon to repeat its words, again and again, in order to meet the deaf man's infirmity. Jehovah thought of this, and provided for it. And what is the provision? "Thou shalt fear thy God." When tried by a deaf person, remember the Lord, and look to Him for grace to enable you to govern your temper.

The second part of this statute reveals a most humiliating amount of wickedness in human nature. The idea of laying a stumbling-block in the way of the blind, is about the most wanton cruelty imaginable; and yet man is capable of it, else he world not be warned against it. No doubt, this, as well as many other statutes, admits of a spiritual application; but that in nowise interferes with the plain literal principle set forth in it. Man is capable of placing a stumbling block in the way of a fellow-creature afflicted with blindness. Such is man! Truly, the Lord knew what was in man when He wrote the statutes and judgments of the Book of Leviticus.

I shall leave my reader to meditate alone upon the remainder of our section. He will find that each statute teaches a double lesson – namely, a lesson with respect to nature's evil tendencies, and also a lesson as to Jehovah's tender care.[22]

---

[22] Verses 16 and 17 demand special attention. "Thou shalt not go up and down as a talebearer among thy people." This is a most seasonable admonition for the people of God, in every age. A talebearer is sure to do incalculable mischief. It has been well remarked that a talebearer injures three persons – he injures himself, he injures his hearer, and he injures the subject of his tale. All this he does directly; and as to the indirect consequences, who can recount them? Let us carefully guard against this horrible evil. May we never suffer a tale to pass our lips; and let us never stand to hearken to a talebearer. May we always know how to drive away a backbiting tongue with an angry countenance, as the north wind driveth away rain.

In verse 17, we learn what ought to take the place of tale bearing. "Thou shalt in anywise rebuke thy neighbour, and not suffer sin upon him." In place of carrying to another a tale about my neighbour, I am called upon to go directly to himself and rebuke him, if there is anything wrong. This is the divine method. Satan's method is to act the talebearer.

Chapters 21 & 22

PURITY OF THE PRIESTS

Position and state

These chapters unfold, with great minuteness of detail, the divine requirements in reference to those who were privileged to draw near as priests to "offer the bread of their God." In this, as in the preceding section, we have conduct as the *result*, not the procuring *cause* of the relationship. This should be carefully borne in mind. The sons of Aaron were, in virtue of their birth, priests unto God. They all stood in this relationship, one as well as another. It was not a matter of attainment, a question of progress, something which one had, and another had not. All the sons of Aaron were priests. They were born into a priestly place. Their capacity to understand and enjoy their position and its attendant privileges was, obviously, a different thing altogether. One might be a babe; and another might have reached the point of mature and vigorous manhood. The former would, of necessity, be unable to eat of the priestly food, being a babe for whom "milk" and not "strong meat" was adapted: but he was as truly a member of the priestly house as the man who could tread, with firm step, the courts of the Lord's house, and feed upon "the wave breast" and "heave shoulder" of the sacrifice.

This distinction is easily understood in the case of the sons of Aaron, and, hence, it will serve to illustrate, in a very simple manner, the truth as to the members of the true priestly house over which our Great High Priest presides, and to which all true believers belong (Heb. 3:6). Every child of God is a priest. He is enrolled as a member of Christ's priestly house. He may be very ignorant; but his position, as a priest, is not founded upon knowledge, but upon life. His experience may be very shallow; but his place as a priest does not depend upon experience, but upon life. His capacity may be very limited; but his relationship as a priest does not rest upon an enlarged capacity, but upon life. He was born into the position and relationship of a priest. He did not work himself thereinto. It was not by any efforts of his own that he became a priest. He became a priest by birth. The spiritual priesthood, together with all the spiritual functions attaching thereunto, is the necessary appendage to spiritual birth. The capacity to enjoy the privileges and to discharge the functions of a position must not be confounded with the position itself. They must ever be kept distinct. Relationship is one thing; capacity is quite another.

Furthermore, in looking at the family of Aaron, we see that nothing could break the relationship between him and his sons. There were many things which would interfere with the full enjoyment of the privileges attaching to the relationship. A son of Aaron might "defile himself by the dead." He might defile himself by forming an unholy alliance. He might have some bodily "blemish." He might be "blind or lame." He might be "a dwarf." Any of these things would have interfered, very materially, with his enjoyment of the privileges, and his discharge of the functions pertaining to his relationship, as we read, "No man that hath a blemish of the seed of Aaron the priest shall come nigh to offer the offerings of the Lord made by fire: he hath a blemish: he shall not come nigh to offer the bread of his God. He shall eat the bread of his God, both of the most holy and the holy; only he shall not go in unto the veil, nor come nigh unto the altar, because he hath a blemish; that he profane not my sanctuaries: for I the Lord do sanctify them" (chap. 21:21-23). But none of these things could possibly touch the fact of a relationship founded upon the established principles of human nature. Though a son of Aaron were a dwarf, that dwarf was a son of Aaron. True, he was, as a dwarf, shorn of many precious privileges and lofty dignities pertaining to the priesthood; but he was a son of Aaron all the while. He could neither enjoy the same measure or character of communion, nor yet discharge the same elevated functions of priestly service, as one who had reached to manhood's appointed stature; but he was a member of the priestly house, and, as such, permitted to "eat the bread of his God." The relationship was genuine, though the development was so defective.

The spiritual application of all this is as simple as it is practical. To be a child of God, is one thing; to be in the enjoyment of priestly communion and priestly worship, is quite another. The latter is, alas! interfered with by many things. Circumstances and associations are allowed to act upon us by their defiling influence. We are not to suppose that all Christians enjoy the same elevation of walk, the same intimacy of fellowship, the same felt nearness to Christ. Alas! alas! they do not. Many of us have to mourn over our spiritual defects. There is lameness of walk, defective vision, stunted growth; or we allow ourselves to be defiled by contact with evil, and to be weakened and hindered by unhallowed associations. In a word, as the sons of Aaron, though being priests by birth, were, nevertheless, deprived of many privileges through ceremonial defilement and physical defects; so we, though being priests unto God, by spiritual birth, are deprived of many of the high and holy privileges of our position, by moral defilement and spiritual defects. We are shorn of many of our dignities through defective spiritual development. We lack singleness of eye, spiritual vigour, whole-hearted devotedness. Saved we are, through the free grace of God, on the ground of Christ's perfect sacrifice. "We are all the children of God, by faith in Christ Jesus;" but, then, salvation is one thing; communion is quite another. Sonship is one thing; obedience is quite another.

These things should be carefully distinguished. The section before us illustrates the distinction with great force and clearness. If one of the sons of Aaron happened to be "broken-footed, or broken-handed," was he deprived of his sonship? Assuredly not. Was he deprived of his priestly position? By no means. It was distinctly declared, "He shall eat the bread of his God, both of the most holy and of the holy." What, then, did he lose by his physical blemish? He was forbidden to tread some of the higher walks of priestly service and worship. "Only he shall not go in unto the vail, nor come nigh unto the altar." These were very serious privations; and though it may be objected that a man could not help many of these physical defects, that did not alter the matter. Jehovah could not have a blemished priest at His altar, or a blemished sacrifice thereon. Both the priest and the sacrifice should be perfect. "No man that hath a blemish of the seed of Aaron the priest shall come nigh to offer the offerings of the Lord made by fire" (chap. 21:22). "But whatsoever hath a blemish, that shall ye not offer; for it shall not be acceptable for you" (chap. 22:20).

Our infirmities and our High Priest

Now, we have both the perfect priest, and the perfect sacrifice, in the Person of our blessed Lord Jesus Christ. He, having "offered himself without spot to God," passed into the heavens, as our great High Priest, where He ever liveth to make intercession for us. The Epistle to the Hebrews dwells elaborately upon these two points. It throws into vivid contrast the sacrifice and priesthood of the Mosaic system and the Sacrifice and Priesthood of Christ. In Him we have divine perfectness, whether as the Victim or as the Priest. We have all that God could require, and all that man could need. His precious blood has put away all our sins; and His all-prevailing intercession ever maintains us in all the perfectness of the place into which His blood has introduced us. "We are complete in him" (Col. 2); and yet, so feeble and so faltering are we in ourselves; so full of failure and infirmity; so prone to err and stumble in our onward way, that we could not stand for a moment, were it not that "He ever lives to make intercession for us." These things have been dwelt upon in the earlier chapters of this volume; and it is, therefore, needless to enter further upon them here. Those who have anything like correct apprehensions of the grand foundation truths of Christianity, and any measure of experience in the Christian life, will be able to understand how it is that, though "complete in him who is the head of all principality and power," they, nevertheless, need, while down here amid the infirmities, conflicts, and buffetings of earth, the powerful advocacy of their adorable and divine High Priest. The believer is "washed, sanctified, and justified" (1 Cor. 6). He is "accepted in the beloved" (Eph. 1:6). He can never come into judgment, as regards his person (see John 5:24, where the word is *krisin* and not *katakrisin*). Death and judgment are behind him, because he is united to Christ who has passed through them both, on his behalf and in his stead. All these things are divinely true of the very weakest, most unlettered, and inexperienced member of the family of God; but yet, inasmuch as he carries about with him a nature so incorrigibly bad, and so irremediably ruined, that no discipline can correct it, and no medicine cure it, inasmuch as he is the tenant of a body of sin and death – as he is surrounded, on all sides, by hostile influences – as he is called to cope, perpetually, with the combined forces of the world, the flesh, and the devil – he could never keep his ground, much less make progress, were he not upheld by the all-prevailing intercession of his great High Priest, who bears the names of His people upon His breast and upon His shoulder.

Some, I am aware, have found great difficulty in reconciling the idea of the believer's perfect standing in Christ with the need of priesthood. "If," it is argued, "he is perfect, what need has he of a priest?" The two things are as distinctly taught in the word as they are compatible one with another, and understood in the experience of every rightly-instructed Christian. It is of the very last importance to apprehend, with clearness and accuracy, the perfect harmony between these two points. The believer is perfect in Christ; but, in himself, he is a poor feeble creature, ever liable to fall. Hence, the unspeakable blessedness of having One who can manage all his affairs for him, at the right hand of the Majesty in the heavens – One who upholds him continually by the right hand of His righteousness – One who will never let him go – One who is able to save to the uttermost – One who is "the same yesterday, today, and for ever" – One who will bear him triumphantly through all the difficulties and dangers which surround him; and, finally, "present him faultless before the presence of his glory with exceeding joy." Blessed for ever be the grace that has made such ample provision for all our need in the blood of a Spotless Victim and the intercession of a divine High Priest!

Keeping ourselves pure from every blemish

Dear Christian reader, let it be our care so to walk, so to "keep ourselves unspotted from the world," so to stand apart from all unhallowed associations, that we may enjoy the highest privileges and discharge the most elevated functions of our position as members of the priestly house of which Christ is the Head. We have "boldness to enter into the holiest, through the blood of Jesus" – "we have a great High Priest over the house of God" (Heb. 10). Nothing can ever rob us of these privileges. But, then, our communion may be marred – our worship may be hindered – our holy functions may remain undischarged. Those ceremonial matters against which the sons of Aaron were warned, in the section before us, have their antitypes in the Christian economy. Had they to be warned against unholy contact? So have we. Had they to be warned against unholy alliance? So have we. Had they to be warned against all manner of ceremonial uncleanness? So have we to be warned against "all filthiness of the flesh and spirit" (1 Cor. 7). Were they shorn of many of their loftiest priestly privileges by bodily blemish and imperfect natural growth? So are we, by moral blemish, and imperfect spiritual growth.

Will any one venture to call in question the practical importance of such principles as these? Is it not obvious that the more highly we estimate the blessings which attach to that priestly house of which we have been constituted members, in virtue of our spiritual birth, the more carefully shall we guard against everything which might tend in any wise, to rob us of their enjoyment? Undoubtedly. And this it is which renders the close study of our section so pre-eminently practical. May we feel its power, through the application of God the Holy Ghost! Then shall we *enjoy* our priestly place. Then shall we faithfully discharge our priestly functions. We shall be able "to present our bodies a living sacrifice, holy and acceptable unto God" (Rom. 12:1). We shall be able to "offer the sacrifice of praise to God continually, that is, the fruit of our lips, giving thanks to his name" (Heb. 13:15). We shall be able, as members of the "spiritual house" and the "holy priesthood," to "offer up spiritual sacrifices, acceptable to God by Jesus Christ" (1 Peter 2:5). We shall be able, in some small degree, to anticipate that blissful time when, from a redeemed creation, the hallelujahs of intelligent and fervent praise shall ascend to the throne of God and the Lamb throughout the everlasting ages.

Chapter 23

THE SEVEN FEASTS OF THE LORD

Outline of God's dealings with Israel

One of the most profound and comprehensive chapters in the inspired volume now lies open before us, and claims our prayerful study. It contains the record of the seven great feasts or periodical solemnities into which Israel's year was divided. In other words, it furnishes us with a perfect view of God's dealings with Israel, during the entire period of their most eventful history.

Looking at the feasts separately, we have the Sabbath, the Passover, the feast of unleavened bread, the first-fruits, Pentecost, the feast of trumpets, the day of atonement, and the feast of tabernacles. This would make eight, altogether; but it is very obvious that the Sabbath occupies quite a unique and independent place. It is first presented, and its proper characteristics and attendant circumstances fully set forth; and then, we read "These are the feasts of the Lord, even holy convocations, which ye shall proclaim in their seasons" (ver. 4). So that, strictly speaking, as the attentive reader will observe, Israel's *first* great feast was the Passover, and their *seventh* was the feast of tabernacles. That is to say, divesting them of their typical dress, we have, first, redemption; and, last of all, we have the millennial glory. The paschal lamb typified the death of Christ (1 Cor. 5:7); and the feast of tabernacles typified "the times of the restitution of all things, of which God hath spoken by the mouth of all his holy prophets, since the world began" (Acts 3:21).

Such was the opening and such the closing feast of the Jewish year. Atonement is the foundation, glory the top-stone;

while, between these two points, we have the resurrection of Christ (ver. 10-14), the gathering of the Church, (ver 15-21,) the waking up of Israel to a sense of their long-lost glory (ver. 24-25), their repentance and hearty reception of their Messiah (ver. 27-32.) And that not one feature might be lacking in this grand typical representation, we have provision made for the Gentiles to come in at the close of the harvest, and glean in Israel's fields (ver. 22). All this renders the picture divinely perfect, and evokes from the heart of every lover of Scripture the most intense admiration. What could be more complete? The blood of the Lamb and practical holiness founded thereon – the resurrection of Christ from the dead, and His ascension into heaven – the descent of the Holy Ghost, in pentecostal power, to form the Church – the awakening of the remnant – their repentance and restoration – the blessing of "the poor and the stranger" – the manifestation of the glory – the rest and blessedness of the kingdom. Such are the contents of this truly marvellous chapter, which we shall, now, proceed to examine in detail. May God the Holy Ghost be our Teacher!

The Sabbath

"And the Lord spake unto Moses, saying, Speak unto the children of Israel, and say unto them, concerning the feasts of the Lord, which ye shall proclaim to be holy convocations, even these are my feasts. Six days shall work be done; but the seventh day is the sabbath of rest, an holy convocation; ye shall do no work therein: it is the sabbath of the Lord in all your dwellings." The place which the Sabbath here gets is full of interest. The Lord is about to furnish a type of all His dealings in grace with His people; and, ere He does so, He sets forth the Sabbath as the significant expression of that rest which remaineth for the people of God. It was an actual solemnity, to be observed by Israel; but it was also a type of what is yet to be, when all that great and glorious work which this chapter foreshadows shall have been accomplished. It is God's rest, into which all who believe can enter now in spirit; but which, as to its full and actual accomplishment, yet remains (Heb. 4). We work now. We shall rest by and by. In one sense, the believer enters into rest; in another sense, he labours to enter into it. He has found his rest in Christ; he labours to enter into his rest in glory. He has found his full mental repose in what Christ has wrought for him, and his eye rests on that everlasting Sabbath upon which he shall enter when all his desert toils and conflicts are over. He cannot rest in the midst of a scene of sin and wretchedness. "He rests in Christ, the Son of God, who took the servant's form." And, while thus resting, he is called to labour as a worker together with God, in the full assurance that, when all his toil is over, he shall enjoy unbroken, eternal repose in those mansions of unfading light and unalloyed blessedness where labour and sorrow can never enter. Blessed prospect! May it brighten more and more each hour in the vision of faith! May we labour all the more earnestly and faithfully, as being sure of this most precious rest at the end! True, there are foretastes of the eternal Sabbath; but these foretastes only cause us to long more ardently for the blessed reality – that Sabbath which shall never be broken – that "holy convocation" which shall never be dissolved.

We have already remarked that the Sabbath occupies quite a unique and independent place in this chapter. This is evident from the wording of the fourth verse, where the Lord seems to begin afresh with the expression, "These are the feasts of the Lord," as if to leave the Sabbath quite distinct from the seven feasts which follow, though it be, in reality, the type of that rest to which those feasts so blessedly introduce the soul.

The Passover

"These are the feasts of the Lord, even holy convocations, which ye shall proclaim in their seasons. In the fourteenth day of the first month at even is the Lord's passover" (ver. 4, 5). Here, then, we have the first of the seven periodical solemnities – the offering of that paschal lamb whose blood it was that screened the Israel of God from the sword of the destroying angel, on that terrible night when Egypt's firstborn were laid low. This is the acknowledged type of the death of Christ; and, hence, its place in this chapter is divinely appropriate. It forms the foundation of all. We can know nothing of rest, nothing of holiness, nothing of fellowship, save on the ground of the death of Christ. It is peculiarly striking, significant, and beautiful to observe that, directly God's rest is spoken of, the next thing introduced is the blood of the paschal lamb. As much as to say, "There is the *rest*, but here is your *title*." No doubt, labour will *capacitate* us, but it is the blood that *entitles* us to enjoy the rest.

The unleavened bread

"And on the fifteenth day of the same month is the feast of unleavened bread unto the Lord: seven days ye must eat unleavened bread. In the first day ye shall have an holy convocation: ye shall do no servile work therein. But ye shall offer an offering made by fire unto the Lord seven days: in the seventh day is an holy convocation: ye shall do no servile work therein" (ver. 6-8.). The people are here assembled round Jehovah, in that practical holiness which is founded upon accomplished redemption; and, while thus assembled, the fragrant odour of the sacrifice ascends from the altar of Israel to the throne of Israel's God. This gives us a fine view of that holiness which God looks for in the life of His redeemed. It is based upon the sacrifice, and it ascends in immediate connexion with the acceptable fragrance of the Person of Christ. "Ye shall do no *servile work* therein. But ye shall offer *an offering made by fire.*" What a contrast! The servile work of man's hands, and the sweet savour of Christ's sacrifice! The practical holiness of God's people is not servile labour. It is the living unfolding of Christ, through them, by the power of the Holy Ghost. "To me to live is Christ." This is the true idea. Christ is our life; and every exhibition of that life is, in the divine judgment, redolent with all the fragrance of Christ. It may be a very trifling matter, in man's judgment; but, in so far as it is the outflow of Christ our life, it is unspeakably precious to God. It ascends to Him and can never be forgotten. "The fruits of righteousness which are by Jesus Christ" are produced in the life of the believer, and no power of earth or hell can prevent their fragrance ascending to the throne of God.

It is needful to ponder deeply the contrast between "servile work," and the outflow of the life of Christ. The type is very vivid. There was a total cessation of manual labour throughout the whole assembly; but the sweet savour of the burnt offering ascended to God. These were to be the two grand characteristics of the feast of unleavened bread. Man's labour ceased, and the odour of the sacrifice ascended; and this was the type of a believer's life of practical holiness. What a triumphant answer is here to the legalist, on the one side, and the antinomian on the other! The former is silenced by the words, "no servile work;" and the latter is confounded by the words, "Ye shall offer an offering made by fire." The most elaborate works of man's hands are "servile" but the smallest cluster of "the fruits of righteousness" is to the glory and praise of God. Throughout the entire period of the believer's life, there must be no servile work; nothing of the hateful and degrading element of legality. There should be only the continual presentation of the life of Christ, wrought out and exhibited by the power of the Holy Ghost. Throughout the "seven days" of Israel's second great periodical solemnity, there was to be "no leaven;" but, instead thereof, the sweet savour of "an offering made by fire" was to be presented to the Lord. May we fully enter into the practical teaching of this most striking and instructive type!

The sheaf of the first-fruits

"And the Lord spake unto Moses, saying, Speak unto the children of Israel, and say unto them, When ye be come into the land which I give unto you, and shall reap the harvest thereof, then ye shall bring a sheaf of the first-fruits of your harvest unto the priest; and ye shall wave the sheaf before the Lord, to be accepted for you: on the morrow after the Sabbath the priest shall wave it. And ye shall offer that day, when ye wave the sheaf, an he lamb without blemish of the first year, for a burnt offering unto the Lord. And the meat offering thereof shall be two tenth deals of fine flour mingled with oil, an offering made by fire unto the Lord for a sweet savour: and the drink offering thereof shall be of wine, the fourth part of an hin. And ye shall eat neither bread, nor parched corn, nor green ears, until the selfsame day that ye have brought an offering unto your God: it shall be a statute for ever throughout your generations, in all your dwellings" (ver. 9-14).

"But now is Christ risen from the dead, and become the *firstfruits* of them that slept" (1 Cor. 15:20). The beautiful ordinance of the presentation of the sheaf of first fruits typified the resurrection of Christ, who, "at the end of the Sabbath, as it began to dawn toward the first day of the week," rose triumphant from the tomb, having accomplished the glorious work of redemption. His was a "resurrection *from among* the dead;" and, in it, we have, at once, the earnest and the type of the resurrection of His people. "Christ the first fruits; afterwards they that are Christ's at his coming." When Christ comes, His people will be raised "from among the dead" (*ek nekrōn*); that is those of them that sleep in Jesus. "But the rest of the dead lived not again until the thousand years were finished" (Rev. 20:5). When, immediately after the transfiguration, our blessed Lord spoke of His rising "*from among the dead,*" the disciples questioned among themselves what that could mean (see Mark 9). Every orthodox Jew believed in the doctrine of the "resurrection of the dead" (*anastasis nekrōn*). But the idea of a "resurrection from among the dead" (*anastasis ek nekrōn*), was what the disciples were unable to grasp and, no doubt, many disciples since then have felt considerable difficulty with respect to a mystery so profound.

However, if my reader will prayerfully study and compare 1 Cor. 15 with 1 Thess. 4:13-18, he will get much precious instruction upon this most interesting and practical truth. He can also look at Romans 8:11, in connexion. "But if the Spirit of him that raised up Jesus from the dead (*ek nekrōn*) dwell in you, he that raised up Christ from the dead shall also quicken your mortal bodies by his Spirit that dwelleth in you." From all these passages it will be seen that the resurrection of the Church will be upon precisely the same principle as the resurrection of Christ. Both the Head and the body are shown to be raised "from among the dead." The first sheaf and all the sheaves that follow after are morally connected.

It must be evident to any one who carefully ponders the subject, in the light of scripture, that there is a very material difference between the resurrection of the believer and the resurrection of the unbeliever. Both shall be raised; but Revelation 20:5, proves that there will be a thousand years between the two, so that they differ both as to the principle, and as to the time. Some have found difficulty, in reference to this subject, from the fact that, in John 5:28, our Lord speaks of "the *hour* in the which *all* that are in the graves shall hear his voice." "How," it may be asked, "can there be a thousand years between the two resurrections when both are spoken of as occurring in an 'hour'?" The answer is very simple. In verse 28, the quickening of dead souls is spoken of as occurring in an "hour;" and this work has been going on for over eighteen hundred years. Now, if a period of nearly *two* thousand years can be represented by the word "hour," what objection can there be to the idea of *one* thousand years being represented in the same way? Surely, none whatever, especially when it is expressly stated that "the rest of the dead lived not again until the thousand years were finished."

But, furthermore, when we find mention made of "a *first* resurrection," is it not evident that all are not to be raised together? Why speak of a "first" if there is but the one? It may be said that "the first resurrection" refers to the soul; but where is the scripture warrant for such a statement? The solemn fact is this: when the "shout of the archangel and the trump of God" shall be heard, the redeemed who sleep in Jesus will be raised to meet Him in the glory. The wicked dead, whoever they be, from the days of Cain down, will remain in their graves, during the thousand years of millennial blessedness; and, at the close of that bright and blissful period, they shall come forth and stand before "the great white throne," there to be "judged every man according to his works," and to pass from the throne of judgment into the lake of fire. Appalling thought!

Oh! reader, how is it in reference to your precious soul. Have you seen, by the eye of faith, the blood of the paschal Lamb shed to screen you from this terrible hour? Have you seen the precious sheaf of firstfruits reaped and gathered into the heavenly garner, as the earnest of your being gathered in due time? These are solemn questions, deeply solemn. Do not put them aside. See that you are, *now*, under the cover of the blood of Jesus. Remember, you cannot glean so much as a single ear in the fields of redemption until you have seen the true sheaf waved before the Lord. "Ye shall eat neither bread, nor parched corn, nor green ears, until *the selfsame day* that ye have brought an offering unto your God." The harvest could not be touched until the sheaf of first fruits had been presented, and, with the sheaf, a burnt offering and a meat offering.

Pentecost

"And ye shall count unto you from the morrow after the sabbath, from the day that ye brought the sheaf of the wave offering: seven sabbaths shall be complete: even unto the morrow after the seventh sabbath shall ye number fifty days; and ye shall offer a new meat offering unto the Lord. Ye shall bring out of your habitations two wave loaves, of two tenth deals: they shall be of fine flour; they shall be baken *with leaven*; they are the firstfruits unto the Lord" (ver. 15-17). This is the feast of Pentecost – the type of God's people, gathered by the Holy Ghost, and presented before Him, in connexion with all the preciousness of Christ. In the Passover, we have the death of Christ; in the sheaf of firstfruits, we have the resurrection of Christ; and in the feast of Pentecost, we have the descent of the Holy Ghost to form the Church. All this is divinely perfect. The death and resurrection of Christ had to be accomplished, ere the Church could be formed. The sheaf was offered and then the loaves were baked.

And, observe, "They shall be baken *with leaven.*" Why was this? Because they were intended to foreshadow those who, though filled with the Holy Ghost, and adorned with His gifts and graces, had, nevertheless, *evil* dwelling in them. The assembly, on the day of Pentecost, stood in the full value of the blood of Christ, was crowned with the gifts of the Holy Ghost; but there was leaven there also. No power of the Spirit could do away with the fact that there was evil dwelling in the people of God. It might be suppressed and kept out of view; but it was there. This fact is foreshadowed in the type, by the leaven in the two loaves; and it is set forth in the actual history of the Church; for, albeit God the Holy Ghost was present in the assembly, the flesh was there likewise to lie unto Him. Flesh is flesh, nor can it ever be made anything else than flesh. The Holy Ghost did not come down, on the day of Pentecost, to improve nature or do away with the fact of its incurable evil, but to baptise believers into one body, and connect them with their living Head in heaven.

Allusion has already been made, in the chapter on the peace offering, to the fact that leaven was permitted in connexion therewith. It was the divine recognition of the evil in the worshipper. Thus is it also in the ordinance of the "two wave loaves;" they were to be "baken with *leaven,*" because of the *evil* in the antitype.

But, blessed be God, the evil which was divinely recognised was divinely provided for. This gives great rest and comfort to the heart. It is a comfort to be assured that God knows the worst of us; and, moreover, that He has made provision according to *His* knowledge, and not merely according to *ours.* "And ye shall offer *with the bread,* seven lambs *without blemish,* of the first year, and one young bullock, and two rams; they shall be for a burnt offering unto the Lord, with their meat offering and their drink offerings, even an offering made by fire, of a sweet savour unto the Lord" (ver. 18). Here, then, we have, in immediate connexion with the leavened loaves, the presentation of an unblemished sacrifice, typifying the great and all-important truth that it is Christ's perfectness and not our sinfulness that is ever before the view of God. Observe, particularly, the words, "ye shall offer *with the bread,* seven lambs *without blemish.*" Precious truth! Deeply precious, though clothed in typical dress! May the reader be enabled to enter into it, to make his own of it, to stay his conscience upon it, to feed and refresh his heart with it, to delight his whole soul in it. Not I, but Christ.

It may, however, be objected that the fact of Christ's being a spotless lamb is not sufficient to roll the burden of guilt from a sin-stained conscience – a sweet-savour offering would not, of itself, avail for a guilty sinner. This objection might be urged; but our type fully meets and entirely removes it. It is quite true that a burnt offering would not have been sufficient where "leaven" was in question; and hence we read, "Then ye shall sacrifice one kid of the goats for *a sin offering,* and two lambs of the first year for a sacrifice of peace offerings" (ver. 19). The "sin offering" was the answer to the "leaven" in the loaves – "peace" was established, so that communion could be enjoyed, and all went up in immediate connexion with the "sweet savour" of the "burnt offering" unto the Lord.

Thus, on the day of Pentecost, the church was presented, in all the value and excellency of Christ, through the power of the Holy Ghost. Though having in itself the leaven of the old nature, that leaven was not reckoned, because the divine Sin Offering had perfectly answered for it. The power of the Holy Ghost did not remove the leaven, but the blood of the Lamb had atoned for it. This is a most interesting and important distinction. The work of the Spirit in the believer does not remove indwelling evil. It enables him to detect, judge, and subdue the evil; but no amount of spiritual power can do away with the fact that the evil is there – though, blessed be God, the conscience is at perfect ease, inasmuch as the blood of our Sin Offering has eternally settled the whole question; and, therefore, instead of our evil being under the eye of God, it has been put out of sight for ever, and we are accepted in all the acceptableness of Christ, who offered Himself to God as a sweet-smelling sacrifice, that He might perfectly glorify Him in all things, and be the food of His people for ever.

The stranger's portion

Thus much as to Pentecost – after which a long period is entered to roll on ere we have any movement amongst the people. There is, however, the notice of "the poor and stranger" in that beautiful ordinance which has already been referred to in its moral aspect. Here we may look at it in a dispensational point of view. "And when ye reap the harvest of your land, thou shalt not make clean riddance of the corners of thy field when thou reapest, neither shalt thou gather any gleaning of thy harvest; thou shalt leave them unto the poor, and to the stranger: I am the Lord your God" (ver. 22). Provision is here made for the stranger to glean in Israel's fields. The Gentile is to be brought in to participate in the overflowing goodness of God. When Israel's storehouse and winepress have been fully furnished, there will be precious sheaves and rich clusters for the Gentile to gather.

We are not, however, to suppose that the spiritual blessings with which the Church is endowed in the heavenlies with Christ are set forth under the figure of a stranger gleaning in Israel's fields. These blessings are as new to the seed of Abraham as they are to the Gentile. They are not the gleanings of Canaan, but the glories of heaven – the glories of Christ. The Church is not merely blessed *by* Christ, but *with* and *in* Christ. The bride of Christ will not be sent forth to gather up, as a stranger, the sheaves and clusters in the corners of Israel's fields, and from the branches of Israel's vines. No; she tastes of higher blessings, richer joys, nobler dignities, than anything that Israel ever knew. She is not to glean as a stranger on earth, but to enjoy her own wealthy and happy home in heaven to which she belongs. This is the "better thing" which God hath, in His manifold wisdom and grace, "reserved" for her. No doubt, it will be a gracious privilege for "the stranger" to be permitted to glean after Israel's harvest is reaped; but the church's portion is incomparably higher, even to be the bride of Israel's King, the partner of His throne, the sharer of His joys, His dignities, and His glories; to be like Him, and with Him, for ever. The eternal mansions of the Father's house on high, and not the ungleaned corners of Israel's fields below, are to be the church's portion. May we ever bear this in mind, and live, in some small degree, worthy of such a holy and elevated destination!

The feast of trumpets

"And the Lord spake unto Moses, saying, Speak unto the children of Israel, saying, In the seventh month, in the first day of the month, shall ye have a sabbath, a memorial of blowing of trumpets, an holy convocation. Ye shall do no servile work; but ye shall offer an offering made by fire unto the Lord" (ver. 23-25). A new subject is introduced here, by the words, "the Lord spake unto Moses," which, let me remark in passing, affords an interesting help in classifying the subjects of the entire chapter. Thus, the Sabbath, the Passover, and the feast of unleavened bread, are given under the first communication. The wave sheaf, the wave loaves, and the ungleaned corners, are given under the second; after which we have a long unnoticed interval, and then comes the soul-stirring feast of trumpets, on the first day of the seventh month. This ordinance leads us on to the time, now fast approaching, when the remnant of Israel shall "blow up the trumpet" for a memorial, calling to remembrance their long-lost glory, and stirring up themselves to seek the Lord.

The Day of Atonement

The feast of trumpets is intimately connected with another great solemnity, namely, "the day of atonement." *"Also* on the tenth day of this seventh month there shall be a day of atonement: it shall be an holy convocation unto you; and ye shall afflict your souls, and offer an offering made by fire unto the Lord. And ye shall do no work in that same day; for it is a day of atonement, to make an atonement for you before the Lord your God . . . it shall be unto you a sabbath of rest, and ye shall afflict your souls: in the ninth day of the month at even, from even unto even shall ye celebrate your sabbath" (ver. 27-32). Thus, after the blowing of the trumpets, an interval of eight days elapses, and then we have the day of atonement, with which these things are connected, namely, affliction of soul, atonement for sin, and rest from labour. All these things will find their due place in the experience of the Jewish remnant, by and by. "The harvest is past, the summer is ended, and we are not saved" (Jer. 8:20). Such will be the pathetic lament of the remnant when the Spirit of God shall have begun to touch their heart and conscience. "And they shall look upon me whom they have pierced, and they shall mourn for him, as one mourneth for his only son, and shall be in bitterness for him, as one that is in bitterness for her firstborn. In that day shall there be a great mourning in Jerusalem, as the mourning of Hadadrimmon in the valley of Megiddon. And the land shall mourn, every family apart," &c. (Zech. 12:10-14).

What deep mourning, what intense affliction, what genuine penitence there will be, when, under the mighty action of the Holy Ghost, the conscience of the remnant shall recall the sins of the past, the neglect of the Sabbath, the breach of the law, the stoning of the prophets, the piercing of the Son, the resistance of the Spirit! All these things will come in array on the tablets of an enlightened and exercised conscience, and produce keen affliction of soul.

But the blood of atonement will meet all. "In that day there shall be a fountain opened to the house of David, and to the inhabitants of Jerusalem, for sin and for uncleanness" (Zech. 13:1). They will be made to feel their guilt and be afflicted, and they will also be led to see the efficacy of the blood and find perfect peace – a Sabbath of rest unto their souls.

Now, when such results shall have been reached, in the experience of Israel, in the latter day, for what should we look? Surely, THE GLORY. When the "blindness" is removed, and "the vail" is taken away, when the heart of the remnant is turned to Jehovah, then shall the bright beams of the "Sun of righteousness" fall, in healing, restoring, and saving power upon a truly penitent, afflicted, and poor people. To enter elaborately upon this subject would demand a volume in itself. The exercises, the experiences, the conflicts, the trials, the difficulties, and the ultimate blessings of the Jewish remnant are fully detailed throughout the Psalms and Prophets. The existence of such a body must be clearly seen, ere the Psalms and Prophets can be studied with intelligence and satisfaction. Not but that we may learn much from those portions of inspiration, for "all scripture is profitable." But the surest way to make a right use of any portion of the Word of God, is to understand its primary application. If, then, we apply scriptures to the Church or heavenly body which belong, strictly speaking, to the Jewish remnant or earthly body, we must be involved in serious error as to both the one and the other. In point of fact, it happens, in many cases, that the existence of such a body as the remnant is completely ignored, and the true position and hope of the Church are entirely lost sight of. These are grave errors which my reader should sedulously seek to avoid. Let him not suppose, for a moment, that they are mere speculations fitted only to engage the attention of the curious, and possessing no practical power whatever. There could not be a more erroneous supposition. What! is it of no practical value to us to know whether we belong to earth or heaven? Is it of no real moment to us to know whether we shall be at rest in the mansions above, or passing through the apocalyptic judgments down here? Who could admit anything so unreasonable? The truth is, it would be difficult to fix on any line of truth more practical than that which unfolds the distinctive destinies of the earthly remnant and the heavenly Church. I shall not pursue the subject further, here; but the reader will find it well worthy of his calm and prayerful study. We shall close this section with a view of the feast of tabernacles – the last solemnity of the Jewish year.

The feast of tabernacles

"And the Lord spake unto Moses, saying, Speak unto the children of Israel, saying, The fifteenth day of this seventh month shall be the feast of tabernacles for seven days unto the Lord . . . Also in the fifteenth day of the seventh month, when ye have gathered in the fruit of the land, ye shall keep a feast unto the Lord seven days: on the first day shall be a sabbath, and on the eighth shall be a sabbath. And ye shall take you on the first day the boughs of goodly trees, branches of palm trees, and the boughs of thick trees, and willows of the brook; and ye shall rejoice before the Lord your God seven days. And ye shall keep it a feast unto the Lord seven days in the year: it shall be a statute for ever in your generations; ye shall celebrate it in the seventh month. Ye shall dwell in booths seven days: all that are Israelites born shall dwell in booths; that your generations may know that I made the children of Israel to dwell in booths, when I brought them out of the land of Egypt: I am the Lord your God" (ver. 33-43).

This feast points us forward to the time of Israel's glory in the latter day, and, therefore, it forms a most lovely and appropriate close to the whole series of feasts. The harvest was gathered in, all was done, the storehouses were amply furnished, and Jehovah would have His people to give expression to their festive joy. But, alas! they seem to have had but little heart to enter into the divine thought in reference to this most delightful ordinance. They lost sight of the fact that they had been strangers and pilgrims, and hence their long neglect of this feast. From the days of Joshua down to the time of Nehemiah, the feast of tabernacles had never once been celebrated. It was reserved for the feeble remnant that returned from the Babylonish captivity to do what had not been done even in the bright days of Solomon. "And all the congregation of them that were come again out of the captivity made booths, and sat under the booths: for since the days of Joshua the son of Nun, unto that day, had not the children of Israel done so. And there was very great gladness" (Neh. 8:17). How refreshing it must have been to those who had hung their harps on the willows of Babylon, to find themselves beneath the shade of the willows of Canaan! It was a sweet foretaste of that time of which the feast of tabernacles was the type, when Israel's restored tribes shall repose within those millennial bowers which the faithful hand of Jehovah will erect for them in the land which He sware to give unto Abraham and to his seed for ever. Thrice happy moment when the heavenly and the earthly shall meet, as intimated, in "the first day" and "the eighth day" of the feast of tabernacles! "The heavens shall hear the earth, and the earth shall hear the corn and the wine, and the oil, and they shall hear Jezreel."

There is a fine passage in the last chapter of Zechariah which goes to prove, very distinctly, that the true celebration of the feast of tabernacles belongs to the glory of the latter day. "And it shall come to pass, that every one that is left of all the nations which came against Jerusalem, shall even go up from year to year to worship the King, the Lord of hosts, and to keep the feast of tabernacles" (chap. 14:16). What a scene! Who would seek to rob it of its characteristic beauty by a vague system of interpretation falsely called spiritualizing? Surely, Jerusalem means Jerusalem; nations mean nations; and the feast of tabernacles means the feast of tabernacles. Is there anything incredible in this? Surely, nothing save to man's reason which rejects all that lies beyond its narrow range. The feast of tabernacles shall yet be celebrated in the land of Canaan, and the nations of the saved shall go up thither to participate in its glorious and hallowed festivities. Jerusalem's warfare shall then be accomplished, the roar of battle shall cease. The sword and the spear shall be transformed into the implements of peaceful agriculture; Israel shall repose beneath the refreshing shade of their vines and fig-trees; and all the earth shall rejoice in the government of "the Prince of Peace." Such is the prospect presented in the unerring pages of inspiration. The types foreshadow it; the prophets prophesy of it; faith believes it; and hope anticipates it.

NOTE. – At the close of our chapter we read, "And Moses declared unto the children of Israel *the feasts of the Lord.*" This was their true character, their original title; but in the Gospel of John, they are called *"feasts of the Jews."* They had long ceased to be Jehovah's feasts. He was shut out. They did not want Him; and, hence, in John 7, when Jesus was asked to go up to *"the Jews' feast of tabernacles,"* He answered, "My time is not yet come;" and when He did go up it was "privately," to take His place outside of the whole thing, and to call upon every thirsty soul to come unto Him and drink. There is a solemn lesson in this. Divine institutions are speedily marred in the hands of man; but, oh! how deeply blessed to know that the thirsty soul that feels the barrenness and drought connected with a scene of empty religious formality, has only to flee to Jesus and drink freely of His exhaustless springs, and so become a channel of blessing to others.

Chapter 24

FIGURES OF ISRAEL

There is very much to interest the spiritual mind in this brief section. We have seen in chapter 23 the history of the dealings of God with Israel, from the offering up of the true paschal Lamb, until the rest and glory of the millennial Kingdom. In the chapter now before us, we have two grand ideas – namely, first, the unfailing record and memorial of the twelve tribes, maintained before God, by the power of the Spirit, and the efficacy of Christ's priesthood; and, secondly, the apostasy of Israel after the flesh, and divine judgment executed thereon. It is the clear apprehension of the former that will enable us to contemplate the latter.

The light which burnt continually

"And the Lord spake unto Moses, saying, Command the children of Israel, that they bring unto thee *pure* oil olive, *beaten* for the light, to cause the lamps to burn *continually*. Without the vail of the testimony, in the tabernacle of the congregation, shall Aaron order it *from the evening unto the morning* before the Lord *continually*; it shall be a statute for ever in your generations. He shall order the lamps upon the *pure* candlestick before the Lord *continually*" (ver. 1-4). The "pure oil" represents the grace of the Holy Spirit, founded upon the work of Christ, as exhibited by the candlestick of "beaten gold." The "olive" was *pressed* to yield the "oil," and the gold was "*beaten*" to form the candlestick. In other words, the grace and light of the Spirit are founded upon the death of Christ, and maintained, in clearness and power, by the priesthood of Christ. The golden lamp diffused its light throughout the precincts of the sanctuary, during the dreary hours of night, when darkness brooded over the nation and all were wrapped in slumber. In all this we have a vivid presentation of God's faithfulness to His people whatever might be their outward condition. Darkness and slumber might settle down upon them, but the lamp was to burn "continually." The high priest was responsible to keep the steady light of testimony burning during the tedious hours of the night. "Without the vail of the testimony, in the tabernacle of the congregation, shall Aaron order it from the evening unto the morning, before the Lord continually." The maintenance of this light was not left dependent upon Israel. God had provided one whose office it was to look after it and order it continually.

The twelve loaves and the unity of the people

But, further, we read, "And thou shalt take fine flour, and bake twelve cakes thereof: two-tenth deals shall be in one cake. And thou shalt set them in two rows, six in a row, upon the *pure* table before the Lord. And thou shalt put *pure* frankincense upon each row, that it may be on the bread for a memorial, even an offering made by fire unto the Lord. Every sabbath he shall set it in order before the Lord *continually*, being taken from the children of Israel by an everlasting covenant. And it shall be Aaron's and his sons'; and they shall eat it in the holy place: for it is most holy unto him of the offerings of the Lord made by fire, by a perpetual statute" (ver. 5-9). There is no mention of leaven in these loaves. They represent, I doubt not, Christ in immediate connexion with "the twelve tribes of Israel." They were laid up in the sanctuary before the Lord, on the pure table, for seven days, after which they became the food of Aaron and his sons, furnishing another striking figure of Israel's condition in the view of Jehovah, whatever might be their outward aspect. The twelve tribes are ever before Him. Their memorial can never perish. They are ranged in divine order in the sanctuary, covered with the fragrant incense of Christ, and reflected from the pure table whereon they rest beneath the bright beams of that golden lamp which shines, with undimmed lustre, through the darkest hour of the nation's moral night.

Now, it is well to see that we are not sacrificing sound judgment or divine truth on the altar of fancy, when we venture to interpret, after such a fashion, the mystic furniture of the sanctuary. We are taught, in Hebrews 9, that all these things were "the patterns of things in the heavens;" and again, in Hebrews 10:1, that they were "a shadow of good things to come." We are, therefore, warranted in believing that there are "things in the heavens" answering to the "patterns" – that there is a substance answering to the "shadow". In a word, we are warranted in believing that there is that "in the heavens" which answers to "the seven lamps," "the pure table," and the "twelve loaves." This is not human imagination, but divine truth on which faith has fed, in all ages. What was the meaning of Elijah's altar of "twelve stones," on the top of Carmel? It was nothing else than the expression of his faith in that truth of which the "twelve loaves" were "the pattern" or "the shadow." He believed in the unbroken unity of the nation, maintained before God in the eternal stability of the promise made to Abraham, Isaac, and Jacob, whatever might be the external condition of the nation. Man might look in vain for the manifested unity of the twelve tribes; but faith could always look within the hallowed enclosure of the sanctuary, and there see the twelve loaves, covered with pure frankincense, ranged in divine order on the pure table; and even though all without were wrapped in midnight's gloomy shades, yet could faith discern, by the light of the *seven* golden lamps, the same grand truth foreshadowed – namely, the indissoluble unity of Israel's twelve tribes.

Thus it was then; and thus it is now. The night is dark and gloomy. There is not, in all this lower world, so much as a single ray by which the human eye can trace the unity of Israel's tribes. They are scattered among the nations, and lost to man's vision. But their memorial is before the Lord. Faith owns this, because it knows that "all the promises of

God are yea and amen in Christ Jesus." It sees in the upper sanctuary, by the Spirit's perfect light, the twelve tribes faithfully memorialised. Hearken to the following noble accents of faith: "And now I stand and am judged for the hope of the promise made of God unto our fathers: unto which promise *our twelve tribes,* instantly serving God night and day (*nukta kai hēmeran*), hope to come" (Acts 26:6, 7). Now, if King Agrippa had asked Paul, "Where are the twelve tribes?" could he have shown them to him? No. But why not? Was it because they were not to be seen? No; but because Agrippa had not eyes to see them. The twelve tribes lay far beyond the range of Agrippa's vision. It needed the eye of faith and the gracious light of the Spirit of God to be able to discern the twelve loaves, ordered upon the pure table in the sanctuary of God. There they were, and Paul saw them there; though the moment in which he gave utterance to his sublime conviction was as dark as it well could be. Faith is not governed by appearances. It takes its stand upon the lofty rock of God's eternal word, and, in all the calmness and certainty of that holy elevation, feeds upon the immutable word of Him who cannot lie. Unbelief may stupidly stare about and ask, Where are the twelve tribes? or, How can they be found and restored? It is impossible to give an answer. Not because there is no answer to be given; but because unbelief is utterly incapable of rising to the elevated point from which the answer can be seen. Faith is as sure that the memorial of the twelve tribes of Israel is before the eye of Israel's God, as it is that the twelve loaves were laid on the golden table every Sabbath day. But who can convince the sceptic or the infidel of this? Who can secure credence for such a truth from those who are governed, in all things, by reason or sense, and know nothing of what it is to hope against hope? Faith finds divine certainties and eternal realities in the midst of a scene where reason and sense can find nothing. Oh! for a more profound faith! May we grasp, with more intense earnestness, every word that proceedeth out of the mouth of the Lord, and feed upon it in all the artless simplicity of a little child.

The man who blasphemed the name of the LORD

We shall now turn to the second point in our chapter – namely, the apostasy of Israel, after the flesh, and the divine judgment thereon.

"And the son of an Israelitish woman, whose father was an Egyptian, went out among the children of Israel; and this son of an Israelitish woman and a man of Israel strove together in the camp. And the Israelitish woman's son blasphemed the name of the LORD, and cursed. And they brought him unto Moses . . . And they put him in ward, that the mind of the LORD might be showed them. And the LORD spake unto Moses, saying, Bring forth him that hath cursed without the camp; and let all that heard him lay their hands upon his head, and let all the congregation stone him . . . And Moses spake to the children of Israel, that they should bring forth him that had cursed out of the camp, and stone him with stones. And the children of Israel did as the LORD commanded Moses" (ver. 10-23).

The peculiar place assigned by the inspired penman to this narrative is striking and interesting. I have no doubt whatever but that it is designed to give us the opposite side of the picture presented in the opening verses of the chapter. Israel after the flesh has grievously failed and sinned against Jehovah. The name of the Lord has been blasphemed amongst the Gentiles. Wrath has come upon the nation. The judgments of an offended God have fallen upon them. But the day is coming when the dark and heavy cloud of judgment shall roll away; and then shall the twelve tribes, in their unbroken unity, stand forth before all the nations as the amazing monument of Jehovah's faithfulness and loving-kindness, "And in that day thou shalt say, O Lord, I will praise thee; though thou wast angry with me, thine anger is turned away, and thou comfortedst me. Behold, God is my salvation: I will trust, and not be afraid: for the Lord JEHOVAH is my strength and my song, he also is become my salvation. Therefore with joy shall ye draw water out of the wells of salvation. And in that day shall ye say, Praise the Lord, call upon his name, declare his doings among the people, make mention that his name is exalted. Sing unto the Lord; for he hath done excellent things: this is known in all the earth. Cry out and shout, thou inhabitant of Zion: for great is the Holy One of Israel in the midst of thee" (Isa. 12). "For I would not, brethren, that ye should be ignorant of this mystery, lest ye should be wise in your own conceits, that blindness in part is happened to Israel, until the fullness of the Gentiles be come in. And so all Israel shall be saved: as it is written, There shall come out of Sion the Deliverer, and shall turn away ungodliness from Jacob. For this is my covenant unto them, when I shall take away their sins. As concerning the gospel, they are enemies for your sakes: but as touching the election, they are beloved for the fathers' sakes. For the gifts and calling of God are without repentance. For as ye in times past have not believed God, yet have now obtained mercy through their unbelief: even so have these also now not believed in your mercy, that they also may obtain mercy. For God hath concluded them all in unbelief, that he might have mercy upon all. O the depth of the riches both of the wisdom and knowledge of God! How unsearchable are his judgments, and his ways past finding out! For who hath known the mind of the Lord? or who hath been his counsellor? Or who hath first given to Him, and it shall be recompensed to him again? For of him, and through him, and to him, are all things: to whom be glory for ever. Amen" (Rom. 11. 25-36).

Passages might be multiplied to prove that though Israel is suffering the divine judgment because of sin, yet "the gifts and calling of God are without repentance" – that though the blasphemer is being stoned without the camp, the twelve loaves are undisturbed within the sanctuary. "The voices of the prophets" declare, and the voices of apostles re-echo the glorious truth that "all Israel shall be saved;" not because they have not sinned, but because "the gifts and calling of God are without repentance." Let Christians beware how they tamper with "the promises made unto the fathers." If these promises be explained away or misapplied, it must, necessarily, weaken our moral sense of the divine integrity and accuracy of Scripture, as a whole. If one part may be explained away, so may another. If one passage may be vaguely interpreted, so may another; and thus it would come to pass that we should be deprived of all that blessed certainty which constitutes the foundation of our repose in reference to all that the Lord hath spoken. But more of this as we dwell upon the remaining chapters of our book.

THE SABBATICAL YEAR AND THE YEAR OF JUBILEE

The decrees of the Lord of all the earth

The intelligent reader will discern a strong moral link between this and the preceding chapter. In chapter 24 we learn that the house of Israel is preserved for the land of Canaan. In chapter 25 we learn that the land of Canaan is preserved for the house of Israel. Taking both together, we have the record of a truth which no power of earth or hell can obliterate. "All Israel shall be saved," and "the land shall not be sold forever." The former of these statements enunciates a principle which has stood like a rock amid the ocean of conflicting interpretations; while the latter declares a fact which many nations of the uncircumcised have sought in vain to ignore.

The reader will, I doubt not, observe the peculiar way in which our chapter opens. "And the Lord spake unto Moses in *Mount Sinai.*" The principal part of the communications contained in the Book of Leviticus is characterised by the fact of its emanating "from the tabernacle of the congregation." This is easily accounted for. Those communications have special reference to the service, communion, and worship of the priests, or to the moral condition of the people, and hence they are issued, as might be expected, from "the tabernacle of the congregation," that grand centre of all that appertained, in any way, to priestly service. Here, however, the communication is made from quite a different point. "The Lord spake unto Moses in *Mount Sinai.*" Now, we know that every expression in Scripture has its own special meaning, and we are justified in expecting a different line of communication from "Mount Sinai" from that which reaches us from "the tabernacle of the congregation." And so it is. The chapter at which we have now arrived treats of Jehovah's claims as Lord of all the earth. It is not the worship and communion of a priestly house, or the internal ordering of the nation; but the claims of God in government, His right to give a certain portion of the earth to a certain people to hold as tenants under Him. In a word, it is not to Jehovah in "the tabernacle" – the place of *worship*; but Jehovah in "Mount Sinai" – the place of *government*.

The sabbatical year

"And the Lord spake unto Moses in Mount Sinai, saying, Speak unto the children of Israel, and say unto them, When ye come into the land which I give you, then shall the land keep a sabbath unto the Lord. Six years thou shalt sow thy field, and six years thou shalt prune thy vineyard, and gather in the fruit thereof; but in the seventh year shall be a sabbath of rest unto the land, a sabbath for the Lord: thou shalt neither sow thy field, nor prune thy vineyard. That which groweth of its own accord of thy harvest thou shalt not reap, neither gather the grapes of thy vine undressed: for it is a year of rest unto the land. And the sabbath of the land shall be meat for you; for thee and for thy servant, and for thy maid, and for thy hired servant, and for thy stranger that sojourneth with thee, and for thy cattle, and for the beast that are in thy land, shall all the increase thereof be meat" (ver. 1-7).

Here, then, we have the special feature of the Lord's land. He would have it to enjoy a sabbatical year, and in that year there was to be the evidence of the rich profusion with which He would bless those who held as tenants under Him. Happy, highly privileged tenantry! What an honour to hold immediately under Jehovah! No rent! No taxes! No burdens! Well might it be said, "Happy is the people that is in such a case; yea, happy is the nation whose God is Jehovah." We know, alas! that Israel failed to take full possession of that wealthy land of which Jehovah made them a present, He had given it *all*. He had given it *forever*. They took but *a part*, and that for *a time*. Still, there it is. The property is there, though the tenants are ejected for the present. "The land shall not be sold *for ever*: for *the land is mine;* for ye are strangers and sojourners *with me*." What does this mean, but that Canaan belongs specially to Jehovah, and that He will hold it through the tribes of Israel? True, "the earth is the Lord's," but that is quite another thing. It is plain that He has been pleased, for His own unsearchable purposes, to take special possession of the land of Canaan, and to submit that land to a peculiar line of treatment, to mark it off from all other lands, by calling it His own, and to distinguish it by judgments, and ordinances, and periodical solemnities, the mere contemplation of which enlightens the understanding and affects the heart. Where, throughout all the earth, do we read of a land enjoying a year of unbroken repose – a year of richest abundance? The rationalist may ask, "How can these things be" The sceptic may doubt if they could be; but faith finds a satisfying answer from the lips of Jehovah: "And if ye shall say, What shall we eat the seventh year? behold, we shall not sow, nor gather in our increase: then I will command my blessing upon you in the sixth year, and it shall bring forth fruit for three years. And ye shall sow the eighth year, and eat yet of old fruit until the ninth year; until her fruits come in ye shall eat of the old store" (ver. 20-22). Nature might say, "What shall we do for *our sowing?*" God's answer is, "I will command *My blessing*." God's "blessing" is better far than man's "sowing." He was not going to let them starve in His sabbatic year. They were to feed upon the fruits of His blessing, while they celebrated His year of rest – a year which pointed forward to that eternal Sabbath that remains for the people of God.

The year of Jubilee

"And thou shalt number seven sabbaths of years unto thee,

seven times seven years; and the space of the seven sabbaths of years shall be unto thee forty and nine years. Then shalt thou cause the trumpet of the jubilee to sound on the tenth day of the seventh month; in the day of atonement shall ye make the trumpet sound throughout all your land" (ver. 8, 9). It is peculiarly interesting to note the various methods in which the millennial rest was held up to view, in the Jewish economy. Every seventh day was a sabbatical day; every seventh year was a sabbatical year; and every seven times seven years there was a jubilee. Each and all of these typical solemnities held up to the vision of faith the blessed prospect of a time when labour and sorrow should cease; when "the sweat of the brow" would no longer be needed to satisfy the cravings of hunger; but when a millennial earth, enriched by the copious showers of divine grace, and fertilised by the bright beams of the Sun of righteousness, should pour its abundance into the storehouse and winepress of the people of God. Happy time! Happy people! How blessed to be assured that these things are not the pencillings of imagination, or the flights of fancy, but the substantial verities of divine revelation, to be enjoyed by faith which is "the substance of things hoped for, the conviction of things not seen."

Of all the Jewish solemnities the jubilee would seem to have been the most soul-stirring and enrapturing. It stood immediately connected with the great day of atonement. It was when the blood of the victim was shed, that the emancipating sound of the jubilee trump was heard through the hills and valleys of the land of Canaan. That longed-for note was designed to wake up the nation from the very centre of its moral being, to stir the deepest depths of the soul, and to send a shining river of divine and ineffable joy through the length and breadth of the land. "In the day of atonement shall ye make the trumpet sound throughout *all* your land." Not a corner was to remain unvisited by "the joyful sound." The aspect of the jubilee was as wide as the aspect of the atonement on which the jubilee was based.

"And ye shall hallow the fiftieth year, and proclaim liberty throughout all the land unto all the inhabitants thereof: it shall be a jubilee unto you; and ye shall return every man unto his possession, and ye shall return every man unto his family. A jubilee shall that fiftieth year be unto you: ye shall not sow, neither reap that which groweth of itself in it, nor gather the grapes in it of thy vine undressed. For it is the jubilee; it shall be holy unto you: ye shall eat the increase thereof out of the field. In the year of this jubilee ye shall return every man unto his possession" (ver. 8-13). All estates and conditions of the people were permitted to feel the hallowed and refreshing influence of this most noble institution. The exile returned; the captive was emancipated; the debtor set free; each family opened its bosom to receive once more its long-lost members; each inheritance received back its exiled owner. The sound of the trumpet was the welcome and soul-stirring signal for the captive to escape; for the slave to cast aside the chains of his bondage; for the manslayer to return to his home; for the ruined and poverty-stricken to rise to the possession of their forfeited inheritance. No sooner had the trumpet's thrice-welcome sound fallen upon the ear, than the mighty tide of blessing rose majestically, and sent its refreshing undulations into the most remote corners of Jehovah's highly-favoured land.

The land is mine, says the Lord

"And if thou sell anything unto thy neighbour, or buyest anything of thy neighbour's hand, ye shall not oppress one another: according to the number of years after the jubilee thou shalt buy of thy neighbour, and according unto the number of years of the fruits he shall sell unto thee. According to the multitude of years thou shalt increase the price thereof, and according to the fewness of years thou shalt diminish the price of it: for according to the number of the years of the fruits doth he sell unto thee. Ye shall not therefore oppress one another; but thou shalt fear thy God: for I am the Lord your God" (ver. 14-17). The year of jubilee reminded both buyer and seller that the land belonged to Jehovah, and was not to be sold. "The fruits" might be sold, but that was all – Jehovah could never give up the land to any one. It is important to get this point well fixed in the mind. It may open up a very extensive line of truth. If the land of Canaan is not to be sold – if Jehovah declares it to be His for ever, then for whom does He want it? Who is to hold under Him? Those to whom He gave it by an everlasting covenant, that they might have it in possession as long as the moon endureth – even to all generations.

There is no spot in all the earth like unto the land of Canaan in the divine estimation. There Jehovah set up His throne and His sanctuary; there His priests stood to minister continually before Him; there the voices of His prophets were heard testifying of present ruin and future restoration and glory; there the Baptist began, continued, and ended his career as the forerunner of the Messiah; there the Blessed One was born of a woman; there He was baptised; there He preached and taught; there He laboured and died; from thence He ascended in triumph to the right hand of God; thither God the Holy Ghost descended, in Pentecostal power; from thence the overflowing tide of gospel testimony emanated to the ends of the earth; thither the Lord of glory will descend, ere long, and plant His foot "on the mount of Olives;" there His throne will be re-established and His worship restored. In a word, His eyes and His heart are there continually; its dust is precious in His sight; it is the centre of all His thoughts and operations, as touching this earth; and it is His purpose to make it an eternal excellency, the joy of many generations.

It is, then, I repeat, immensely important to get a firm hold of this interesting line of truth with respect to the land of Canaan. Of that land Jehovah hath said, "IT IS MINE." Who shall take it from Him? Where is the king or the emperor, where the power, human or diabolical, that can wrest "the pleasant land" out of Jehovah's omnipotent grasp? True, it has been a bone of contention, an apple of discord to the nations. It has been, and it will yet be, the scene and centre of cruel war and bloodshed. But far above all the din of battle and the strife of nations, these words fall with divine clearness, fullness, and power, upon the ear of faith – *"the land is mine!"* Jehovah can never give up that land, nor those "twelve tribes," through whom He is to inherit it for ever. Let my reader think of this. Let him ponder it deeply. Let him guard against all looseness of thought and vagueness of interpretation, as to this subject. God hath not cast away His people, or the land which He sware to give unto them for an everlasting possession. "The twelve loaves" of Leviticus 24 bear witness to the former; and "the jubilee" of Leviticus 25 bears witness to the latter. The memorial of the "twelve tribes of Israel" is ever before the Lord; and the moment is rapidly approaching when the trump of jubilee shall be heard upon the mountains of Palestine. Then, in reality, the captive shall cast off the ignominious chain which, for ages, has bound him. Then shall the exile return to that happy home from which he has so long been banished. Then shall every debt be cancelled, every burden removed, and every tear wiped away. "For thus saith the Lord, Behold, I will extend peace to her (Jerusalem) like a river, and the glory of the Gentiles like a flowing stream: then shall ye suck, ye shall be borne upon her sides, and be dandled upon her knees. As one whom his mother comforteth, so will I comfort you; and ye shall be comforted in Jerusalem. And when ye see this, your heart shall rejoice, and your bones shall flourish like an herb; and the hand of the Lord shall be known toward his servants, and his indignation toward his enemies. For, behold, the Lord will come with fire, and with his chariots like a whirlwind, to render his anger with fury, and his rebuke with flames of fire. For by fire and by his sword will the Lord plead with all flesh: and the slain of the Lord shall be many . . . For I know their works and their thoughts; it shall come, that I will gather all nations and tongues; and they shall come and see my glory. And I will set a sign among them, and I will send those that escape of them unto the nations, to Tarshish, Pul, and Lud, that draw the bow; to Tubal and Javan, to the isles afar off, that have not heard my fame, neither have seen My glory; and they shall declare my glory among the Gentiles. And they shall bring all your brethren for an offering unto the Lord, out of all nations, upon horses, and in chariots, and in litters, and upon mules, and upon swift beasts, to my holy mountain Jerusalem, saith the Lord, as the children of Israel bring an offering in a clean vessel into the house of the Lord. And I will also take of them for priests and for Levites, saith the Lord. For as the new heavens and the new earth, which I will make, shall remain before me, saith the Lord, so shall your seed and your name remain. And it shall come to pass, that from one new moon to another, and from one sabbath to another, shall all flesh come to worship before me, saith the Lord" (Isaiah 66:12-23).

And, now, let us look for a moment at the practical effect of the jubilee – its influence upon the transactions between man and man. "And if thou sell aught unto thy neighbour, or buyest aught of thy neighbour's hand, ye shall not oppress one another. According to the number of years after the jubilee thou shalt buy of thy neighbour, and according to the number of years of the fruits he shall sell unto thee." The scale of prices was to be regulated by the jubilee. If that glorious event were at hand, the price was low; if far off, the price was high. All human compacts as to land were broken up the moment the trump of jubilee was heard, for the land was Jehovah's; and the jubilee brought all back to its normal condition.

This teaches us a fine lesson. If our hearts are cherishing the abiding hope of the Lord's return, we shall set light by all earthly things. It is morally impossible that we can be in the attitude of waiting for the Son from heaven, and not be detached from this present world. "Let your moderation be known unto all men. The Lord is at hand" (Phil. 4). A person may hold "the doctrine of the millennium," as it is called, or the doctrine of "the second advent," and be a thorough man of the world; but one who lives in the habitual expectation of Christ's appearing must be separated from that which will be judged and broken up when He comes. It is not a question of the shortness and uncertainty of human life, which is quite true; or of the transitory and unsatisfying character of the things of time, which is equally true. It is far more potent and influential than either or both of these. It is this, *"The Lord is at hand."* May our hearts be affected and our conduct in all things influenced by this most precious and sanctifying truth!

Chapter 26

THE GOVERNMENT OF GOD TOWARDS ISRAEL

Blessings and punishments

This chapter requires little in the way of note or exposition. It contains a most solemn and affecting record of the blessings of obedience, on the one hand, and the terrible consequences of disobedience, on the other. Had Israel walked in obedience, they would have been invincible. "I will give peace in the land, and ye shall lie down, and none shall make you afraid: and I will rid evil beasts out of the land, neither shall the sword go through your land. And ye shall chase your enemies, and they shall fall before you by the sword. And five of you shall chase an hundred, and an hundred of you shall put ten thousand to flight: and your enemies shall fall before you by the sword. For I will have respect unto you, and make you fruitful, and multiply you, and establish my covenant with you. And ye shall eat old store, and bring forth the old because of the new. And I will set my tabernacle among you: and my soul shall not abhor you. And I will walk among you and will be your God, and ye shall be my people. I am the Lord your God, which brought you forth out of the land of Egypt, that ye should not be their bondsmen; and I have broken the bands of your yoke, and made you go upright" (ver. 6-13).

The presence of God should ever have been their shield and buckler. No weapon formed against them could prosper. But, then, the divine presence was only to be enjoyed by an obedient people. Jehovah could not sanction by His presence disobedience or wickedness. The uncircumcised nations around might depend upon their prowess and their military resources. Israel had only the arm of Jehovah to depend upon, and that arm could never be stretched forth to shield unholiness or disobedience. Their strength was to walk with God in a spirit of dependence and obedience. So long as they walked thus, there was a wall of fire round about them, to protect them from every enemy and every evil.

But, alas! Israel failed altogether. Notwithstanding the solemn and appalling picture placed before their eyes, in verses 14-33 of this chapter, they forsook the Lord and served other gods, and thus brought upon themselves the sore judgments threatened in this section, the bare record of which is sufficient to make the ears tingle. Under the heavy weight of these judgments they are suffering at this very hour. Scattered and peeled, wasted and outcast, they are the monuments of Jehovah's inflexible truth and justice. They read aloud, to all the nations of the earth, a most impressive lesson on the subject of the moral government of God – a lesson which it would be profitable for these nations to study deeply, yea, and a lesson which it would be salutary for our own hearts to ponder likewise.

Grace and the final restoration

We are very prone to confound two things which are clearly distinguished in the word, namely, God's *government* and God's *grace*. The evils which result from this confusion are various. It is sure to lead to an enfeebled sense of the dignity and solemnity of government, and of the purity, fullness, and elevation of grace. It is quite true that God in government reserves to Himself the sovereign right to act in patience, long-suffering, and mercy; but the exercise of these attributes, in connexion with His throne of government, must never be confounded with the unconditional actings of pure and absolute grace.

The chapter before us is a record of divine government, and yet, in it we find such clauses as the following: "If they shall confess their iniquity, and the iniquity of their fathers, with their trespass which they trespassed against me; and that also they have walked contrary unto me, and that I also have walked contrary unto them, and have brought them into the land of their enemies; if then their uncircumcised hearts be humbled, and they then accept of the punishment of their iniquity: then will I remember my covenant with Jacob, and also my covenant with Isaac, and also my covenant with Abraham will I remember; and I will remember the land. The land also shall be left of them, and shall enjoy her sabbaths, while she lieth desolate without them; and they shall accept of the punishment of their iniquity: because, even because they despised my judgments, and because their soul abhorred my statutes. And yet, for all that, when they be in the land of their enemies, I will not cast them away, neither will I abhor them, to destroy them utterly, and to break my covenant with them: for I am the Lord their God. But I will for their sakes remember the covenant of their ancestors, whom I brought forth out of the land of Egypt in the sight of the heathen, that I might be their God: I am the Lord" (ver. 40-45).

Here we find God in government, meeting, in long-suffering mercy, the very earliest and faintest breathings of a broken and penitent spirit. The history of the judges and of the kings presents many instances of the exercise of this blessed attribute of the divine government. Again and again, the soul of Jehovah was grieved for Israel (Judges 10:16), and He sent them one deliverer after another, until at length there remained no hope, and the righteous claims of His throne demanded their expulsion from that land which they were wholly incompetent to keep.

All this is *government*. But, by and by, Israel will be brought into possession of the land of Canaan on the ground of unqualified and unchangeable *grace* – grace exercised in divine righteousness through the blood of the cross. It will not be by works of law; nor yet by the institutions of an evanescent economy, but by that grace which "reigns through righteousness, by Jesus Christ our Lord." Wherefore, they shall never again be driven forth from their possession. No enemy shall ever molest them. They shall enjoy undisturbed repose behind the shield of Jehovah's favour. Their tenure of the land will be according to the eternal stability of divine grace, and the efficacy of the blood of the everlasting covenant. "They shall be saved in the Lord with an everlasting salvation."

May the Spirit of God lead us into more enlarged apprehensions of divine truth, and endow us with a greater capacity to try the things that differ, and rightly to divide the word of truth!

Chapter 27

THE VOWS

Persons or things devoted to the LORD

This closing section of our book treats of the "singular vow," or the voluntary act whereby a person devoted himself or his property unto the Lord. "And the Lord spake unto Moses, saying, Speak unto the children of Israel, and say unto them, When a man shall make a singular vow the persons shall be for the Lord by thy estimation. And thy estimation shall be . . . after the shekel of the sanctuary."

Now, in the case of a person devoting himself, or his beast, his house, or his field, unto the Lord, it was obviously a question of capacity or worth; and, hence, there was a certain scale of valuation, according to age. Moses, as the representative of the claims of God, was called upon to estimate, in each case, according to the standard of the sanctuary. If a man undertakes to make a vow, he must be tried by the standard of righteousness; and, moreover, in all cases, we are called upon to recognise the difference between *capacity* and *title*. In Exodus 30:15, we read, in reference to the atonement money, "The rich shall not give more, and the poor shall not give less, than half a shekel, when they give an offering unto the Lord, to make an atonement for your souls." In the matter of atonement all stood upon one common level. Thus it must ever be. High and low, rich and poor, learned and ignorant, old and young, all have one common title. "There is no difference." All stand alike on the ground of the infinite preciousness of the blood of Christ. There may be a vast difference as to capacity, as to title there is none. There may be a vast difference as to experience – as to title there is none. There may be a vast difference as to knowledge, gift, and fruitfulness – as to title there is none. The sapling and the tree, the babe and the father, the convert of yesterday and the matured believer, are all on the same ground. "The rich shall not give more, and the poor shall not give less." Nothing more could be given, nothing less could be taken. "We have boldness to enter into the holiest by the blood of Jesus." This is our title to enter. Our capacity to worship, when we have entered, will depend upon our spiritual energy. Christ is our title. The Holy Ghost is our capacity. Self has nothing to do with either the one or the other. What a mercy! We get in by the blood of Jesus; we enjoy what we find there by the Holy Ghost. The blood of Jesus opens the door; the Holy Ghost conducts us through the house. The blood of Jesus opens the casket; the Holy Ghost unfolds the precious contents. The blood of Jesus makes the casket ours; the Holy Ghost enables us to appreciate its rare and costly gems.

But, in Leviticus 27, it is entirely a question of ability, capacity, or worth. Moses had a certain standard from which he could not possibly descend. He had a certain rule from which he could not possibly swerve. If any one could come up to that, well; if not, he had to take his place accordingly.

What, then, was to be done in reference to the person who was unable to rise to the height of the claims set forth by the representative of divine righteousness? Hear the consolatory answer: "But if he be *poorer* than thy estimation, then he shall present himself before *the priest,* and the priest shall value him; *according to his ability* that vowed shall the priest value him" (ver. 8). In other words, if it be a question of man's undertaking to meet the claims of *righteousness*, then he must meet them. But if, on the other hand, a man feels himself wholly unable to meet those claims, he has only to fall back upon *grace*, which will take him up, just as he is. Moses is the representative of the claims of divine righteousness. The priest is the exponent of the provisions of divine grace. The poor man who was unable to stand before Moses fell back into the arms of the priest. Thus it is ever. If we cannot *"dig"* we can "*beg*;" and directly we take the place of a beggar, it is no longer a question of what we are able to *earn*, but of what God is pleased to *give*. "Grace all the work shall crown, through everlasting days." How happy it is to be debtors to grace! How happy to take when God is glorified in giving! When man is in question, it is infinitely better to dig than to beg; but when God is in question, the case is the very reverse.

Application to the nation of Israel

I would just add, that I believe this entire chapter bears, in an especial manner, upon the nation of Israel. It is intimately connected with the two preceding chapters. Israel made "a singular vow" at the foot of Mount Horeb; but were quite unable to meet the claims of law – they were far "poorer than Moses' estimation." But, blessed be God, they will come in under the rich provisions of divine grace. Having learnt their total inability "to dig," they will not be "ashamed to beg;" and, hence, they shall experience the deep blessedness of being cast upon the sovereign mercy of Jehovah, which stretches, like a golden chain, "from everlasting to everlasting." It is well to be poor, when the knowledge of our poverty serves but to unfold to us the exhaustless riches of divine grace. That grace can never suffer any one to go empty away. It can never tell any one that he is too poor. It can meet the very deepest human need; and not only so but it is glorified in meeting it. This holds good in every case. It is true of any individual sinner; and it is true with respect to Israel, who, having been valued by the Lawgiver, have proved "poorer than his estimation." Grace is the grand and only resource for all. It is the basis of our salvation; the basis of a life of practical godliness; and the basis of those imperishable hopes which animate us amid the trials and conflicts of this sin-stricken world. May we cherish a deeper sense of grace, and more ardent desire for the glory!

We shall here close our meditations upon this most profound and precious book. If the foregoing pages should be used of God to awaken an interest in a section of inspiration which has been so much neglected by the Church, in all ages, they shall not have been written in vain.

C. H. M.

CONTENTS

Preface 5
Preface to the Second Edition 15

Chapter 1
The sacrifices - Introduction 17
   God speaks out of the tabernacle 17
   The order of the different offerings 19
The burnt offering 21
   Christ's offering of Himself to God 21
   The types in Leviticus 22
   The essential glory of Christ 23
   The value of the cross of Christ to God 24
   A voluntary offering 24
   The identification of the worshipper with the burnt offering 28
   The place of the priests 30
   Atonement 32
   The preparation of the sacrifice 33
   A sacrifice by fire: a sweet savour 35
   The law of the burnt offering 36

Chapter 2
The meal offering 39
   Christ in His life 39
   The humanity of Christ 40
   The perfect man 42
   Fine flour mingled with oil 44
   The truth concerning the person of Christ 47
   Fine flour anointed with oil 51
   Frankincense 53

Salt	54
Leaven	56
Honey	57
A sweet savour	59
Suffering for righteousness' sake	60
Suffering in sympathy	61
Suffering by anticipation	63
Communion with the sufferings of Christ	64
The priests' portion	66

Chapter 3
The peace offering 70

What distinguishes this sacrifice from the burnt offering	70
A portion in communion with God	72
The joy of communion	73
The peace offering and the meat offering	74
The sin in us and the sin on us	77
Confessing sins	79
Leavened bread with the sacrifice	83
The Lord's Supper	85
Worship	87

Chapter 4-5:1-13
The sin offering 92

The relation of the people to God and the individual conscience	92
Sinning through ignorance or error	93
The sin offering and the burnt offering	96
The laying on of hands	100
Differences between the burnt offering and the sin offering	102
The fat offered upon the altar	104
The body of the victim burnt outside the camp	105
The value of Christ's blood	106
Christ dead and resurrected	108
Let us go forth unto Him without the camp	111

Chapter 5:14-6:7
The trespass offering 116
The holiness of God 116
Restitution and a fifth part added 118
Trespasses against God and trespasses against man 122

Chapter 6:8-30 & Chapter 7
The law of various offerings 127

Chapters 8 & 9
The priesthood 130
Christ, sacrifice and priest 130
A high priest in the heavens 131
Priests on earth? 132
The consecration of Aaron before all the assembly 133
Christ, our great high Priest 134
This is the thing which the LORD has commanded 136
The eighth day 138
The blood of the victim 139
Aaron and his sons: Christ and the church 141
The glory of the millennial reign 144

Chapter 10
Nadab and Abihu offer strange fire 147
Man corrupts the divine institutions 147
The judgment of God in His house 149
The attitude of the priests in the face of this judgment . 152
Neither wine nor strong drink in the presence of God .. 157
The inalienable portion of the priests 160
Omission in service 162

Chapter 11
The law concerning clean and unclean animals 165
God gives adequate directions 165
Animals which chew the cud and which divide the hoof 168
The internal life and the external walk 170
Creatures living in water 171

Birds	173
The holiness of God and the holiness of the believer	174
Obsolete ordinances	177

Chapter 12
Purification of the woman who has had a child ... 179
- *Man conceived and born in sin* ... 179
- *The blood of atonement within the reach of all* ... 181
- *The downstooping of the Lord Jesus* ... 183

Chapters 13 & 14
The leper ... 185
- *The responsibility of the priest* ... 185
- *Leprosy in a man* ... 186
- *A man totally covered in leprosy* ... 190
- *Leprosy in a garment* ... 194
- *The cleansing of the leper* ... 195
- *The two birds* ... 197
- *The cedar wood, scarlet and hyssop* ... 200
- *Sprinkling the blood on the leper* ... 201
- *He shall tarry abroad out of his tent seven days* ... 204
- *The eighth day and its offerings* ... 207
- *Leprosy in a house* ... 214
- *Judgment of evil in an assembly* ... 215

Chapter 15
Ceremonial uncleanness ... 218
- *What is inherent in human nature* ... 218
- *The water and the blood* ... 221

Chapter 16
The great Day of Atonement ... 224
- *A way still closed* ... 224
- *Aaron, a type of Christ* ... 225
- *Aaron and his house* ... 227
- *Two goats – one lot for the* LORD ... 228

  The consequence of the atonement for the whole
   of humanity.. 230
  God is glorified and is able to show grace.................. 231
  The blood of atonement carried within the veil.......... 234
  The way into the holiest of all is open....................... 236
  The goat Azazel or the goat let go 238
  The prophetic aspect for Israel............................. 240

Chapter 17
The blood.. 243
  Life belongs to God... 243
  It is the blood which makes atonement for the soul 244

Chapters 18-20
Detailed instructions... 247
  The holiness required of those who belong to the
   people of God.. 247
  What man is capable of doing............................. 250
  Consideration for the poor and the stranger............. 251
  The worker's just wages 253
  The attitude towards the deaf and the blind............... 256

Chapters 21 & 22
Purity of the priests 258
  Position and state.. 258
  Our infirmities and our High Priest 261
  Keeping ourselves pure from every blemish............. 263

Chapter 23
The seven feasts of the Lord................................... 265
  Outline of God's dealings with Israel....................... 265
  The Sabbath... 266
  The Passover... 267
  The unleavened bread 268
  The sheaf of the first-fruits 269
  Pentecost... 272
  The stranger's portion.. 275

    The feast of trumpets 276
    The Day of Atonement 277
    The feast of tabernacles 279

Chapter 24
Figures of Israel 282
    The light which burnt continually 282
    The twelve loaves and the unity of the people 283
    The man who blasphemed the name of the L<small>ORD</small> 286

Chapter 25
The sabbatical year and the year of Jubilee 289
    The decrees of the Lord of all the earth 289
    The sabbatical year 290
    The year of Jubilee 291
    The land is mine, says the L<small>ORD</small> 293

Chapter 26
The government of God towards Israel 298
    Blessings and punishments 298
    Grace and the final restoration 299

Chapter 27
The vows 302
    Persons or things devoted to the L<small>ORD</small> 302
    Application to the nation of Israel 304